Inside the Bureaucracy:
The View from the
Assistant Secretary's Desk

Westview Special Studies in Public Policy and Public Systems Management

Inside the Bureaucracy:
The View from the Assistant Secretary's Desk
Thomas P. Murphy, Donald E. Nuechterlein,
and Ronald J. Stupak

In recent years the enhanced role of political executives in the White House has tended to overshadow the contributions of assistant secretaries and other political executives in the Cabinet and other agencies. However, President Carter's determination to reestablish the primacy of the Cabinet has opened up the possibility that the assistant secretary's role will be reinvigorated. Assistant secretary positions, originally established for the direction of presidential programs, have evolved over time to encompass many additional roles.

This is the first substantial analysis in more than a decade of the assistant secretaries' roles, relationships, and career patterns—as well as those of other presidential appointees. Based on the specific experiences of twenty-one assistant secretaries and three under secretaries who served during the Nixon, Ford, and Carter administrations, it provides invaluable insights into the background against which political executives carry out the president's programs and help formulate his policies.

Thomas P. Murphy, director of the Federal Executive Institute, founded graduate programs in public administration at the University of Missouri–Kansas City and in urban studies at the University of Maryland. Dr. Murphy's government service includes positions with NASA, the Federal Aviation Administration, the Internal Revenue Service, the General Accounting Office, and the U.S. Air Force. Donald E. Nuechterlein joined the faculty of the Federal Executive Institute in 1968. He specializes in U.S. foreign policy and international affairs and in executive development, and has worked with the U.S. Information Agency in Washington and in U.S. embassies overseas. Dr. Nuechterlein has published four books, including *National Interests and Presidential Leadership*. Ronald J. Stupak is professor of political science and contemporary affairs at the Federal Executive Institute; he previously taught at Miami University (Ohio). Dr. Stupak's most recent book is *Understanding Political Science*.

Inside the Bureaucracy:
The View from the
Assistant Secretary's Desk

Thomas P. Murphy,
Donald E. Nuechterlein,
and Ronald J. Stupak

Westview Press / Boulder, Colorado

Westview Special Studies in Public Policy and Public Systems Management

Published in 1978 in the United States of America by
Westview Press, Inc.
5500 Central Avenue
Boulder, Colorado 80301
Frederick A. Praeger, Publisher

Library of Congress Cataloging in Publication Data
Murphy, Thomas P.   1931-
   Inside the bureaucracy.
   (Westview special studies in public policy and public systems management)
   Includes index.
   1. Governmental executives—United States. I. Nuechterlein, Donald Edwin, 1925-
joint author. II. Stupak, Ronald J., joint author. III. Title.
JK723.E9M87   353   78-7425
ISBN 0-89158-154-5

Printed and bound in the United States of America

Contents

Tables and Figures

Preface

This volume is the result of new directions undertaken by the Federal Executive Institute (FEI) during fiscal years 1977 and 1978. In December 1976, a symposium on "The President's Program Directors: The Assistant Secretaries" was held at the Federal Executive Institute in Charlottesville, Virginia. The objective of that program was to encourage and enrich communication among political and career executives in the federal bureaucratic environment. Program objectives included sharing of experiences and improved communication among assistant secretaries and improvement of FEI's capability to communicate the viewpoints of political executives to career executives.

The three major themes of the symposium were the roles of the assistant secretary, the political-career interface, and the processes of policy formulation and implementation. The assistant and under secretaries met both in plenary sessions and in small discussion groups, in which FEI faculty members served as facilitators. The timing of the symposium—during the transition from the Ford to the Carter administration—contributed substantially to the candor with which participants expressed their opinions. It was clear to all concerned that a major objective was to capture their knowledge as a base for orienting future assistant secretaries to their new jobs. All plenary sessions were videotaped as well as recorded, and the three authors prepared and edited a transcript which was published in 1977 as a monograph entitled *The President's Program Directors: The Assistant Secretaries* (Washington, D.C., U.S. Government Printing Office). Symposium discussions relating to this volume's three major themes are reprinted at the ends of Chapters 2, 3, and 4.

This volume represents an analytic approach to the whole question of assistant secretaries in the federal bureaucracy. Although it draws extensively upon symposium materials, it extends beyond that to include an introductory discussion of the American political environment and the impact of that environment upon bureaucracy, along with an analytic treatment of the comments and opinions of these political executives from the conceptual standpoint of academics with significant practical experience.

By focusing on real actors in the policy process, our analysis attempts to systematically blend some of the theoretical tools of the political scientist with the practical experience of operating officials to achieve a fuller understanding of the policy process. In recognition of the persistent difficulty of social scientists (breadth versus depth, generalization versus bases, or the number of instances on which generalization rests), this book was developed on the assumption that the greater the breadth of analysis and the greater the number of participants, the easier it would be to isolate and magnify the crucial factors for an assistant secretary's success in the policy making process.

The fact that this book is based on the perceptions of particular personalities may raise some questions about the generalizations that have been extracted from it. Nonetheless, we feel that our analysis of the 1976 symposium at the Federal Executive Institute was invaluable because the assistant secretaries who participated were able to speak candidly, honestly, and openly about their jobs. Indeed, for many the session became almost a group exit interview.

We believe that the primary data, taken directly from discussions with assistant secretaries with substantial experience in the federal government, and its analysis by academically qualified interpreters will contribute much to the dialogue on this important subject.

We wish to thank our colleagues Ralph C. Bledsoe, Patrick J. Conklin, and Nancy Dalton for their support on this project, from the planning of the symposium to the preparation of this book. The project would not have been possible without the additional support of our competent staff assistants: Joyce Carter, Fay Davis, Susan Houchens, Jane Pender, and Barbara Rexrode, as well as our graduate assistant, Doug Hastings. Laurin Henry read the full manuscript and offered numerous helpful suggestions.

Thomas P. Murphy
Donald E. Nuechterlein
Ronald J. Stupak

Abbreviations

CBO	Congressional Budget Office
CSC	Civil Service Commission
EEO	Equal Employment Opportunity
EPA	Environmental Protection Agency
FEI	Federal Executive Institute
GAO	General Accounting Office
GSA	General Services Administration
HEW	Department of Health, Education, and Welfare
HUD	Department of Housing and Urban Development
LEA	Limited Executive Assignment
NEA	Noncareer Executive Assignment
NIH	National Institutes of Health
NIMH	National Institute of Mental Health
OMB	Office of Management and Budget

Introduction

The American political system has been characterized since its founding by an emphasis on limiting the power of those who govern. One school of thought (mostly identified with Alexander Hamilton) wanted to locate extensive executive power in the hands of the President, but this approach was rejected by the framers of the constitution, who did not intend to create an imperial presidency. Distrustful of the executive as a result of their experiences with royal mandates and colonial governors, a majority of the delegates to the Constitutional Convention expected Congress to be the heart of the new government. They spelled out in considerable detail the powers of the legislative branch, while leaving the presidency in wholesome ambiguity. Yet, if they did not grant many specific powers to the executive branch, neither did they withhold many. Partly as a result of this, the history of twentieth-century America has been marked by the gradual expansion of presidential prerogatives—from Theodore Roosevelt's idea that the president should act as a steward in the national interest to Richard Nixon's notion that a president, once elected, should be able to govern almost unchallenged. The growth of presidential powers since 1900 can be attributed to personality as well as crisis. Woodrow Wilson, Franklin Roosevelt, and Harry Truman each left a distinctive mark on the office; two world wars, a national depression, and a cold war that placed tremendous emphasis on foreign affairs helped them to do it.

Since assistant secretaries really are extensions of presidential power and presidential administrations, an understanding of the presidency is crucial to an understanding of the role of the assistant secretary. Though American political philosophy emphasizes limited government and the legislative arena, it is actually the presidential arena that dominates the contemporary American governmental scene. (Congress is attempting to regain some of its lost control in the political process, thus demonstrating how powerful the presidency has grown.) Understanding the historical development of the presidency will enable us to achieve a fuller appreciation of the context within which assistant secretaries—whose numbers have increased tremendously as presidential power has increased—have been operating.

The Growth of Presidential Authority

Of the many historical forces that have contributed to the rise of "presidential government," four are especially important. First, the office has been democratized. The election of presidents in the early years of the nation was removed from the people. Presidents were nominated by congressional caucuses and elected by presidential electors chosen by state legislatures. With the rise of democratic sentiment that accompanied the Jacksonian period, however, the choice of electors was turned over to the populace, and the convention system replaced "king caucus."

Second, with the advent of the New Deal and widespread federal involvement in domestic affairs, the president acquired a new job: that of managing the national prosperity. Unlike the pre-1930 period, modern government expects to keep the economy healthy as well as to solve social problems. The president, as head of a far-reaching bureaucracy of three million employees, has the chief responsibility for directing this.

Third, since the Constitution assigns chief responsibility for the conduct of foreign affairs to the president, the emergence of the United States as a world power spearheaded the growth of presidential prerogatives. This has been particularly true because of the changing nature of warfare in the twentieth century. Since 1900, political conditions and military techniques both have developed to such an extent that entire societies (not just people in the armed forces) have been active participants in conflict. Consequently, presidents have been recognized as stewards of national defense deserving broad powers to protect the country's interest in international affairs.

Fourth, the mass media, especially television, have given the president a sophisticated means of influencing public opinion. Although chief executives are limited in their ability to sell their programs over television, as Lyndon Johnson learned with Vietnam, no one has more power over the airways than the president of the United States.

The centrality of the presidency in the American political system is due to the factor of leadership. The president more than any other figure has prime responsibility for setting the national agenda and for acting on national problems in the name of a national constituency. Despite efforts by Congress to establish a more significant role for itself in the policy formulation process, most of the bills introduced in Congress originate not with a legislator but with the executive branch. Most of the legislators' time is spent debating, amending, and rewording issues and measures proposed and promoted by the chief executive. Although there are notable exceptions, such as the Taft-Hartley Act and the Civil Rights Acts of 1957 and 1960, much of the principal reform legislation enacted in this century has been initiated by the president. In domestic crises, such as the Great Depression, Congress has been quick to yield to White House guidance. Virtually all of Franklin Roosevelt's requests in the first three months of his first administration, from stringent economy measures to the Tennessee Valley Authority, received quick and favorable congressional action.

Although the president has large potential powers, limitations and restraints on that power are built into the Constitution. Those who fear an imperial presidency, such as reared its head in the Johnson and Nixon administrations, are watching for any new signs of it. Nonetheless, the president and his programs set the direction that an administration pursues, and assistant secretaries appointed by the president become his representatives in the larger program designs he wants implemented. The parameters within which the assistant secretary must operate are primarily presidential parameters.

But assistant secretaries are not simply neutral conduits for the president; four factors may alter the policy directions a president gives them, either directly or through a cabinet officer. First, the president often cannot spend much time on an assistant secretary's programs. Therefore, an assistant secretary can exercise considerable discretion in pushing for certain kinds of policies. An assistant secretary may use this freedom to champion positions that may compete with other priorities of the president or of other presidential appointees.

Second, the assistant secretary must present the president's program to a bureaucracy of career officials and dedicated professionals, who often have their own ideas of what is best for the American people and what is best in terms of the agency's organization and its delivery capabilities. These negotiations often result in changes in the program.

Third, many assistant secretaries accept their positions because they have something special to bring to the role or because special programs they are interested in are included in the president's overall program design. These individuals champion certain policies and programs based on their own philosophies, personalities, and status needs.

Fourth, many assistant secretaries have their own political sponsors outside the executive branch, which gives them some degree of autonomy. In fact, some listen more intently to their outside patrons than they do to their formal superiors within an administration.

Although the growth of presidential power has resulted in more assistant secretaries to direct the increased number of presidential programs, it has not increased their power and status. Many decisions are now made in the White House, not in cabinet departments, and certainly not at the assistant secretary level. Thus, on many occasions, assistant secretaries have to bargain with the president's White House staff for their departments, their programs, and themselves in order to get "a piece of the policy action" that is available at the presidential level.

Historical Development of the Assistant Secretary Position

The title of "assistant secretary" in the executive departments was not conferred by legislation until the middle of the nineteenth century. Prior to that time, cabinet secretaries had clerks and "assistants to the secretary" as their aides. From 1789 until 1828, these positions, as well as the cabinet posts, were assigned to members of elite groups in American society: the well-born, well-educated, and "respectable" men of the community. This was in keeping with the dominant role exercised in American politics by eastern aristocrats and the commercial class, represented by the first six presidents. When Andrew Jackson won the presidency in 1828, the locus of American politics moved westward and the individuals assigned to key government jobs reflected the different social background of the new political leadership. Introduction of the "spoils system" so politicized the bureaucracy for the next fifty years that it made a sham of both continuity and quality in the public service. The first civil service legislation, the Pendleton Act of 1883, therefore, was designed to improve the quality of public service by reducing political patronage.

Although the first "assistant to the secretary" appointments were made in the Post Office Department shortly after the federal government was formed in 1789, the designation of assistant postmaster general dates from the 1830s. In 1849, Congress authorized the first assistant secretary of the treasury, and in the next fifteen years most of the other departments were given this new position: the State Department in 1853, the War and Navy Departments in 1861, the Department of the Interior in 1862, and the Justice Department (assistant attorney general) in 1859. Newer departments were given at least one assistant secretarial position when they were created later in the nineteenth and twentieth centuries. These were, of course, presidential appointments subject to confirmation by the Senate. The responsibilities of the early appointees were generally not specified in legislation and their duties were, therefore, assigned by the incumbent cabinet officer. While the number of assistant secretaries increased somewhat during the 1870s and 1880s—from thirteen in 1870 to seventeen in 1890—they were abolished in the War and Navy Departments after the Civil War and were not reestablished until the 1890s.

In January 1900, there were 21 assistant secretary–level positions in the federal government, divided as follows: State Department, 3; Treasury, 3; War, 1; Justice, 7; Post Office, 4; Navy, 1; Interior, 1; and Agriculture, 1. By 1910 the number had grown to 25, and in 1930 there were 37 such positions as well as a few under secretaries. The first under secretary post was created in 1919 in the State Department, followed in 1921 by the creation of a similar position in the Treasury Department. In 1933, there were only 4 under secretaries.

Despite the enormous expansion of the federal government during the 1930s and the great number of new employees hired into the Civil Service, there was no change between 1930 and 1940 in the number of assistant and under secretaries; it remained at 37. The large increase came between 1940 and 1950, caused principally by World War II's demands on the federal government and by postwar decisions by President Truman and Congress that the United States would assume a worldwide role in international politics. By 1950, the number of under secretaries, deputy under secretaries, and assistant secretaries stood at 55, with the State and Defense Departments showing sizable increases: State, 12; Treasury, 5; Defense, 9; Justice, 7; Post Office, 6; Interior, 4; Agriculture, 3; Commerce, 4; and Labor, 5. The proliferation of these presidential appointments accelerated in the 1950s and 1960s, resulting principally from a large expansion of existing domestic departments and agencies and the creation of new ones. In 1960 the total had reached 84, and by 1970 it had climbed to 113, divided as follows: State, 16; Treasury, 9; Defense, 12; Justice, 11; Post Office, 8; Interior, 8; Agriculture, 7; Commerce, 7; Labor, 7; HEW, 9; HUD, 11; and Transportation, 8.

The expansion continued in the 1970s and by 1978 the total was 145. The breakdown, in alphabetical order, was as follows: Agriculture, 8; Air Force, 3; Army, 6; Commerce, 14; Defense, 11; Energy, 10; HEW, 11; HUD, 10; Interior, 7; Justice, 11; Labor, 11; Navy, 6; State, 21; Transportation, 6; and Treasury, 10.

The large increase in the number of presidential appointees since World War II has had several important effects on the way the president runs the executive branch of government. First, prestige and influence have declined for the assistant secretary and grown for the under secretary and deputy secretary. In the 1940s, when there were only 55 assistant secretaries, the job was considered an important position of influence in Washington, and the incumbents were given the perquisites that went with high offices—chauffeur-driven cars, high pay, invitations to White House dinners, travel with the president, etc. Today, the growth of the deputy secretary and under secretary positions has removed assistant secretaries from their former key role in the policymaking process and made them in many cases chief managers for implementing presidential and cabinet decisions in their areas of responsibility. In addition, the growth of the White House staff and the increasing importance of the Office of Management and Budget in determining budget and program limits has further eroded their authority and feeling of self-importance.

Resulting from the great increase in the number of presidential appointees and the declining influence of the assistant secretary is another important consequence: presidents beginning with Eisenhower have had to set up special machinery in the White House to recruit good talent from across the country to fill these positions. But the attractiveness of the jobs has declined to the point where it is not always possible to get the best people, and presidential recruiters have therefore settled for "the best available" candidates from among the thousands who apply.

Another factor is that many of these top political jobs now require a good knowledge of the substantive area in which the assistant secretary will devote his or her energies, and a person with this kind of talent very often can earn far more money in the private sector. When they weigh the financial sacrifice of moving to Washington for two years, the reduced influence of most assistant secretaries, and the ever-increasing scrutiny (and even harassment) by congressional committees, many of the best-qualified people in the private sector simply are not willing to take on these jobs. The Carter administration may have made the talent scouts' search even more difficult by asking presidential appointees to remain in their jobs for the full term of the president.

The inevitable point then comes when the best-trained talent for assistant secretary jobs may be in the top ranks of the career civil service. Nearly half of all assistant secretaries in the mid-1970s were officials who had previously served in the career civil service and had moved up the ranks to the point where they were deemed capable of taking on the responsibilities of assistant secretary. Attendance at a symposium of assistant secretaries held at the Federal Executive Institute in Charlottesville, Virginia, bore witness to this trend. The question is whether the trend is good or bad.

Put another way, has not the erosion of the influence and prestige of the assistant secretary's job now made it desirable to place the emphasis on managerial competence and continuity, rather than on freshness of ideas and willingness to take risks? Some feel that the U.S. government should now move in the direction of the Canadian and British systems and select the best career executives for assistant secretary jobs, thus opening up the career ladder to supergrade-level officials who have demonstrated managerial ability but whose promotion to higher positions is usually blocked. The new Senior Executive Service proposed by President Carter in 1978 (discussed later in this volume) opens up the possibility that the president may move in this direction.

The Creative Interface between Political and Career Executives

Relationships between the career bureaucrats and assistant secretaries is a subject which has long interested scholars and management specialists in government. Although these relationships vary widely among the departments and agencies, several generalizations can be made here (the symposium highlighted most of them). The interface has three obvious characteristics: (1) There is inevitable and understandable tension between the career civil servants and their politically appointed superiors, with the degree of tension related to the amount of previous government experience the political appointee has had. (2) Political appointees can usually overcome the skepticism of the career people working under them if they have the complete confidence of their cabinet secretary and the White House. (3) Conversely, an assistant secretary without previous experience in government and without solid backing from his or her secretary will have to build respect among subordinates on the basis of managerial ability. A participant in the symposium observed that a political appointee can afford to know nothing about the culture of government, or to know little about administration policy, but he or she can't afford to be ignorant of both.[1] These three aspects of the interface are worth further discussion here.

Bureaucrats harbor a natural suspicion of any person assigned to the assistant secretary job who has not previously served in that organization. Career officials know it will take six months to train the appointee (if he or she will let them), and that the appointee will probably leave after about eighteen months—just when he or she is becoming fully effective. Those who do not learn the ropes of government, or make some grievous mistake, usually will not stay longer than twelve months. Many political appointees arrive in office with the conviction that they are going to make significant changes during their tenure, and then become aggravated when subordinates who are cognizant of the legal and administrative constraints attempt to point out these difficulties. What the assistant secretary often perceives as overcautiousness and preoccupation with rules and traditions may well be the accumulation of wisdom by career executives who have seen ambitious political executives come and go and make mistakes they would not make if they listened to good counsel from their careerists.

Integrity is essential in a political appointee who wishes to gain respect and support from subordinates. This point was demonstrated time and again during the Nixon administration, when some political appointees obviously were involved in unethical and illegal activities. The career service is rarely corrupted in the performance of its duties, and civil servants are quick to observe tendencies of political appointees to succumb to corruption from outside—or within—government. In a word, the effectiveness of a political executive is largely determined by the confidence he or she generates through integrity, competence, and managerial ability.

The best assistant secretary, from the careerist's point of view, is one who has served previously in that department in another role. For example, a bright young lawyer or business executive may first serve as an assistant to a cabinet secretary or an assistant secretary, and then be moved up to deputy assistant secretary. He or she may then leave government for a few years but come back as an assistant secretary. The best of these might eventually end up as secretary of a department in a new administration. Cabinet secretaries Vance, Brown, Blumenthal, and Califano of the Carter administration all served in lower political jobs in the Kennedy and (or) Johnson administrations. The advantage such people have over appointees without previous service in government is that they know how government operates and can begin the first day in office to get their organizations rolling; career executives do not have to spend a great deal of time explaining the elementary facts of bureaucratic life to them.

It must be added, however, that even if a political executive—old or new to government—establishes excellent relations with subordinate career employees, this will not help if his or her relationship with the White House or Congress is poor. Appointees who simply cannot get along with the chairman of their appropriations subcommittee or with a key White House assistant will find their days in Washington numbered.

Some political appointees come to their jobs with the attitude that their primary responsibility is to "conceptualize" government programs and policies, and that the job of career civil servants is to implement them. This attitude sets up immediate barriers between the political and career levels and may cause difficulty for the political appointee. Many career executives believe they too are capable of asking the "why" questions and should be consulted before major decisions are made to shift programs, personnel, or budgets to carry out administration policy.

The quality that may be lacking most often in new political appointees is humility. Too many political appointees think that if they give the impression that they are brighter, more energetic, and more assertive than other people, they will instill respect among subordinates even though the substance of their decisions may not be superior. Career civil servants usually see through these masks; they respect the person who shows self-confidence but is not afraid to seek advice and occasionally is willing to admit, "I don't know."

When the so-called "whiz kids" were running the Department of Defense in the early 1960s, they were not criticized by the career staff for their intelligence, but rather for their attitude of having the answers before the questions were asked. Judging by the poor decisions many of them made about U.S. policies in Southeast Asia, the careerists may well have been right when they argued that having brains is no guarantee of making wise decisions.

In *A Government of Strangers*, Hugh Heclo states that, since bureaucratic government is a fact of contemporary life, it is essential in a functioning democracy to make sure that political representatives not only be formally installed in government posts, but that they in some sense be capable of gaining control of the large bureaucracies that constitute the modern stage.[2] It is in this context that the assistant secretaries are seen as one of the key linchpins for effective government. For between the politician's intentions and the government's final actions passes the shadow of the bureaucracy. Hence, it is important to find political leadership that can make the bureaucracy respond effectively to the demands and guidelines established by the American electorate at the polls. As bureaucracy becomes politicized and political leadership becomes more bureaucratized in the contemporary American environment, it is important that we try in this book to analyze a key political position in American government—the assistant secretary.

We realize that assistant secretaries are not at the pinnacles of power. But we are aware also that they are at the vital interface between the political and the bureaucratic elements of our government. Furthermore, they are at the interface of interest group and electoral demands on the bureaucratic system where the quest for delivery of services and allocation of resources is most intense. By focusing on the assistant secretary's role, we hope to bring to light many of the tensions, conflicts, and problems of our democratic processes. At the same time, we trust that this book will demonstrate the creative capabilities of assistant secretaries in government, emphasizing the high ideals of those who have chosen to serve as assistant secretaries, as well as pointing out some of the frustrations of their interface position.

In sum, through the symposium that serves as the basis for this book, through the book itself, and through the programs and philosophy of the Federal Executive Institute, we hope to highlight some of the excitement, as well as some of the frustration, that exists in a post-industrial democratic society as it tries to achieve both dignity for the individual and harmony among many complex parts.

Notes

1. Some of the views expressed here are similar to the findings of Hugh Heclo in his recent volume *A Government of Strangers* (Washington, D.C.: Brookings Institution, 1977) but were arrived at independently as a result of the symposium discussions at the Federal Executive Institute in Charlottesville, Virginia, in December 1976.

2. Heclo, *A Government of Strangers*, passim.

1
Ranges and Types
of Political Executives

The people are entitled to the most efficient public service we can devise. The way to provide such service is to make sure that all Government employees, except those in top policy jobs, are under the merit system.

—Harry S Truman

To fully understand the impact political appointees have in the federal bureaucracy, we must overcome the false impression that federal political positions by definition involve top executives. The term "political positions" covers all positions, from cabinet secretaries down to chauffeurs. Because most of these other political positions are at least indirectly tied to the assistant secretaries, it is important to understand their functions and how they are distributed. At the other end of the spectrum, it is important to understand the categories of executive positions that occupy a position superior to that of the assistant secretaries. This chapter will examine the range of political executives and political appointees and will also review in more detail the specific types of assistant secretary positions.

The Political Positions: Executive and Support

Table 1.1 indicates the number of noncareer positions in the United States government by rank. As the table shows, there are 2,453 positions at the supergrade and executive levels (1,708 and 745, respectively), including the entire cabinet, the under secretaries, the agency heads, the assistant secretaries, and all of their top assistants. This is not really a very large number considering all the agencies and departments to be managed.

Another way of looking at this is that the 745 Executive Schedule political positions are supported by only 1,708 excepted and political positions below GS-16. Many of these positions generally are of the special assistant, specialist, or secretarial variety. Thus, there are only 3,028 political positions, an average of just about four support

Table 1.1   Noncareer Positions, U.S. Government,
             by Rank, 1975-76

Schedule	Approximate number of political or excepted noncareer positions*	
Executive Schedule		
Level I	12	
Level II	71	
Level III	115	
Level IV	353	
Level V	194	
Total executive level positions		745
General Schedule supergrades		
GS 18	246	
GS 17	386	
GS 16	646	
Subtotal	1,278	
Public Law 313 supergrades		
(GS 16-18 equivalents)	430	
Total supergrades and equivalents		1,708
Other General Schedule grades		
GS 15	310	
GS 14	150	
GS 13	140	
GS 12 and below	720	
Total GS 1-15s		1,320
Total political and excepted noncareer positions		3,773

Source: Adapted from Hugh Heclo, A Government of
Strangers (Washington, D.C.: Brookings Institution,
1977), p. 38, who compiled his data from White House
and Civil Service Commission sources.

* Includes all presidential appointments, Schedule C,
and NEA and miscellaneous noncareer appointments excepted from competitive civil service examinations.

executives of staff assistants for each top political executive position. The category for GS-12 and below includes virtually all the confidential secretaries and drivers, and accounts for one-fourth of the 3,028 noncareer positions supporting the 745 top political executives.

While the total number of political executives is about 2,450, the number of civil service executives at the same supergrade levels and at

Table 1.2   Probability of a Top Executive
Being Noncareer or Political

Category	Probability of a political or excepted noncareer position	Total positions in category
Executive Schedule		
Level I	100%	12
Level II	100%	71
Level III	100%	115
Level IV	99%	357
Level V	90%	213
Total for levels I-V	97%	768
General Schedule supergrades		
GS 18	53%	467
GS 17	33%	1,157
GS 16	17%	3,859
	23%	5,483
Public Law 313 supergrades	35%	1,238
Total executives (political, excepted, and career)	33%	7,489

Source: Derived from Table 1.1 and Heclo, p. 38.

executive levels IV and V totals just over 5,000. The total number of political and career executives in the federal establishment therefore is about 7,500. Almost exactly one-third of these are political executives. Obviously, the higher the level, the more likelihood that a federal executive would be a political or an excepted noncareer appointee. Table 1.2 indicates by grade level the probability of a top executive being a noncareer appointee.

The other footnote which is needed to understand the actual number of political positions at key executive levels is that many of the noncareer Public Law 313 and General Schedule supergrade appointees in positions categorized as political or excepted are actually just as nonpolitical as many of their career counterparts. Often these people are passing through the government and are needed for specific jobs, but since they have not come up through the career route they are considered political or excepted, even if the political executives are former career employees. This tends to be especially true toward the end of a presidential term when persons outside the government are less willing to take positions that are likely to be abolished if a new president should be elected.

It is also essential to understand that "political" is not a synonym for "unqualified." In fact, the qualifications of persons appointed to executive-level positions through the political route have been improving in recent years, and most of them are very highly qualified for their positions. Further, many of them have really had no significant political party activity. To be sure, they are trusted by the leadership of the political party in power. But they have won their positions through professional competence and personal recommendations rather than through direct political activity. The reverse of this may also be true. Some career employees have had strong political sponsorship and loyalties and this has advanced some of their careers.

Categories of Political and Excepted Appointments

Political and excepted employees fall into a number of categories: (1) presidential appointees; (2) noncareer executive assignments (NEAs); (3) limited executive assignments (LEAs); (4) Schedule A; (5) Schedule B; and (6) Schedule C.

Noncareer executive assignments (NEAs) refer to supergrade-level appointments of persons to positions that are not part of the career service. They enjoy all the benefits of supergrades except that they do not have career status and therefore can be removed rather easily. Nevertheless, they tend to stay in service significantly longer than presidential appointees. The average time for an NEA to serve in the supergrade levels is eight years. Roughly 45 percent of these NEAs have in fact been former career employees or have had some prior federal experience. Overall, at the time he or she finally leaves the government, an NEA executive is likely to have averaged fifteen years, including eight years in the NEA category. Those who entered the government at the NEA level tend to stay a shorter period of time (four years) than those with prior government service.[1]

Until 1978, to make an NEA supergrade appointment, the department or agency had to propose the person for policy, confidential, or advocacy-type duties. These proposals were made to the Bureau of Executive Personnel of the U.S. Civil Service Commission, which had the responsibility of recommending to the three commissioners whether the request should be granted. The criteria depended upon whether the position included "noncareer" duties and whether the individual was in fact qualified for the level proposed. On occasion, the recommendation stated that the position was appropriately political but that the grade level was too high for the person's qualifications. In some of these cases, counteroffers were made to the agencies so that an individual being considered for a GS-18 NEA position might in fact be hired for a GS-17 position.

The Civil Service Commission experienced a great deal of pressure in making these decisions. Consequently, in 1977, it signed an agency order providing that the decision on an individual's capability for the level proposed would be heavily influenced by personal certification by the cabinet secretary or agency head that the candidate is qualified. The basic point is that if a cabinet or agency head persists in proposing someone for an NEA-level position, the Civil Service Commission does not want to be in the position of second-guessing the choice. If that person turns out to be weak, the department or agency will suffer. But the responsibility for making such decisions should be with the cabinet or agency head, who ought to be better qualified to evaluate the qualifications of the individual for fitting into that particular organization's policy machinery.

Limited executive assignments (LEAs) are appointments of noncareer people, not to exceed five years, generally to perform reasonably specific assignments. In 1975 there were 123 of these appointments. In the three prior years (1972-74) there were 138, 175, and 186 respectively, showing a steady flow but no drastic changes in the appointment pattern. LEAs may apply for career supergrade positions, but their credentials must be individually approved by the Civil Service Commission on the same basis as other applicants for such positions.

The conversion of LEAs and NEAs became quite controversial in 1976 as Democratic Party leaders in Congress, including Congressman Morris Udall, the ranking majority member of the House Post Office and Civil Service Committee, warned the Civil Service Commission not to permit large-scale conversion of political executives to career ranks in anticipation of President Carter's election victory. In the past, it has been charged that outgoing administrations have attempted to blanket their political appointees into the top career ranks. In fact, a review in 1977 by the Civil Service Commission showed that there were fewer such conversions (19) in 1976 than in previous administrations.[2]

Schedule A positions include those for which it is not practical to give examinations and which are not of a confidential or policy-determining nature. These generally involve specialized fields, especially law. The general counsel's offices in most agencies and departments of the federal government are staffed with Schedule A

Table 1.3   Distribution of Schedule C Positions
by Selected Agency, 1977

Department or agency	Total Schedule Cs	GS 1 to GS 6	GS 7 to GS 12	GS 13 to GS 15	Above GS 15
USDA	97	0	54	38	5
Commerce	92	1	43	43	5
Defense	110	2	80	16	12
Air Force	7	0	6	0	1
Army	12	0	10	2	0
Navy	10	0	9	1	0
OSD	81	2	55	13	11
HEW	70	1	33	36	0
HUD	91	0	38	53	0
Interior	53	2	23	28	0
Justice	50	1	36	13	0
Labor	67	10	24	33	0
State	52	1	36	15	0
DOT	54	2	22	22	8
Treasury	29	0	13	16	0
EPA	15	0	5	10	0
GSA	17	0	9	8	0
NASA	10	0	7	3	0
SBA	20	0	10	10	0
VA	17	0	7	10	0
Total	844	20	440	354	30

Source: U.S. Civil Service Commission, Washington, D.C.

attorneys. These positions are not career appointments—although in practice many of them become such, and a Schedule A attorney who is also a veteran has essentially the same protections against removal as a career employee. In 1976 about 95,300 people held Schedule A appointments, including chaplains, certain interpreters, specially qualified scientific, professional, or academic personnel, and many part-time and seasonal employees.

Schedule B is a category of excepted appointments which are not of a confidential or policy-determining nature and for which it is not feasible to hold a competitive examination. But noncompetitive examinations may apply. It includes professors at the National War College and the Federal Executive Institute as well as numerous work-study students. Faculty appointments normally are made on a term basis such as three or five years, and in some cases are subject to renewal. As in Schedule A, a veteran in one of these positions has essentially the same protections as a career employee. Obviously, most of the positions in Schedule B, while excepted, are not what we normally would consider to be political appointments. In fact, positions in Schedules A and B are generally referred to as "career type."

Schedule C consists almost exclusively of positions which are in fact political. These are the appointments to positions from GS-1 through GS-15, which are excepted from the career service and in which appointees are removable at the will of the appointing authority. Even veteran's status is not sufficient to sustain a person in a Schedule C position when the appointing authority wishes an employee to vacate such a position. Schedule C includes chauffeurs, confidential secretaries, and personal aides to noncareer appointees. Many special assistants to bureau and agency heads also are classified in the Schedule C category. Table 1.3 indicates the distribution of Schedule C positions by grade and by department. It is easy to see that there are wide differences in the use of Schedule C by the various departments and agencies, with the science agencies tending to have the fewest Schedule C positions. Also, few Schedule C's qualify as "executives." However, a small number of them are specifically authorized at the supergrade level by statutes which never have been revised to convert them to NEAs.

Presidential Appointees

The most significant political executives are presidential appointees. The president appoints the secretaries of the twelve cabinet departments, as well as their under secretaries, deputy under secretaries, and assistant secretaries. He also appoints the heads of various agencies not in the cabinet and the commissioners of the regulatory agencies, the so-called fourth branch of the government (Federal Communications Commission, Interstate Commerce Commission, National Labor Relations Board, etc.). The president also appoints ambassadors, some of whom are career and some of whom are political.

All twelve cabinet heads are classified in Level I of the Executive Schedule. The only other position classified at Level I is the special representative for trade negotiations. Salary for these positions is $65,000 per year. Heads of agencies such as the Agency for International Development, the National Aeronautics and Space Administration, the United States Information Agency, and the Veterans Administration are classified at Level II of the Executive Schedule. Likewise, the director of the Office of Management and Budget, the deputy secretaries of the major agencies, and the secretaries of the three military departments (Air Force, Army, and Navy) are at Level II.

Level III includes the heads of smaller agencies, such as the Secret Service and the U.S. Civil Service Commission, deputies of the executives in Level II, and deputy under secretaries of cabinet departments. The chairpersons of most regulatory agencies are at Level III and the other commissioners of these agencies are at Levels IV or V. Top assistant secretaries with line responsibilities, including the following, are pegged at Level IV: assistant secretary of commerce for science and technology; assistant secretary of HEW for health; assistant secretary of interior for energy and minerals; assistant secretary of treasury for enforcement, operations, and tariff affairs; assistant secretary of state for European affairs; assistant secretary of labor for labor-management relations; and assistant attorney general for the criminal division.

All of the assistant secretaries for administration are at Level V (except in the Defense Department, where they are at Level IV). Cabinet department general counsels usually are graded at Level IV, while agency general counsels are at Level V.

The White House Staff and the Executive Office

A number of the key political appointments made by the president are to the White House staff. The White House staff includes presidential counselors, assistants, and special assistants. For example, Donald Rumsfeld and Robert Finch held counselor rank with President Nixon; Robert Hartmann, John Marsh, and Rogers Morton held counselor rank with President Ford. In the first year of the Carter administration no one held this rank. Instead, President Carter had a number of assistants to the president: assistant for national security (Zbigniew Brzezinski), assistant for domestic affairs and policy (Stuart Eizenstat), assistant to the president, political (Hamilton Jordan), assistant for congressional liaison (Frank Moore), assistant for reorganization (Richard Pettigrew), assistant for public liaison (Margaret Costanza), press secretary to the president (Jody Powell), assistant for cabinet and intergovernmental relations (Jack Watson), and counsel to the president (Robert Lipshutz).

Most of these people were classified at the Level II rank in the Executive Schedule. Below them were a variety of special assistants for specialized areas such as administration, health, consumer affairs, media and public affairs, appointments, special projects, and personnel, among others.

In addition to the immediate White House staff, the Executive Office of the President also includes the Office of the Vice-President, the Council of Economic Advisors, the National Security Council, the Domestic Council, the Office of Management and Budget, and a variety of other specialized offices for science, energy, environment, and international economic policy. All of these offices have key political appointees at the executive levels. Figure 1.1 is a representation of the organization of the Executive Office of the President following President Carter's 1977-1978 reorganization.

The Career and Political Executive Mix

To demonstrate the kinds of relationships that NEA and LEA appointees have with career executives in the federal government, the Office of the Assistant Secretary for Fish, Wildlife, and Parks of the U.S. Department of the Interior has been analyzed (Figure 1.2). It was selected as a good example because it has a significant mix of political and career executives, is a line assistant secretary position, and is large enough to be of interest. The political and career positions at the top levels in that office fall into the categories described in Table 1.4. As can be seen, the assistant secretary, the assistant secretary's two deputies, all three bureau heads, their deputies, and all the special assistants have political or noncareer appointments. Yet the other areas of management responsibility were dominated by career appointees, with only one GS-16 exception. In addition, at the lower grade levels the secretaries to the top political executives were in Schedule C positions. The roles of political and career executives

FIGURE 1.1

Executive Office Reorganization

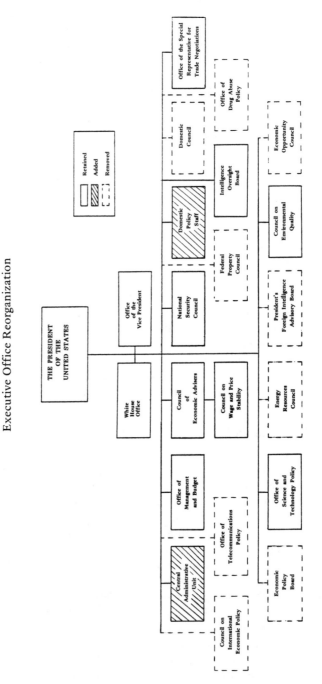

SOURCE: U. S. Office of Management and Budget

FIGURE 1.2

Organization of the Office of the Assistant
Secretary for Fish, Wildlife, and Parks
U.S. Department of the Interior

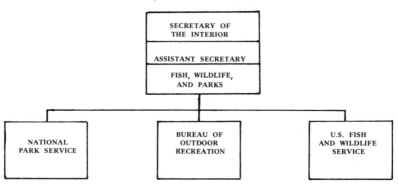

seemed to be clearly separated.

Of the 265 supergrade employees in the Department of the Interior in 1977, 60 were noncareer and 9 of those were in the Office of the Assistant Secretary for Fish, Wildlife, and Parks. However, analysis of the employees in the three bureaus reporting to the assistant secretary showed a drastic difference. Career employees held 25 of the 30 supergrade positions in the headquarters bureau offices. There were no Schedule C employees in the bureaus with the exception of the bureau heads' secretaries.

This suggests that there is a special role for the political executive that may not be appropriate for the career executive. The mix of the two types of executives, however, can create difficulties if the attitudes of the top leadership at the secretary level are not conducive to close collaboration. Nevertheless, if the secretary is to be effective in the long run, ways must be found to mesh the special talents of these two groups.

Types of Assistant Secretaries

Today, there are three major categories of assistant secretaries: staff, line or operational, and those with a combination of roles. It may be helpful to understand which roles are common to all three types.

All three types of assistant secretaries are responsible for representing the president's program to the bureaucracy. Essentially, they serve as bridges between the political and career levels in the

Table 1.4   Political-Career Executive Balance in the Fish, Wildlife, and Parks Units of the Department of the Interior

	Executive level	NEA	LEA	Career supergrades	Schedule C GS 13-15	GS 8-11
The Assistant Secretary for Fish, Wildlife, and Parks	1 (Level IV)					
Deputy assistant secretaries	0	2 (GS 17)	0	0	0	0
Bureau heads	2 (Level V)	1 (GS 17)	0	0	0	0
Deputy bureau heads	0	3 (GS 16) 1 (GS 17)	0	0	0	0
Special assistants	0	1 (GS 16)	0	0	6	4
Assistant and associate directors of major program areas	0	1 (GS 16)	0	3 (GS 17) 6 (GS 16)	0	0
Deputy associate directors	0	0	0	2 (GS 16)	0	0
Regional directors	0	0	0	9 (GS 16)	0	0
Scientific advisors	0	0	0	3 (CS 16)	0	0
Directors (DWRC and NCP)	0	0	0	2 (GS 16)	0	0
Miscellaneous (Western Field Coordinator FWS)	0	0	0	1 (GS 16)	0	0
Total	3	9	0	26	6	4

Source: U.S. Civil Service Commission and Department of the Interior, Washington, D.C.

federal executive branch. They explain the president's actions; they provide leadership for the president's programs; they motivate the bureaucracy, make major administrative decisions, and protect the bureaucracy against unwarranted attacks by Congress, the White House, or outside groups. At times the assistant secretary must "take the rap" for the president or the secretary and sometimes must even resign to solve a political problem. The role always involves listening, feedback, and attempts to establish a working relationship in spite of the mutual suspicions of political and career executives and employees. In some agencies it also involves extensive contact with employee unions.

Depending upon the type of agency and the particular position, an assistant secretary may interact frequently with other assistant secretaries in the department and perhaps in other departments. The nature of the assistant secretary's relationship with the secretary can be crucial to a program's success, as well as to the effectiveness of the assistant secretary's relationship to the bureaucracy. In many cases his or her relationship with regional offices is important in ensuring that the field people are not cut off from the policy level.

Assistant secretaries also have major external responsibilities in representing the president. Selling the president's program to external actors such as the authorization or appropriations committees of the House or Senate is a special challenge. There may also be contact with state and local governments, which sometimes administer federal programs. Assistant secretaries spend considerable time dealing with the media, public interest groups, and various constituencies related to particular programs, as well as with professional associations, industry associations, and individual companies having important ties to the White House, the Congress, or the program.

In all cases, assistant secretaries are involved in translating the president's programs into reality. Promises made or goals set on the campaign trail, in press conferences, or in speeches are rarely thought through; and careful planning of potential programs must be done at a later date. Even after programs have been designed and established, it is important to monitor and evaluate them in terms of the stated objectives and goals.

Another experience that assistant secretaries share is the overcoming of a variety of barriers, organizational and policy conflicts, and simple ambiguities in the context of the particular political climate that relates to their program. This is true whether the assistant secretary is concerned with personnel policy or maritime policy. Often, attempting to respond to these influences leads to conflicts in which the assistant secretary may have difficulty surviving, much less prevailing. Challenges from the bureaucratic system, central agency reviewers, the White House, external powers, and even the Office of the Secretary test the mettle of assistant secretaries.

The titling practices of the federal government are essentially arbitrary. They have grown up over time and may overstate or understate the responsibility of the incumbent in a position. A bureau head who reports to an assistant secretary may in fact be more influential with Congress and outside constituencies than is the assistant secretary. Because of this, the bureau head may even be more influential with the cabinet secretary. On the other hand, sometimes a bureau head or administrator reports directly to the cabinet secretary on the same basis as the assistant secretaries in the same department and really ought to be titled an assistant secretary. In the end, the real differences depend on the abilities of the individuals, the political context in which their department and program are operating, and the specific point in history.

Assistant secretaries, almost by definition, are members of the secretary's own "little cabinet." And just as all secretaries are members of the president's cabinet, but are not necessarily equal in the eyes of the president, the same is true within departments. The cabinet secretary's style and ability are significant factors in the potential success of an assistant secretary, as is the relationship of that secretary with the president and the White House staff. An extremely talented secretary may be frozen out of a particular administration in such a way that his or her assistant secretaries cannot be effective. On the other hand, a secretary with only mediocre personal talents may be able to open up channels of communication with the White House that will facilitate major successes for the assistant secretaries in spite of the secretary. It is a very subjective situation, and each assistant secretary position must be examined on its own terms and in the context of the political climate.

The Staff Assistant Secretaries

Staff assistant secretaries serve as means to the department's ends. That is, they administer programs under the supervision of line or operational assistant secretaries. Most staff assistant secretaries deal with external matters such as congressional relations, public affairs, and international affairs, or with infrastructural matters such as administration, evaluation, and resource allocation.

Assistant Secretary for Administration

All but one of the cabinet departments have an assistant secretary for administration. In some departments, the assistant secretary for administration is responsible for the full range of administrative functions. In others, such as the Department of Health, Education, and Welfare (HEW), other assistant secretaries share that responsibility. During the Ford administration, HEW had an assistant secretary (comptroller). In the Carter administration, this position has been merged with the position of assistant secretary for administration and retitled assistant secretary for administration and management. However, a new position, assistant secretary for personnel and training, was created. Thus, the assistant secretary for administration at HEW, once not responsible for the budget, later was responsible for the budget but not for personnel. Yet budget and personnel are two major concerns for which the position was created.

On the other hand, in the Department of Energy, the director of administration has all the functions of an assistant secretary for administration, including budget and personnel. In submitting its legislative package, the Department of Energy chose to have directors instead of assistant secretaries for the personnel and public affairs positions. Positions as director are not presidential appointments, and the secretary has a bit more flexibility in selecting them. At the same time, this makes the positions somewhat more available to career executives.

Table 1.5 indicates the functions handled by the assistant secretary for administration in the various cabinet departments. It can be seen from the table that differences in titles are arbitrary. Likewise, the table indicates the scope of the responsibility of the director of administration in the Department of Energy. The most common functions of assistant secretaries are management analysis (12), administrative services (12), automated data processing services (11), procurement (11), personnel (10), finance or budget (10), audit or program evaluation (6), and equal employment opportunity enforcement (5). Unique arrangements include the Department of Defense's position of assistant secretary (comptroller), which handles most of the administrative functions; the State Department's arrangement in which the deputy under secretary for management and the assistant secretary for administration share administrative responsibilities; the HEW situation already discussed; and the Department of Energy, where the deputy under secretary and the

Table 1.5 Scope of Departmental Chief Administrator's Duties

Department	Management analysis	Automated data processing services	Administrative services	Equal employment opportunity enforcement	Personnel	Audit/program evaluation	Finance/budget	Procurement
Agriculture	Y	Y	Y	Y	Y	Y	Y	Y
Commerce	Y	Y	Y	Y	Y	Y	Y	Y
Defense	Y	Y	Y	N	N	N	Y	Y
Energy	Y	Y	Y	N	Y	N	N	N
HEW	Y	Y	Y	N	N	N	Y	Y
HUD	Y	Y	Y	N	Y	N	Y	Y
Interior	Y	Y	Y	N	Y	Y	Y	Y
Justice	Y	Y	Y	N	Y	Y	Y	Y
Labor	Y	Y	Y	Y	Y	Y	Y	Y
State	Y	Y	Y	Y	Y	N	Y	Y
Transportation	Y	N	Y	N	Y	N	N	Y
Treasury	Y	Y	Y	Y	Y	Y	Y	Y

Note: Y = yes; N = no. Titles are "assistant secretary for administration" except Defense, assistant secretary (comptroller); Energy, director of administration; HEW, assistant secretary for management and budget; Interior, assistant secretary for policy, budget, and administration; Justice, assistant attorney general for management and finance; Labor, assistant secretary for administration and management; State, deputy under secretary for management and assistant secretary for administration.

director of administration each have major responsibility for administration.

In addition, there is a growing movement to establish the position of "inspector general." The Departments of Energy, Housing and Urban Development (HUD), and HEW already have such positions. Further, a number of members of Congress have proposed legislation that would accomplish this objective. Investigation and internal audits are handled by the inspector general, thus changing the responsibility of the assistant secretary for administration. Indeed, in those agencies with an inspector general, the function of ombudsman tends to develop and be handled there, whereas it might otherwise be handled in some office reporting to the assistant secretary for administration.

In some agencies, equal opportunity enforcement is the responsibility of the assistant secretary for administration. Other agencies have a special assistant to the secretary for equal employment opportunity. Through the special assistant, contractors or persons in the agency with a grievance have direct access to the Office of the Secretary without being screened by the assistant secretary for administration, whose office very likely contains the organizational unit that is the object of the complaint.

President Carter's 1977-1978 Personnel Reorganization Project recommended that the position of assistant secretary for personnel and training be established in each department. This was an attempt by the leadership of the U.S. Civil Service Commission to ensure that personnel management would receive more direct attention from cabinet secretaries. Considering that the people in the various departments are the major resource available to a secretary, it was argued, it made little sense to subordinate the personnel function. The project therefore recommended that the cabinet secretary provide direct leadership and orders for the person responsible for implementing personnel management in the department. This was the model selected in the Department of Health, Education, and Welfare.

Yet it certainly may be argued that personnel is so directly related to other functions—such as management analysis, budget, and equal opportunity—that it ought not be separated, and that some official below the secretary should be responsible for integrating and balancing all the forces that influence administration, including personnel. It may also be argued that the departments have such different missions, and the cabinet secretaries have such different personal management styles, that it would be best to leave them free to

Table 1.6. Types of Roles for
Administrative Assistant Secretaries

	Leader/ motivator	Advocate with/ for?	No-sayer for secretary
External			
Congress	---	---	---
White House	---	---	---
Office of Management and Budget	---	X	---
Civil Service Commission/ General Services Admin.	---	X	---
Other agencies	---	---	X denying use of facilitator
Agency constituencies	---	---	---
State and local grants	---	---	---
Private industry	---	---	---
Nonprofit public interest groups (nongovernment: Nader, Common Cause)	---	X example: the CSC reform	---
Internal			
Staff:			
Career	X	X	X
Political	X	---	X
Other assistant secretaries:			
Staff	X	X	X
Program	X	---	X
The secretary and under secretary	X	X to some extent	---

Table 1.6. (cont.)

Explainer/ apologist/ communicator	Lightning rod for secretary	Mediator/ negotiator	Resolver/ decision maker	Enforcer	Policy formulator
X	X contracting out for	---	---	---	---
X	X	---	---	---	---
X	X	X	X	---	X
X	X	X	X	X	X
X	---	X	X	---	X
---	---	---	---	---	---
---	---	---	---	---	---
---	---	---	---	---	---
---	---	---	---	---	---
X	X	X	X	X	X
X	X	X	X	--- (sec'ys)	--- shared with sec'y
X	X	X	X	---*	X
X	X	X	X	---*	X
--- for CSC, OMB, GSA, etc.	---	---	X	---*	---

* covered in no-sayer.

organize their departments in the way they found best.

Nevertheless, functional specialists historically have little patience with such arguments and believe that structural considerations, such as having direct access to the secretary, will strengthen the hand of the person responsible for a function. This is undoubtedly true where the secretary is receptive; however, some cabinet secretaries are unreceptive and do not want to spend the time required for a particular function. In the latter case, even the title of assistant secretary will not necessarily lead to more contact or more leverage within the organization.

Table 1.6 shows the various roles of the assistant secretary for administration and indicates the substantial emphasis on interaction with central agencies such as the Civil Service Commission, the Office of Management and Budget, and the General Services Administration. There is a less direct relationship to outside pressure groups since the policies being determined by an assistant secretary for administration concern procedural matters rather than broader questions affecting interest groups. It has been said that while substantive assistant secretaries must cope with outside pressure groups, the assistant secretary for administration must cope with the numerous books of rules promulgated by agencies such as CSC, OMB, and GSA.

Assistant Secretary for Congressional Relations

Ten of the twelve cabinet agencies have an assistant secretary for congressional relations. Titles used by the various departments include the following: assistant secretary for legislative affairs (Defense Department), assistant secretary for legislation (HEW, Labor), and assistant secretary for legislative affairs and intergovernmental relations (HUD). The two departments without an assistant secretary in this capacity (Agriculture and Interior) have a director for congressional affairs.

The assistant secretary for congressional relations spends most of his or her time representing the interests of the secretary and the department on Capitol Hill and with the White House congressional relations staff. The fact that the president has his own assistant for congressional liaison means that no major department or agency can afford to carry on its congressional relationship independent of the White House. In many cases the department may be asked to subordinate its own interests to the broader interests of the White House, which may be attempting to work out a trade or a compromise of some sort with a key congressional committee. Often departmental congressional offices are asked to support White House legislative objectives, thus harnessing the special relationships the department may have with key members of Congress.

The assistant director for congressional relations in the Office of Management and Budget is important to assistant secretaries for congressional relations. Again, when a department of the federal government deals with Congress, it must do so in the context of representing the president. But historically, departments and agencies have developed their own relationships with authorization and appropriations committees and subcommittees, often to the detriment of the president's program. In an attempt to control some of this departmental entrepreneurship, the process of legislative clearance with the assistant director of OMB was established, in which departments responding to questions from Capitol Hill must clear their responses with OMB if the response has any financial implications. Even if it does not, departments must clear policy proposals or responses to Congress with the OMB legislative office to ensure compatibility with the president's overall program.

An annual problem is testifying on the department's budget. Departmental witnesses must insist to Congress that they are appearing in defense of the President's budget, which normally includes a reduction in the department's request. However, subcommittee members in Congress frequently attempt to elicit from departmental witnesses testimony to the effect that they consider a particular cutback by OMB or the president to be against the best interests of their program and the nation's welfare. The White House view is that all witnesses are there to defend the president's budget and that only the president has the overview and the comprehensive responsibility to weigh the needs of one program against another. In many cases, departments can get into hot water if the White House questions their allegiance during budget testimony. The temptation is strong to respond to congressional questions in ways that will lead to additional funding. The president's confidence in a department can be severely shaken if he suspects that the department has, for its own benefit, armed members of Congress with questions embarrassing to the White House.

Departmental activities with regard to the congressional function are restricted in certain ways. For example, Section 18 of the U.S. Code 1913 provides that agencies are not permitted to lobby with public money. In some cases departments have abused this, and Congress has responded sharply by cutting appropriations or otherwise restricting the agencies. The only justification for the existence of departmental congressional offices is to process congressional requests for information or to provide information and services for their constituents.

Assistant Secretary for Public Affairs

Four cabinet agencies have an assistant secretary for public affairs. The Departments of Energy, Agriculture, Commerce, Interior, Justice, and Transportation have elected to designate their officials responsible for this function as director of public affairs. The Department of Housing and Urban Development calls the position assistant to the secretary for public affairs, and Labor has a special assistant for public affairs.

As the result of various "sunshine" laws, federal agencies must conduct their business in full public view. Major newspapers, television stations, magazines, and other representatives of the media have significant staffs stationed in Washington whose daily function is to get information from agency media and public information specialists about departmental programs considered by the media to be of interest to the public.

Since all agency action and inaction, decisions and indecision can expect to come under the glare of the public spotlight, numerous matters require the talents of a communications specialist. For example, media representatives compete to get the story of a major event, and the cabinet department must be very careful that the representatives feel that they have had a fair shake in getting the information. If an inside story is leaked to one newspaper, magazine, or television network, the benefit of the favorable treatment by that media outlet is soon offset by criticism from the others regarding the process and the reasons why such favorable treatment was sought or provided.

The demand for media relations is so extensive that a very large office is sometimes necessary. The Department of Defense has 296 employees reporting to the assistant secretary for public affairs, and the State Department has 129 employees (according to information obtained from telephone calls to the appropriate offices on February 9, 1978). However, strong congressional forces oppose the establishment of large public affairs offices. Congress is not interested in funding a gigantic propaganda machine to promote the programs of any particular federal department. On the other hand, the public needs information, and the media certainly demands service. Therefore, from time to time, departments have attempted to "hide" public affairs personnel in operating departments to prevent Congress from knowing how much they were spending on the mission of providing public information. The impact on Congress, of course, is that an effective public affairs office can help generate very favorable public opinion toward a program or department, which can then be used to pressure Congress for larger appropriations or for the approval of programs that it otherwise might be inclined to reject.

Public affairs offices are responsible not only for handling questions from the press and public, but also for taking the initiative by preparing pamphlets and press releases for public consumption. Many public affairs offices write the speeches of the department's top representatives. Very often the departments provide exhibits to shopping centers, educational institutions, and other organizations with the intention, naturally, of creating a favorable impression for its programs.

A close relationship exists between the programs of the assistant secretary for public affairs and the assistant secretary for congressional relations. Often requests received by a department from Congress can be satisfied with an exhibit, a pamphlet, or an explanation already prepared by public affairs personnel. Frequently, members of Congress call or write to secure a speaker from the department, and this may fit in with the assistant secretary's plans to publicize a particular departmental position.

Another task of media specialists in the Office of the Assistant Secretary for Public Affairs is to make recommendations to the secretary about where he or she should spend time making speeches. It is the business of this office to know what organizations are likely to have the most influence on public opinion and where media coverage will be the best.

Assistant Secretary for International Affairs

While most cabinet agencies have some international involvement, only six have an assistant secretary for that function. In the State Department, of course, essentially all the assistant secretaries deal with international affairs. While in many cases they have line authority over international programs, the kinds of functions that other cabinet departments delegate to an international staff position are handled in the State Department by the assistant secretary for educational and cultural affairs or the assistant secretary for international organizational affairs.

Some agencies have programs that require participation by foreign scientists and engineers (Commerce, Defense, Transportation). Some require access to foreign facilities (Defense); others have an impact on foreign markets (Agriculture, Commerce, Labor, and Transportation) or foreign policy (Defense and State). Conversely, involvement with citizens or governments of foreign countries may result from a need to defend American interests, as when high unemployment levels or trade deficits focus attention on foreign imports.

The assistant secretary for international affairs often serves as a specialized public affairs officer dealing with the foreign media and attempting to influence foreign public opinion. To this extent, he or she may lean rather heavily on the assistant secretary for public affairs or the United States Information Agency.

In many cases departmental programs depend upon cooperative efforts in the international scientific community. A weather satellite to be launched from Cape Canaveral, for example, may include experiments from French, Japanese, and American scientists. The success of the experiments may lead to programs that require the use of ground facilities throughout the world. Securing approval for such facilities may depend upon convincing other countries, particularly those in the Third World, that the facilities will be used strictly for peaceful scientific rather than military purposes. This requires influencing foreign opinion through the media as well as negotiating directly with the foreign governments.

Assistant Secretary for Evaluation

This position now exists in five departments (Defense, Energy, HEW, HUD, and Labor), and it is relatively new in all cases. Its development is an attempt to respond to congressional and public criticism of the expensive programs of some agencies and departments. In many cases the amount of money involved is so great that assurance is necessary that the program is achieving its objectives and that there are no unforeseen negative consequences.

Accomplishing this requires the establishment of an independent office to measure a program's results and evaluate its effectiveness. To some extent it is analogous to the financial audit, which requires an independent auditor. (Those with the most to gain from a favorable report naturally will be tempted to evaluate their own programs through rose-colored glasses.)

Another factor influencing the establishment of this position has been the gradual expansion of the role of the General Accounting Office in evaluating the effectiveness of federal programs. Agencies that want to improve their ability to respond to criticism from GAO find it useful to have an office capable of anticipating GAO audit people's reactions and providing Congress with measures for evaluating departmental expenditures.

Some departments have elected not to establish a central position for program evaluation. An alternative approach is to establish a unit in each major operating program that reports independently to the assistant secretary or the bureau director in charge of the program. In other cases, the function exists in the department but has not yet attained assistant secretary status. In the Departments of Commerce and Treasury, the person in charge of evaluation reports to the assistant secretary for administration.

General Counsels

No department has a position titled "assistant secretary for legal affairs." However, the general counsel is essentially a staff assistant secretary responsible for the legal affairs of the department and for advising the secretary in a variety of ways. Yet there are some differences. For example, the job in the Department of Justice, handled by the assistant attorney general in charge of the Office of Legal Counsel, is really a hybrid position: although it is the department's legal office, it also issues policy statements that guide activities of general counsels in other departments, especially with regard to questions of civil and criminal law. Likewise, although the General Accounting Office is an agency of Congress, not a cabinet department, its general counsel serves in a hybrid role. In addition to being the legal office within GAO, the general counsel is responsible for rendering decisions that guide all other government agencies in procedures and policies for expenditure of public funds.

There should be no mistaking the fact that the internal operating programs of a major department are heavily affected by legal considerations arising out of staff work of the general counsel. For example, John Rhinelander, the under secretary of HUD, who had been general counsel of HEW, has pointed out that when he took on the job "we had the impoundment lawsuits; we had half of our civil rights offices being run by the district court judges. We had Social Security with its problems with the computer and which gave us such legal problems that today over ten percent of the cases in the federal courts now come from the Social Security Administration."* Given such a situation, the value of the office of the general counsel is

---

*All quoted material in this chapter, unless otherwise noted, is from Thomas P. Murphy, Donald E. Nuechterlein, and Ronald J. Stupak, eds., *The President's Program Directors: The Assistant Secretaries* (Charlottesville, Va.: Federal Executive Institute, 1977).

obvious. It would be foolish to develop a. program without attempting to anticipate the legal problems that might result.

Another factor that leads to major involvement by the general counsel is that there is much more personnel flexibility in the office of the general counsel. Lawyers there hold Schedule A appointments, an exception from the regular career service. This means that it is easier to reassign and hire attorneys to get things done. John Rhinelander pointed out that

> one reason . . . that the general counsel's office frequently assumes greater power than they probably should have is that you have a lot of flexibility in hiring the general counsel's staff. Lawyers by tradition either are, or think they are, great generalists; and you find out that people look to the general counsel to pick up a lot of things that ought to be handled elsewhere. The Defense Department is a classic case. The deputy there . . . has been acting general counsel more than he's been deputy. The general counsel at DOD has frequently been the key special assistant to the secretary of defense, handling hot situations all over the place.

Miscellaneous Staff Assistant Secretaries

A number of new staff assistant secretary positions have developed in recent years. For example, under the Nixon and Ford administrations there was an assistant secretary for environment, safety, and consumer affairs in the Department of Transportation. This position has been abolished in the Carter administration and its functions reassigned. Consumer affairs are now the responsibility of the director of the Office of Public and Consumer Affairs, a staff office. Environmental and safety affairs are now the responsibility of the assistant secretary for policy, plans, and international affairs. Another position is HUD's assistant secretary for neighborhoods, voluntary associations, and consumer protection. (Given sufficient resources, this office would branch out to conduct programs, and in that case it would become a hybrid staff-line position.)

Operational Assistant Secretaries

Most early assistant secretaries were persons known to the president and loyal to him. They acted as general assistants, aiding the secretary in managing and directing the department's various branches. However, by 1978 almost all assistant secretaries had specialized areas of responsibility, either in a staff or line capacity. But line responsibility does not mean watching over just one program. Most single programs are administered by bureau chiefs, directors, or persons with titles other than assistant secretary. For the most part, line assistant secretaries are like group vice presidents in industry in that they oversee several line operations headed by bureau directors or administrators.

To show this transition over time, it may help to see how some cabinet departments have developed. In the Department of Agriculture, the number of assistant secretaries and number of programs have increased substantially since 1950, as shown below:

	Number of assistant secretaries	Average no. program chiefs reporting to each assistant secretary	Total
1950	1	0	1
1960	4	3	16
1978	7	4	35

Another example is the Department of Labor:

	Number of assistant secretaries	Average no. program chiefs reporting to each assistant secretary	Total
1950	4	0	4
1960	4	2	12
1970	6	4	30

For the Treasury Department, the data are as follows:

	Number of assistant secretaries	Average no. program chiefs reporting to each assistant secretary	Total
1950	3	0	3
1960	5	2	15
1977	8	3	32

At Treasury, the number of people between the assistant secretaries and the secretary has also increased. In 1960 the assistant secretaries and bureau directors reported to a secretary and an under secretary; by 1978 the secretary was assisted by a deputy secretary and two under secretaries. The various assistant secretaries report to one of the under secretaries, both of whom report to the deputy secretary and the secretary. Treasury almost had three under secretaries, because when Laurence Woodworth was recruited from the Senate Finance Committee staff to handle tax programs, it was expected that the position would be designated under secretary for tax affairs. But the title remained unchanged—assistant secretary for tax policy.

The assistant secretary for enforcement, operations, and tariff affairs in the Treasury Department is a good example of an operational assistant secretary. Three major organizational segments reported to this assistant secretary—the Bureau of Customs, the Secret Service, and the Bureau of Alcohol, Tobacco, and Firearms. Each program was headed by a strong executive, a political appointee whose background was that of a career executive. Thus, the assistant secretary functioned basically as a group vice president. He did not directly control any of the line programs, yet he was clearly a line official since the executives reported to him and he was responsible to the secretary for all the substantive policies of the bureaus.

David Macdonald, who held this position from 1975 to 1976, made a key point regarding the position and the role of the assistant secretary:

> One of the things that the political appointee, and particularly the assistant secretary, can do is to utilize his own expendability. The fact that he doesn't have to stay around, and in fact won't stay around, is an asset which permits him to be an advocate for his own bureau where advocacy is appropriate; and to protect his people, and be the politically expendable appointee when the bureau is attacked by Congress or by individual congressmen or women. I remember when Congresswoman Bella Abzug came after the Secret Service which she felt was attacking individual rights. The Secret Service felt it was using procedures which were proper and required in order to protect the president. The Secret Service is an excellent organization, but like most career-oriented organizations, it is not conditioned to respond to that kind of political attack. At that point, I think it is essential for the political appointee to stand up and defend his agency if that is, in fact, his judgment.

One interesting development in cabinet departments has been that some assistant secretaries play both staff and line roles. Such hybrid responsibilities in some cases are established from the start, while in others they evolve over time. For example, the assistant secretary for health in the Department of Health, Education, and Welfare was converted from a strictly staff position to a more line-oriented position in the 1970s. While it was a staff position, the assistant secretary reported directly to the secretary of HEW, but a number of very strong organizations such as the Food and Drug Administration, the U.S. Public Health Service, and the National Institutes of Health (NIH) had commissioners or directors who also reported directly. Strength in such a staff role was impossible unless the secretary either gave the assistant secretary clear-cut support or had so little interest in the whole field that he or she chose to deal primarily with the assistant secretary as a way of limiting the secretary's exposure to the bureau heads.

Ted Cooper, who held this position from 1975 to 1977, noted that the bureaucracy seriously questioned "whether an Assistant Secretary of Health [was] really even necessary" when it was a staff position. When the secretary revised the organization and made the assistant secretary a line official, he then looked to the assistant secretary to coordinate and evaluate the activities of these major operating bureaus. The change had a major effect internally in the sense that "the character and the strength of the office were really strengthened in the eyes of the inside constituency. The interests of our Secretary were being expressed organizationally."

Nevertheless, even with this official expression of the secretary's desires, the changeover was not automatic or total. Heads of prestigious operating units with a history of direct contact with the secretary were not about to give up that channel of communication. They used a variety of techniques to maintain some contact. Further, the director of NIH and the commissioner of the Food and Drug Administration had very powerful outside constituencies who did not see it in their interests to report to the assistant secretary instead of to the secretary. All this meant that the assistant secretary for health had to tread very carefully.

In a comment on his change from a staff to a line role, Cooper noted, "My role is an evolving one that is greatly marked by its superiors, is greatly marked by the political climate, is greatly marked by the public constituencies, and is traditionally evaluated and either supported or opposed by a very strong bureaucracy with great constituencies of its own."

When HEW Secretary David Matthews left office and was replaced

under the Carter administration by Joseph Califano, the nature of the
position of assistant secretary changed further. The secretary
appointed a new assistant, and the three unit heads were left with no
direct relationship to the secretary. Among the many major internal
decisions the new secretary made was one to fire the long-time director of the National Institute of Mental Health (NIMH). This took
time and involved a great deal of attention by the media and reaction
from the professional mental health community. Nevertheless, in
January 1978, NIMH Director Bertram Brown was reassigned to the
position of assistant to the assistant secretary for health, following
Secretary Califano's announcement in December that Brown was no
longer the head of the NIMH. It had taken several months of
negotiations for HEW to find an appropriate medical position to
which Brown, a career medical officer, could be assigned so that a new
director of NIMH could be selected.

This lengthy and touchy personnel process indicates that even an
aggressive secretary in the second-largest cabinet department cannot
make high-level changes in a major operating bureau without
considering the effect of powerful external forces. One can imagine,
therefore, the frustration of an HEW assistant secretary who attempts
to make a change about which the secretary is not particularly
concerned. Assistant secretaries need to be able to mobilize the
bureaucracy and collaborate with entrenched career executives, who,
in most cases, will survive several assistant secretaries before retiring
or leaving.

A major distinction between staff assistant secretaries and those
with line or operating responsibilities is that the latter are much more
likely to have extensive involvement with outside constituencies.
This is true in the Departments of Agriculture, Commerce, Interior,
Labor, and Treasury as well as in the various health bureaus of the
Department of Health, Education, and Welfare. Representing the
president and the secretary to these outside constituencies is one of the
continuing primary roles of the assistant secretary. If the constituency
is powerful enough, the assistant secretary occasionally will be
responsible for bringing in the secretary, the vice-president, or even
the president to demonstrate the administration's stand on issues important to that constituency.

As Bill Kolberg, assistant secretary of labor for Employment and
Training, put it, strong influences come from

> both ends of Pennsylvania Avenue—the White House (and all the
> associated agencies there) and in Congress. All of us, I think, have

powerful outside constituencies which must be satisfied. There are certain places where you must appear; certain clientele groups you must speak before; and if you don't understand your role and your job, you will be "punished" for it in one way or another. Your role is circumscribed in the sense that there are expectations from outside groups which you must meet. There are certain congressional committees where no one else can appear and do a decent job because of the role that is expected of an assistant secretary.

David Taylor, assistant secretary for Manpower and Reserve Affairs in the Department of Defense, agreed that

an assistant secretary is operating at his hazard if he dismisses any group of constituents that is necessary for the performance of his role. Surely, in our business we have a wide variety of special interest groups—the reserves, the National Guard, the Veterans Association, the association that represents active duty people—to be concerned about, but it's important for these people to know that they are respected. You have to get that message across to them, and it's just one of the things you have to do so that it does not necessarily become a burden. But it's very easy for a newcomer, I would suppose, to come in and say, "I don't need you, I can send somebody else; I can send a subordinate to deal with this crowd or that crowd." But, I say, I think it's done at that individual's peril.

* * *

Assistant secretary positions are not alike. They vary depending upon the president and secretary served, societal pressures, and precedents relating to the job, the department, and the department's relationship to the public, to Congress, and to the White House. These factors influence the position, which in turn is shaped by the background and energies of the individual assistant secretary. In the next chapter we shall explore in greater depth the art of playing the role of assistant secretary—using the assistant secretaries' own words.

Notes

1. U.S. Civil Service Commission, Bureau of Executive Personnel, "Career Patterns of Executive Branch Supergrades and Public Law Equivalents Under CSC Purview," Washington, D.C.: U.S. Government Printing Office, 1972.

2. U.S. Civil Service Commission, Bureau of Executive Personnel, "Non-Career Supergrade Government Employees Who Have Moved Directly into Career Government Positions," 1977. This report was prepared at the request of the House Committee on Government Operations. See also the bureau's report titled "Reports on Supergrades Who Have Served in Schedule C or Non-Career Executive Assignments and Have Moved into Career Positions," June 1977.

2
Playing the Role
of Assistant Secretary

The requirements of today and those of the future are so great that the services of the best minds in the Nation must be secured if governmental affairs are to be conducted in the manner demanded by modern conditions and at the high level of ability which a democratic Government owes to the people of the United States.

— Franklin D. Roosevelt

Some assistant secretary positions require very specific qualifications that influence behavior and role. It would be unthinkable to have an assistant secretary for labor management who had not had extensive involvement with labor relations. Likewise, the Commerce Department's assistant secretary for maritime affairs, who is in charge of the entire federal program relating to the maritime industry, must have a background in that industry. The same is true of the assistant secretary for energy and minerals in the Department of Interior. A legal education and experience are absolutely essential for any general counsel position. Very often the general counsel also has experience in applying the law to the particular areas of the department.

On the other hand, an assistant secretary for administration in the Department of Housing and Urban Development need not have a background in housing and could have earned his or her experience in fields such as budgeting, personnel, procurement, administrative services, or information systems. Likewise, HEW's assistant secretary for planning and evaluation is likely to be someone with extensive experience in health, education, or welfare—but probably not in all three areas; the scope of the department is just too broad. Yet the primary criteria for such a position is analytic ability, and it is conceivable that a person with a social science, business, or even an engineering or scientific background may be considered.

Specific criteria for an assistant secretary position may vary over time depending upon the issues that are expected to predominate. Sometimes general knowledge is the most valuable trait, and at other times very specific substantive knowledge may be essential. In positions such as assistant secretary for administration, government experience is very helpful. Yet, sometimes a line assistant secretary in a department with frequent and intense policy disputes would find prior government experience a hindrance, because it might affect his or her credibility with insecure constituent groups. Generally, line assistant secretaries have a wider range of backgrounds than do staff assistant secretaries. In some departments experience in state or local governments is very helpful, because many federal programs are implemented by state and local program managers.

The British approach of using broad generalists to fill top policy positions is not the normal practice in the American system. It may be that the top political offices in the United States are filled by people whose backgrounds are as elite as those of the British generalists. However, at the secondary level of the assistant secretary, a much higher percentage of political executives are specialists. Further, in the American system, the opportunity is greater for career executives to work their way from the bottom to the top.

The Representation Role and the Other Political Executives

One of the most significant relationships of an assistant secretary is with the department secretary. As Labor Assistant Secretary Fred Clark stated, "The strategies or techniques that an assistant secretary must of necessity develop depend to a large degree on the style of the boss . . . and the ability of that assistant secretary to learn that style as rapidly as possible and to be flexible enough to adjust to that style. If any change is necessary, it is the assistant secretary—not the secretary—who must change."*

Michael Moskow, who was an assistant secretary in the Department of Labor and HUD as well as an under secretary in the Department of Labor, pointed out that the relationship between the secretary and the under secretary is very crucial for assistant secretaries:

> In some cases, the secretary does not want to run the agency on a daily basis and he assigns that to his under secretary, thus the under secretary is in constant touch with the secretary so that he can reflect the secretary's views on a daily basis as he deals with the assistant

---

*All quoted material in this chapter, unless otherwise noted, is from Thomas P. Murphy, Donald E. Nuechterlein, and Ronald J. Stupak, eds., *The President's Program Directors: The Assistant Secretaries* (Charlottesville, Va.: Federal Executive Institute, 1977).

secretaries. . . . In other cases, the under secretary performs special assignments or special functions that the secretary has assigned to him, meaning that he does not have that line responsibility for operating the agency on a daily basis.

The question of management style also exists at the assistant secretary level. Some assistant secretaries spend most of their time managing individual programs. Others, however, delegate that responsibility to a deputy assistant secretary and instead spend most of their time working with outside constituencies. It depends upon the assistant secretary's relationship with the secretary and the under secretary, the nature of the program, the political climate, and the nature of the outside constituencies, as well as the backgrounds of the assistant and deputy assistant secretaries.

The distinction made earlier between line and staff assistant secretaries is a real one, despite the fact that many have hybrid roles. An assistant secretary responsible for a major program will have contact with other assistant secretaries in the department whose programs have an impact on his or her program. In many cases there is very little interaction, even in the same agency. Frequently, however, political executives in other departments or agencies run programs that bear significantly on programs for which the assistant secretary is responsible. Often these programs are competitive, and the assistant secretary therefore must be concerned with these relationships and with the potential impact of the programs on their mutual constituencies.

However, no matter whether a particular assistant secretary's programs relate to other programs in or out of the department, he or she certainly will be involved in a substantial number of key decisions involving staff assistant secretaries, especially the assistant secretary for administration and evaluation. The assistant secretary for administration is crucial because of the need to secure the resources to do the job, whether dollars, personnel ceilings, or administrative services. The assistant secretary for evaluation is in the business of second-guessing the line officials, and it is essential that they understand the program so that they will not unnecessarily develop any negative attitudes toward it.

Perspectives of the assistant secretary and the department secretary often differ substantially. For example, in the Department of Transportation, a variety of frequently conflicting interests are represented by the various programs. The Federal Aviation Administration is to some extent in conflict with the Federal

Highway Administration, as well as the Coast Guard, which has its own transportation interests. Further, the U.S. Army Corps of Engineers is closely tied to the waterway transportation industry, which frequently competes with the trucking industry, highway builders, and even the air cargo industry. An assistant secretary or other political executive who heads a program in such a department must operate as a partisan for his or her particular mode of transportation. The secretary of the department, on the other hand, is frequently cast in the role of arbiter among competing interests. To some extent, then, an assistant secretary with a partisan approach to a program will have some difficulty representing the views of the secretary, whether in Congress, with the constituencies, or with the media.

To some extent, there can be a conflict between the policymaking role and the management role for assistant secretaries. Judith Connor, assistant secretary for Environment, Safety, and Consumer Affairs in the Department of Transportation, stated:

> I thoroughly enjoy the policy function and working with a secretary like Bill Coleman. He is so exciting as far as policymaking goes and he is so anxious to be personally involved in the major issues of the Department that you tend to get very much involved in policy yourself. In fact, I think he measures the performance of his political executives relevant to their role in a policymaking function. On the other hand, if you have a long-run interest in management and in strengthening your own organization within the time frame you expect to have, you more or less have to use extra energies.

The Representation Role and the Career Bureaucracy

One major function of an assistant secretary is to represent the secretary and the president to the career bureaucracy. By title and image, the assistant secretary represents to the bureaucracy that part of the executive level with which they may reasonably expect to have some contact. In this regard, Bradley Patterson, a former White House staff member under three presidents, indicated that "in order to be an effective advocate of the president's programs back to the bureaucracy . . . an assistant secretary has to speak credibly about those programs."

Patterson asked twenty assistant secretaries, most of whom had served under President Nixon and all of whom were serving under President Ford, how much contact they had with the president. They said that generally contact with President Ford had been satisfactory, but contact with President Nixon had not. The consensus was that contact had been limited with both presidents, but that President Ford had been more willing to permit a program's top official to explain his case before major decisions were made. A number of assistant secretaries said that although they may have lost the argument, they at least felt they had had a chance to present their case and that the president fully considered it. Jack Young, HEW's assistant secretary (comptroller), reported that President Ford had permitted the secretary to include the appropriate program directors in such discussions. This removed a tremendous burden from the assistant secretary responsible for budgeting, who otherwise would have had total responsibility for convincing the president of the merits of the needs presented by the operating assistant secretaries.

On the other hand, HUD Assistant Secretary Charles Orlebeke noted that he did not believe "an assistant secretary ought to expect regular access to the president. The assistant secretary's representative to the president is normally the secretary." Orlebeke had met only twice with President Ford, but added, "I don't feel deprived on that account. I feel that my boss, Secretary Hills, has had good access to the president."

An assistant secretary must provide dynamism and inject new ideas into an organization. Assistant Secretary of the Army for Manpower and Reserve Affairs Donald Brotzman noted that an assistant secretary ought to be able "to bring something dynamic from his or her experience, knowledgeability, or dedication to this thing called government. Within the charters that we have and how we perceive them, and because of the assistant secretaries' temporariness, we have a special role to play. I think that part of our role is to [provide] the bureaucracy a 'shot in the arm.' " Brotzman had been a member of Congress for ten years and felt that his special contribution might be to point out to other army administrators ways in which members of Congress perceive them as weak.

Another approach was taken by Agriculture Assistant Secretary J. P. Bolduc, who noted:

> I find too few people in the bureaucracy willing to challenge the system. Too few people are willing to take that risk to make it better. I find that there are too many disincentives in the bureaucracy which keep people from trying to change it. . . . We need to encourage risk-taking. . . . Career people look at an assistant secretary to see if he is willing to take that risk. . . . If they find you retreating because you've analyzed it and found that there are so many disincentives, they will get the signal and they will not try to challenge things.

Closely related to the role of providing leadership are motivating the bureaucracy and rewarding quality performance. Al Alm of the Environmental Protection Agency (EPA) pointed out that careerists often outwait their assistant secretaries to accomplish their objectives, and he stressed the need to establish leadership very early in the game. Minimally, he said, an assistant secretary must "get the bureaucracy working with you, but also you must develop a set of priorities and have enough time to really make an impact."

Bill Morrill, who is assistant secretary for evaluation at HEW, stressed the need to "pay attention to 'institution building' and to strengthening and improving that organization for whomever comes after you. . . . One has to pay some attention to specific accomplishments. But it is all too easy to get into the business of doing the sexy political thing of the day while ignoring the longer run." Commenting on the short tenure of assistant secretaries, he added that many "see their roles almost wholly in political terms and what can be accomplished during the course of their tenure. I think a tendency to look at the job in that fashion is in the longer run bound to be a failure."

In addition to providing leadership, an assistant secretary must make decisions and perform administrative functions. Don Brotzman noted that one "must still take care of that paperwork back at the office. You must save time to work with your staff. So, as you serve your secretary, not only do you have responsibility to the public, you have the representational responsibility in the field and on the Hill, but you must also apply yourself to your principal responsibility— the administrative role."

Bill Kolberg expressed a similar opinion:

> The toughest continual conflict and dilemma in these jobs is to try to strike a proper balance between the outside world and your program. It is too easy for someone coming in from the outside and filling a role like this to go on an ego trip and get his kicks giving speeches, appearing on the Hill, and absorbing all the public display. The tough part of this role to me is the disciplined role of administration— insight, motivating people, energizing new ideas, the innovative role; that's what's tough. It is an easy one to overlook. Unless you balance those two roles, I would say that you are not going to be successful.

A number of participants in the conference of assistant secretaries pointed to the problem of overcoming suspicions career people hold regarding political executives. Remarking that "there is a deep and serious distrust between assistant secretaries from the political world and the career staff," Jack Young noted that "if you do not co-opt the bureaucracy effectively as a new political officer, . . . you lose the game."

The Problem of Coordination

Although most conflicts and pressures faced by an assistant secretary derive from his or her interaction with the career bureaucracy and the secretary, other significant pressures include coordination problems within the department and from constituent groups. Assistant Secretary Judith Connor remarked that the powerful bureaus in the Department of Transportation "enjoy a constituency of their own and very often are operating at cross purposes. One of our jobs is to make sure that they are not operating at as many cross purposes as they were prior to consolidating the Department in 1967." Furthermore, HEW Assistant Secretary Bill Morrill remarked that "particularly within a large department, the staff role often is to reconcile department-wide policies or deal with government-wide policies. That leads to clashes in which the leaders themselves—the cabinet secretaries or others—may be a little uncertain as to their authority."

Discussing White House intervention in coordination and policy development, Bradley Patterson noted that many new White House staff positions have been added which have an impact on the role of assistant secretary. White House staff members often are given troubleshooting assignments that require them to delve deeply into the policy development process in cabinet departments. The Domestic Council, he said, is another new institution in the area of cross-departmental policy development. Their involvement in the process raises the question of whether the assistant secretary really can work effectively outside his or her department.

Patterson pointed out specifically that the president has an Office of Public Liaison to deal with minorities, women, and other specialized interests. "These are some of the same client groups that you work with. I am not saying that it is because you can't work with them, or don't, or haven't, that the White House fills in behind you. But, for one reason or another the president feels that he has to have that function in the White House as well." The White House also has an office dealing with state and local governments. Patterson concluded by saying, "it is not any reflection on assistant secretaries, but I think it is partly out of the ambiguities and question marks surrounding the role of cabinet officers and their assistant secretaries, among other reasons, that presidents have felt impelled to pile on machinery in the White House to do some of those tasks.''

Relationships with the Central Administrative Agencies

In terms of total power and access to the president, the Office of Management and Budget (OMB) is the most powerful of the central agencies. The Civil Service Commission (CSC) exists as a quasi-regulatory agency with plural leadership and the sometimes conflicting role of serving as both the president's personal advisor and the protector of the merit system. The General Services Administration (GSA) is headed by a single administrator; but unlike OMB, it is not part of the Executive Office of the President. Instead, it is an independent agency reporting to the president.

All three agencies prescribe numerous procedural steps for agencies and departments operating the federal government. Since the General Accounting Office (GAO) audits to find out if administrative and statutory procedures are followed, there is substantial pressure to conform to the central agencies' requirements. Although they limit the flexibility and discretion of departmental executives, the requirements also protect certain values in the administrative system. The number of interventions by the central agencies in departments' decision-making processes should be reduced without threatening the protection of the values those agencies were established to protect.

Selling the President's Program

A major asset which political executives bring to the bureaucracy is the potential of providing it access to the White House, to OMB, to the secretary, and, in some cases, even to Capitol Hill. Access to Capitol Hill is especially enhanced when a Democrat occupies the White House, since over several decades the congressional committees have been totally controlled by the Democratic Party.

Making the case for the president's program, after achieving OMB support, involves working with Congress and constituencies affected by the program. Besides the appropriations subcommittees, a house of Congress deals with basic legislation, program authorizations, and overseeing the department's operation. Often the agency's major constituency deals with the agency through these congressional channels. As indicated above, the policies and objectives of the agencies and departments frequently are not consistent with those of the president. The same inconsistencies exist on the congressional side of the relationship.

Increasingly, state and local governments have come to depend upon federal money for their programs. This has led to more requests by members of Congress for inclusion in departments' decisions regarding such programs and, at the same time, more complaints about the imposition of federal financial requirements on the programs' operation. Often, assistant secretaries have to explain to state and local governments why presidential policy is what it is.

The media play an essential role in the execution of federal programs. This can create difficulties, because the press, which may not always understand the bureaucratic process or the issues, is free to sit outside the system and criticize compromises that may be essential to secure action. As Under Secretary David Macdonald indicated: "The assistant secretary in particular . . . is the one who has to interpret and translate what is right into what is desirable, and he has to hold his own with the press. I find just holding your own with the media to be a victory."

In almost every case, the major departments have important constituencies concerned with decisions the departments will be making. Some of these groups are organized and powerful, while others are amorphous and unorganized—but all of them need and receive federal aid. For an assistant secretary, "it is very important to learn who the external groups are and what their interests are."

Professional groups are increasingly active in promoting the interests of their members. Although they can be used by the assistant secretary to counter the influence of a specialized constituency such as labor or business, the groups also frequently are aggressive and narrow-minded about their demands. However, since they are comprised of a relatively small number of people with important and needed talents, they are generally able to secure a response to their demands. Assistant secretaries must learn that in many cases these professional associations are advancing their own interests and are not weighing sufficiently the larger public interest. Thus, even though they represent professionals, they must be treated as self-interested parties.

The emerging field of public interest lobbying has had a major impact on the various decisions of Congress as well as on agency operations. In general the influence has been positive, but there are still problems in determining who best represents the public interest and deciding whether such groups are asking for more than is reasonable.

Translating Presidential Initiatives into Programs

Because contact of assistant secretaries with the president and even the White House staff is limited, there often is much confusion about precisely what the president's policy is or should be. Assistant secretaries, along with the rest of the public, can attempt to learn this in a variety of ways.

For example, a new president must cope with his campaign statements. In attempting to secure his party's nomination, a presidential candidate competes against a range of political opponents in a manner designed to show how he is different and how he will provide important leadership. After he wins the nomination, the issues become even more focused, especially when presidential candidates debate each other. After the election, the new president must translate his campaign statements into programs.

The first indication of a president's policies is his first State of the Union message presented in January following the November election. A cafeteria approach to establishing policy priorities, the address is delivered to a joint session of Congress and a national television audience, and so there is a limit to how long the president can talk. Yet all the bureaucratic agencies and all the new appointees to cabinet offices and as heads of agencies, as well as the White House staff and the Office of Management and Budget, have competed for a place in the president's message. Often the address includes only one or two sentences about a specific program for which bureaucrats are responsible.

Especially during the first State of the Union message, the bureaucracy has not created programs to carry out campaign promises, and the president essentially is stating only a policy direction. The job of translating it into a program falls upon line officials in cabinet departments and independent agencies. Many (but not all) of those officials are assistant secretaries, and most assistant secretaries have some role to play in this process.

In the weeks following the State of the Union address, the president submits a series of special messages drafted in the departments under the direction of the assistant secretaries or responsible line officials, cleared by the cabinet secretaries or agency heads, and then run through the gauntlet of the White House staff and the Office of Management and Budget. These messages deal with matters such as financial impact, requirements for additional staffing, and policy considerations as well as questions of political feasibility. After it clears all these barriers, a special message to Congress must be scheduled—a tricky business, because if the president sends up too many special messages at once or when controversial pieces of legislation, nominations, or treaties are being considered, the environment on Capitol Hill may not be appropriate. Further, the workload of the congressional committees that will consider the legislation spawned by the special message must be considered.

The delivery of the special message and even the drafting of the legislation to go with it do not end the development and translation of presidential policy to program. The president continues to refer to the program in speeches in appropriate forums. White House press conferences also communicate his intent to Congress and the public. Further, in his numerous White House meetings with members of Congress, the press, and leaders from business, public interest groups, state and local governments, and foreign nations, the president seeks support for his programs.

Following the approval of a presidential policy and the submission of legislation or a special message or both, the assistant secretaries proceed with detailed program development. Much of this work will already have been done in convincing the White House of the need for the program in the first place. However, as congressional committees begin to conduct public hearings on the question and as organizations with a stake in the new policy make known their feelings about it, assistant secretaries must adjust the implementation plans. Usually several program alternatives are drawn up, and the costs and benefits of each one to each interested party are considered. In some cases, heated debate results, and the assistant secretary must attempt to mediate the positions of the various sides to develop a policy the president can support.

While the matter is being considered in authorization committees and Congress, lobbies or interest groups previously unable to influence the assistant secretary attempt to influence the legislators. This means that the assistant secretary must be prepared to testify frequently, anticipate alternative programs that Congress may suggest, and be able to tell the congressional committees what impact their proposed changes would have on the program's effectiveness.

After the congressional authorization committees, the whole Congress, and eventually the president consider the program, the next step is appropriations. An authorization law is, of course, crucial. However, all it really says is that Congress and the president intend to establish such a program with whatever maximum expenditure level was approved. Authorized totals are often much higher than the amount that can be approved in the appropriations process. The reason for this is simple: people on the authorization committees know more about the program than do the rest of the members of Congress, and generally they are on that committee precisely because they have an interest in the program. Authorization committee members are frequently partisans for the program.

When it comes to a question of dollars, however, the program is no longer competing just in terms of whether it is a good idea; instead, it is competing directly with other programs approved by other authorization committees and the Congress. The plain fact is that there never is sufficient money to pay for all the programs that are approved. Therefore, it is likely that in the appropriations process the authorization level will be reduced substantially. Further, the OMB will get back into the act as the appropriations bill is prepared, and it may advise the president to reduce his request below the authorization.

At this stage, the assistant secretary or another appropriate line official is responsible for dealing with Congress to achieve whatever appropriation is possible. In this respect, the assistant secretary for congressional affairs has an important role: he or she is responsible for strategy, while the assistant secretary for the program actually argues its substantive merits.

Assuming approval of an adequate appropriation, the next problem is to implement the program. Often simplistic assumptions made in the design of the program were not sufficiently challenged during the legislative process, and further adjustments are necessary to make the program realistic. And even a good program plan is not self-executing. The assistant secretary must determine (1) whether the program's objectives are being met and (2) whether the program is being effectively managed so that available resources are adequate. The secretary is also responsible for overseeing the total program of the department. Since critical views often are expressed to the secretary either directly or through Congress, it is essential that these criticisms be communicated back to the program people.

Before and after the program is in full operation, it is essential to devote a substantial amount of time to evaluation. An operating program cannot be evaluated effectively if criteria were not agreed upon earlier. Often congressional committees spell out the kinds of criteria they consider valid which will influence them to approve a program. However, the really intensive program reviews and evaluations must be conducted under the auspices of the executive branch.

Program assistant secretaries are responsible for organizing the evaluation process and for developing clear evaluation criteria. If the department has an assistant secretary for evaluation, the program assistant secretary receives his or her assistance, while still shouldering primary responsibility for the evaluation. In fact, in many cases a central evaluation office means more work for the program assistant secretary. The very fact that the assistant secretary for evaluation reports directly to the secretary and will be intensively analyzing program data demands that the program assistant secretary pay even more attention to the evaluation.

Other influences on the evaluation process include the possibility of an investigation and audit by the GAO of the program's effectiveness. GAO's role has expanded far beyond the simple matter of dollar accountability; it now studies methods of program implementation from the standpoint of efficiency and effectiveness. Even the Congressional Budget Office (CBO), established in 1974, now has a role in evaluation in providing congressional authorization and appropriations committees with analyses of past programs.

Many programs—for example, community development—fall within the jurisdiction of several cabinet departments. For such cases, interdepartmental coordinating committees are often established, with leadership usually vested in the department having the greatest role. This does not work effectively, however, if assistant secretaries from the different departments compete for control of the program or for the job of evaluating it. If such competition exists, the Office of Management and Budget has a greater than normal opportunity to participate in the evaluation.

Barriers, Conflicts, and Ambiguities Influencing Success

An assistant secretary's success depends upon, in addition to personal capabilities, the political climate, the department's relationship with the White House, and the manner in which role conflicts are resolved.

Political and Organizational Environment

Leadership in a cabinet department obviously largely depends on the secretary's personality and style. However, the organizational environment also has an impact on the role of the assistant secretary. The position of an assistant secretary in a department with a strong secretary, little turnover, a good relationship with the White House, and strong congressional support is much different from his position in a department with the opposite characteristics.

Reference has already been made to the significance of a program's constituencies. This matter differs depending on the program area. For example, consider the pressure on the Commerce Department's assistant secretary for maritime affairs. The maritime industry itself is very well organized, the unions in the industry are equally well organized, separate subcommittees in the House and Senate are dedicated totally to maritime affairs, the subject involves negotiations with other nations, and maritime policy is often affected by its real or imagined impact on the defense establishment.

On the other hand, in some other program areas, including ones headed by assistant secretaries, the constituencies are not well organized and the impact is not international or relevant to defense. The constituency served by HEW's Office of Human Development, for example, is diverse, ambiguous, essentially unorganized, and without much political clout. The office's services are important but they do not involve the kinds of pressures associated with international relations and defense. Its programs include services to poor children (Head Start), abused children, runaways, the handicapped, the elderly, the mentally retarded, and native Americans.

The Senate has a subcommittee on child and human development within the Committee on Human Resources, and many other committees and subcommittees are also involved with some aspect of this office's work. The House committee is the Committee on Education and Labor. Especially in the House, issues affecting the Office of Human Development may easily be swallowed up by the broader issues for which the committees and subcommittees are responsible. For maritime affairs, however, members of the relevant subcommittees build much of their reputation in Congress upon what happens in that area, and therefore they are inevitably much more active in pressuring the agency. Further, the assistant secretary who heads a visible and politically potent program area will receive much more attention from the press than will an assistant secretary whose program area is not highly controversial.

All these factors contribute to the organizational environment an assistant secretary faces in attempting to develop and implement program objectives. In many respects, there is not much he or she can do to change that environment. Although assistant secretaries may contribute to the effectiveness of a particular secretary's administration, they have little to say about who the secretary will be. Yet despite the organizational environment, an assistant secretary can do some things to improve relationships with the White House and Congress.

The White House Role

If attention from the press, Congress, and constituent groups is minimal, the White House staff obviously is also less interested in a program. But if interest is high, the White House staff definitely will make its presence felt with the assistant secretary responsible for the program. Bradley Patterson pointed out the following:

> Our presidents . . . have piled on White House machinery for policy development, sometimes including, but often on top of or along side of, the role of assistant secretaries. . . . For example, it was Leonard Garment, rather than the attorney general or the secretary of HEW, who, back in 1970, personally spent three months writing a paper on school busing and the problems of school busing. He spent all three months doing nothing else. And the president didn't turn to any of the assistant secretaries or even secretaries, but instead turned to his White House staff for his policy development role.
>
> The growth of the Domestic Council is another case in the same area. . . . assistant secretaries have their dilemmas, but the president has certain responsibilities and direct concerns as well. . . .
>
> We talked about the role of assistant secretaries vis-à-vis the outside groups as well as the liaison and linkage role they play with outside client groups. Well, the White House evidently must consider that this is not good enough, because the White House has set up an office . . . called the Office of Public Liaison. That office has two or three special officers for liaison with women, two officers for liaison with Spanish-speaking groups, one with Indians, several with blacks, business, veterans, and so forth. These are some of the same client groups that you work with. . . .
>
> You obviously are on the front line in terms of testimony before Congress. But the White House staff, beginning a long time ago, certainly with Eisenhower if not before, has had its own congressional relations staff. . . .
>
> I can think of one other function—the relationship with state and local governments. Again, practically all the programs over which you as assistant secretaries have important line responsibility affect state and local governments. Yet the White House staff also has built into it a special office, as far back as Eisenhower's time and continuing right up until now, for liaison with state and local governments.

Role Conflicts

An assistant secretary may be heavily involved in role conflicts. For example, someone with line responsibility may lose a policy battle within the department, or with the White House or Congress, and yet have the responsibility of implementing the policy. Obviously, if the dispute is serious enough, the assistant secretary may feel that someone else should implement the policy, which may or may not be possible in the department's organizational structure. If it is not, the assistant secretary must decide whether to leave.

Michael Moskow, who had some experience with this problem in HUD and the Department of Labor, said if the assistant secretary handles the situation correctly, he or she should be able to avoid serious difficulties. According to Moskow, assistant secretaries:

> want to have the option; that is, they want to be assured that they will be able to present their views to the person that is making the final decision on a certain policy issue. . . . But obviously the final policy maker—the president or the secretary—is the one making the authoritative decision on the issue. . . . If the policy maker decides against an assistant secretary, then that person has to fall in line and accept the decision of the policy maker in that particular case. Now that's worked out very well in the situations that I've seen. Obviously, if an assistant secretary goes forward with a very strong proposal that his staff has worked on for a long time, and he's ginned everyone up with his confidence that he is going to get it accepted, I think that before he gets to that point, he has to do the base touching that I talked about earlier, otherwise he gets too far out on a limb. In effect, an assistant secretary clearly has problems if he has not performed the intermediate steps that he should have performed.

Another role conflict involves loyalty to the public service as opposed to loyalty to the secretary. Alvin Alm, assistant administrator for Planning and Management at the Environmental Protection Agency, phrased the dilemma as follows:

> Some assistant secretaries have regulatory functions such as being in charge of a merit system within an agency, while on the other hand they are part of the top political management team. These kinds of conflicts are very difficult; for example, dealing with unions and employee groups and the like as an interpreter of the federal personnel system, while on the other hand representing management.

This is the same kind of conflict many study groups have noted regarding the U.S. Civil Service Commission itself. It has attempted to serve both as an impartial arbiter of the merit system and also as the president's personnel management agency. In many respects, these roles conflict, and it is difficult for the agency to perform either one effectively. This was a primary reason that President Carter reorganized the federal personnel system in 1977-1978.

Achieving program objectives with limited resources often causes role conflicts. To attempt to fight inflation or stimulate a sector of the economy, the president may ask his top team to take a general budget cut. Yet, the assistant secretary has come to Washington to develop some pet ideas related to the program area, often with strong support from outside groups, and cutbacks may make his or her plans impossible. The same problem exists regarding implied commitments to career bureaucrats in the program area who are depending on the assistant secretary to represent their interest to the secretary, the White House, and Congress.

Another conflict occurs with attempts to fulfill the commitments of predecessors. In many cases, outside interest groups, potential grant or contract recipients, congressional subcommittees, individual members of Congress, White House staff members, and assistant secretaries in other departments have all received commitments about a program from the assistant secretary's predecessor. Charles Orlebeke noted that

> at the outset, of course, you confront the commitments that have been made by your immediate predecessor. These are commitments which your career officials, as well as other assistant secretaries, have relied upon. You must decide whether simply to go along with these commitments, or assert your right to revoke them. You have to decide whether a commitment made in the last month is as good as one made a year or two previously. A whole range of judgments has to be made of that sort.

Ambiguity also causes role conflict. Very often the uncertainty of his or her standing with the secretary and with other assistant secretaries and departments is a major problem for an assistant secretary. Sometimes the secretary assigns a job to the assistant secretary which other assistant secretaries or program officials believe really should be theirs. In such cases, the secretary should make the assignment very clear—although often the assignment is verbal and no record exists why a particular assistant secretary was selected.

As Bill Morrill of HEW noted,

> particularly within a large department, the staff role often is to reconcile department-wide policies or deal with government-wide policies. That leads to clashes in which the leaders themselves—the cabinet secretaries or others—may be a little uncertain as to their authority. This leaves the assistant secretaries in a wonderful guessing game as to how many issues can in fact be resolved.

Finally, role conflict may involve the bureaucratic drag of the federal system. An assistant secretary with clear ideas of what to do may find it difficult to do them because of the rules of the Civil Service Commission or the Office of Management and Budget. An assistant secretary's great desire to accomplish something specific during his or her short tenure means that some institution building is neglected and some problems are created for future assistant secretaries. John Rhinelander described that problem as follows:

> One of the great problems and one of the great frustrations that people feel when they come into government is the problem which we've been focusing on: the personnel rules, the lack of flexibility, the lack of ability to get people on when you need them, and the lack of the ability to either move them laterally or out if they're not performing. Part of the problem, of course, is the short tenure. People don't wish to spend the time to build the record needed to remove from the service those who are not performing. You'll simply leave it to your successor, and your successor leaves it to his successor, and then this builds up. This is one of the consequences of the short tenure.

Appendix: Excerpts from FEI Symposium Discussion on Executive Roles*

Reports on the Role of the Assistant Secretary

Conklin: The primary question for the first Executive Learning Team report is: "What roles do you perform that are derived from organizational superiors, your subordinates, yourself, outside groups, legislation, and administrative regulations?" The first spokesman for the Red Team will be Bill Kolberg.

Red Team Report

Kolberg: We started out by trying to get behind this question. We talked about the two basic roles that various members of the group had—variations on the line and the staff role. A number of us are not just assistant secretaries in a staff position or policy position but also

---

*From Thomas P. Murphy, Donald E. Nuechterlein, and Ronald J. Stupak, eds., *The President's Program Directors: The Assistant Secretaries* (Charlottesville, Va.: The Federal Executive Institute, 1977).

happen to head an agency in a line sense. It is my understanding that one of my colleagues, Ted Cooper, is in a very similar situation. He is not only an assistant secretary, he is also the top line officer for the health program in HEW. Dave Macdonald served that dual role in Treasury where several major operating programs reported to him. So I think all of us in this room are a mix, and the roles, therefore, differ a great deal. We went around the room and talked across this question. We ended up with a lot of adjectives—about fifteen or twenty of them. Let me just tick off the adjectives and then we'll go back through and see how we got to those various adjectives.

An assistant secretary is as follows: leader, motivator, representer, advocate, mediator/negotiator, enforcer, "no" sayer, cheerleader, resolver, lightning rod, and shock absorber.

Now to get more into the substance, I am going to call on my colleagues to discuss the roles they perform which are derived from their organizational superiors. In most of our cases, what the secretary or the boss wants conditions our behavior in our roles. First let me ask Dick Feltner. Dick used the words "shock absorber," "lightning rod," and "resolver" as related to his secretary and the role that at times the secretary wants him to play.

Feltner: I think that we all agree that different styles of management call for different subordinates to play different roles. In the situation in which I have been operating, Secretary Butz has essentially given his assistant secretaries the freedom, in fact the direction, to operate on their own as much as possible. One of my functions, therefore, is to try to keep as many items as possible from reaching the secretary's level. I must try to resolve everything that I possibly can. As for the shock absorber role, I use that term to indicate that there are times when decisions may in fact be made by the secretary, but then the assistant secretary is the one who is designated to give that decision to someone else. For example, if an outside group has asked for something and the decision is that we cannot respond affirmatively as far as that outside group is concerned, the assistant secretary may be the one who gives them that message. This is done for two or three reasons—the main one being that it provides for an escape hatch. If they are going to be extremely unhappy, then they can always appeal to the secretary if they need to do that.

Kolberg: Ted Cooper is the top health officer in Health, Education, and Welfare, a department which is now headed by an educator. Ted made a comment or two relating to what it might mean if in fact the top officer in the department were a health officer.

Cooper: Many different assistant secretaries have established roles and clear-cut functions. This is not my situation. Both the health system in the country and the program in the Department are evolving. They have been greatly colored by influences both from the character of the secretary and the character of the bureaucracy. And one of the issues that really has been most important is the question of some in the bureaucracy—and I don't use that in a pejorative sense, having come from it—whether an assistant secretary of health is really even necessary. I think there is also some question as to whether the distinctions we make are appropriate. The perception of the health field has been changing and the evolution of the post since 1967 clearly reflects it.

The turning point was when it was converted from just a staff position to a line operating position. In that sense, the character and the strength of the office were really strengthened in the eyes of the inside constituency. The interests of our secretary were being expressed organizationally. There is no question that I have allegedly under my jurisdiction several large inside constituencies, including very distinguished organizations like the National Institutes of Health (NIH). The Director of NIH traditionally would rather talk to the secretary than to any assistant secretary. The commissioner of the Food and Drug Administration is in the same category. If the secretary is not particularly interested in the operations of those agencies and does not talk to those directors, then the role of an aggressive assistant secretary can become much greater. He can be of greater help to the secretary in a large number of ways.

The final point that I think has characterized this evolution is marked by the nature of the public problems and the political situation, particularly since Congress is controlled by one party and the Administration by another. In the field of health, with its growing aspirations and greatly different philosophies, there has been created a tension which has provided a need for a role that has been characterized in our session as the "half-way point." You need to be a translator, a type of conciliator to that important structure. Lack of success in that area automatically decreases the effectiveness of the assistant secretary for Health, at least in this temporal setting. We have an evolving system which in the next several years undoubtedly will undergo several more changes as the national aspirations in health become fixed on either national health insurance or some other mode of operation. So my role is an evolving one that is greatly marked by its superiors, is greatly marked by the political climate, is greatly marked by the public constituencies, and is traditionally evaluated and either supported or opposed by a very strong bureaucracy with great constituencies of its own.

Kolberg: I have had three bosses in my current role and several of them weren't very fond of testifying in congressional hearings. This meant that somebody else had to do it and that somebody turned out to be me. The political officer is the "fall guy" at the bottom of the chain, and therefore our assistant secretaries catch a lot of assignments that they do not seek.

The next thing we want to look at is how subordinates condition our behavior. To me as a career person, coming out of a career bureaucracy, and being a political officer, I find this even more challenging and interesting as a question. Let me get Dave Taylor to comment first on this one. Dave started out in the Labor Department eight years ago as a secretary's executive assistant and he has seen a lot of this—how does the bureaucracy condition political officers' behavior?

Taylor: Well, I think that the tremendous success that George Shultz had in building the Labor Department in the early part of this administration resulted heavily from his ability and willingness to romance the bureaucracy. He would say, "I was closely associated with these people for several years as a professional in labor management relations. I know what they can do, I know the Bureau of Labor Statistics, I know the Manpower Administration, and I know that it is filled with real professionals in the labor relations and the labor field." As a result of this—his sincere ability to get that message across—he was able, I believe, in the first seven or eight months of the Nixon Administration to get the Labor Department into a tremendously positive position. They were pushing through programs that were important, imaginative, and of great significance to the society and the Administration.

Many of the programs that he was urging on the White House and on the Bureau of the Budget at that time were programs that were generated within the bureaucracy, by his subordinates within the Department of Labor. The ability to mobilize that bureaucracy is extremely important—it is impossible to develop a position and to go up to Congress and defend it if you don't have support from within the bureaucracy. So it is our job to have an impact on the programs, yet we have to mobilize the organization and impress it with the importance of the activity. Otherwise, we are not going to accomplish anything.

Brotzman: We are trying to spell out the role of assistant secretaries and obviously that varies a great deal according to each individual's particular view of his role, and what his boss thinks he should be doing. We have a broad charter in most cases, so it would seem to me that one of the items of greatest value to the country from an assistant secretary would be for that individual to bring something dynamic from his or her experience, knowledgeability, or dedication to this thing called government. Within the charters that we have and how we perceive them, and because of the assistant secretaries' temporariness, we have a special role to play. I think that part of our role is to come in and give the bureaucracy a "shot in the arm." I don't say bureaucracy in the pejorative sense—I have a tremendous staff; and I have the highest regard for most of the individuals I have met in governmental service. But, I feel that those of us who are assistant secretaries must bring a little "sparkle," and some new ideas and some leadership to the bureaucracy. So that it is clear that I'm not just talking platitudes, let me say that I served ten years in the Congress— and I'm not saying that defensively either. The point is I now serve the army as an assistant secretary. I feel that in this job that I now have, I should impart my knowledge of the Congress to other army administrators so that they might improve their performance. I want to point out to them some of their shortcomings that I detected as I sat there in Congress. I believe that the army has not portrayed itself as effectively or efficiently as it could. I don't think it has told its story particularly well. So, I deem it my responsibility to help the army improve its presentation of itself.

Macdonald: One of the things that the political appointee, and particularly the assistant secretary, can do is to utilize his own expendability. The fact that he doesn't have to stay around, and in fact won't stay around, is an asset which permits him to be an advocate for his own bureau where advocacy is appropriate; and to protect his people, and be the politically expendable appointee when the bureau is attacked by Congress or by individual congressmen or women. I remember when Congresswoman Bella Abzug came after the Secret Service which she felt was attacking individual rights. The Secret Service felt it was using procedures which were proper and required in order to protect the president. The Secret Service is an excellent organization, but like most career-oriented organizations, it is not conditioned to respond to that kind of political attack. At that point, I think it is essential for the political appointee to stand up and defend his agency if that is, in fact, his judgment.

Kolberg: I would finish off this area of how our behavior is conditioned by our subordinates by saying that the career people are a large part of the equation. Political executives must be aware that nothing succeeds like success. You are judged very quickly by the career people who work for you, and they judge you on how you do in OMB, how you do in Congress, and how you do with the secretary. You are expected to be the advocate, at times the cheerleader, certainly the leader, and sometimes the definer. God help the assistant secretary who loses too many times, because he loses his own staff's confidence as well. It is very important to have a few early victories. They really go a long way; but you also have to stay with it.

Let us move on to how our roles are defined by outside groups. I think some alternatives are pretty obvious. They are at both ends of Pennsylvania Avenue—the White House (and all the associated agencies there) and in Congress. All of us, I think, have powerful outside constituencies which must be satisfied. There are certain places where you must appear; certain clientele groups you must speak before; and if you don't understand your role and your job, you will be "punished" for it in one way or another. Your role is circumscribed in the sense that there are expectations from outside groups which you must meet. There are certain congressional committees where no one else can appear and do a decent job because of the role that is expected of an assistant secretary. In that connection, as we were talking about this, Dave Macdonald reminded us of the role of the outside groups called the media and the press. Dave, do you want to say anything about that or is that kind of an obvious one for us?

Macdonald: Well, the political appointee, and the assistant secretary in particular, is the one who has to interpret and translate what is right into what is desirable, and he has to hold his own with the press. I find just holding your own with the media to be a victory.

Kolberg: Sure the press sets the ground rules, but there certainly are other groups. For instance, Dave Taylor had an experience today that he related to us about appearing before one of those powerful outside interest groups. Dave, would you make a few comments about that?

Taylor: Well, I agree that an assistant secretary is operating at his hazard if he dismisses any group of constituents that is necessary for the performance of his role. Surely, in our business we have a wide variety of special interest groups—the reserves, the National Guard, the Veterans Association, the association that represents active duty people—to be concerned about, but it's important for these people to know that they are respected. You have to get that message across to them, and it's just one of the things you have to do so that it does not necessarily become a burden. But it's very easy for a newcomer, I would suppose, to come in and say, "I don't need you, I can send somebody else; I can send a subordinate to deal with this crowd or that crowd." But, I say, I think it's done at that individual's peril.

Kolberg: The last area that we were asked to talk about and think about was how we as individuals define the roles; how much latitude we have at least on the margin to define our roles.

Brotzman: I think we have a tremendous opportunity. It pretty much gets down to a point of individual commitment. However, there are several parts to these jobs. There are public features to the job. That is, we need to go around and meet the people in the agencies and the various constituencies. Also, the assistant secretary must still take care of that paperwork back at the office. You must save time to work with your staff. So, as you serve your secretary, not only do you have responsibility to the public, you have the representational responsibility in the field and on the Hill, but you must also apply yourself to your principal responsibility—the administrative role. Also, each of us should set certain standards to institutionalize our respective roles, to then pass on to our successors some of these efforts that have worked for us in the interest of the American people.

Kolberg: I will make just one concluding personal comment. It seems to me from where I am, and maybe you've had the same experiences, that the toughest continual conflict and dilemma in these jobs is to try to strike a proper balance between the outside world and your program. It is too easy for someone coming in from the outside and filling a role like this to go on an ego trip and get his kicks giving speeches, appearing on the Hill, and absorbing all the public display. The tough part of this role to me is the disciplined role of administration—insight, motivating people, energizing new ideas, the innovative role; that's what's tough. It is an easy one to overlook. Unless you balance those two roles, I would say that you are not going to be successful.

Conklin: The primary question dealt with by the White Team is: "What conflicts in roles have been the most evident to you in your work? What ambiguities in roles? And what are the most effective ways you have found to deal with the role conflict and ambiguities you have experienced?" To lead off the report the first speaker will be Al Alm.

White Team Report

Alm: We came to a couple of conclusions: One was that our subject tends to be quite ambiguous, which is one of the things that we were supposed to look at. Second, part of our charter was to discuss solutions. We do not have any solutions. Perhaps it is an oversight or perhaps we haven't really come to grips with most of the problem.

The question of the uncertainty of authorities of staff assistant administrators or assistant secretaries was our first problem. One of the issues was relationships with our operational counterparts. The kinds of decisions, coordination, and the like that the staff assistant secretaries have to perform is often very difficult because normally they are only one among a number of equals. A second relationship is the relationship with the secretary. Bill Morrill raised the problem that often,we are given a charter by the secretary, but the charter tends to be rather unclear to our colleagues with whom we have to deal to actually implement the charter. Bill, you may want to comment on that.

Morrill: You have a point in saying that the staff role is a little like some of the Red Team's comments about the balance between the outside constituencies and the inside demands. You're dealing with operational officials with important on-going responsibilities, people who have clear ideas not only about where they are but also about where they ought to be going. Yet, particularly within a large department, the staff role often is to reconcile department-wide policies or deal with government-wide policies. That leads to clashes in which the leaders themselves—the cabinet secretaries or others— may be a little uncertain as to their authority. This leaves the assistant secretaries in a wonderful guessing game as to how many issues can in fact be resolved. As someone noted already, the role is to reconcile as many issues as one can without taking all of the trivia to the top of the heap.

Alm: We discussed the whole issue of relationships of the assistant secretary between, on the one hand, the secretary and the Administration and, on the other hand, the career staff. This issue becomes difficult because often the assistant secretary is in a position of both defining and, in many respects, selling policy downward. On the other hand, the assistant secretary tends to get hit with the concerns the career bureaucracy may have in terms of the policies and decisions of top leadership. Jack Young, do you want to comment on this?

Young: I think that there is a deep and serious distrust between assistant secretaries from the political world and the career staff. I think former Congressman Brotzman intimated that. I think that is one of the most difficult problems that faced the last Administration and will face the next Administration. I think the Red Team effectively made the point that if you do not co-opt the bureaucracy effectively as a new political officer, congressional background or otherwise, you lose the game.

Alm: The third issue we dealt with was what we characterized as the instability of relationships. These relationships grow out of the rather short tenure of the assistant secretaries. I believe it is about eighteen months on the average. Chuck Orlebeke talked about the problem of commitments made by one's predecessors.

Orlebeke: The problem of instability and short tenure runs all through the problems of assistant secretaries. The jobs are typically complex, which means that something on the order of a year is often necessary simply to learn the full range of what your responsibilities are. Yet, your total tenure may be only a year or two years. At the outset, of course, you confront the commitments that have been made by your immediate predecessor. These are commitments which your career officials, as well as other assistant secretaries, have relied upon. You must decide whether simply to go along with these commitments, or assert your right to revoke them. You have to decide whether a commitment made in the last month is as good as one made a year or two previously. A whole range of judgments has to be made of that sort.

Another complicating factor is something many of us have experienced in the last couple of years—that of many changes in cabinet secretaries which have been accompanied by changes in assistant secretaries. In HUD, for example, some assistant secretaries were brought in by the present secretary but others were carried over from her predecessor. This means that you are engaged in a continuous restructuring and rethinking of personal relationships which, in turn, affect very intensely what you must do in carrying out your particular responsibilities.

Alm: The next two points follow along with the point Orlebeke made. One is the point that the careerist often is successful in merely outwaiting the assistant secretary. A second point is whether there is time to do the job. I think the Red Team made a point that political executives must lead the bureaucracy to be effective. That creates the need to establish an almost immediate leadership stance. It is a matter of trust, a matter of demonstrating leadership, of demonstrating a commitment—both a commitment to the employees and to the mission of the agency. The amount of time to do the job is generally very short. Many of us feel it is difficult to get very much done in an assistant secretary level job unless you have about three years. So a couple of things are terribly important to be successful. You have to get the bureaucracy working with you, but also you must develop a set of priorities and have enough time to really make an impact.

We discussed other roles of the assistant secretaries. And one of the roles that we think is particularly ambiguous is the conflict between the "institutional head" role that the assistant secretary plays and the "politician" role. Bill, do you want to comment on that?

Morrill: I think there is some temptation, particularly with the short tenure of assistant secretaries, to see their roles almost wholly in political terms and what can be accomplished during the course of their tenure. I think a tendency to look at the job in that fashion is in the longer run bound to be a failure. You must pay attention to "institution building" and to strengthening and improving that organization for whomever comes after you. The trick of the matter is to get some balance in there. Clearly, some of the time spent on institution building is going to be unsatisfactory both in terms of expectations from superiors and from those outside the organization. So, one has to pay some attention to specific accomplishments. But it is all too easy to get into the business of doing the sexy political thing of the day while ignoring the longer run. I think the governmental institutions around Washington show more than ample evidence of suffering under that kind of an attitude.

Alm: I think in many respects the next point—the conflict between

policy making and management—tends to flow from the comments
Bill just made.

Connor: I think that my own interests are somewhat schizophrenic. I
thoroughly enjoy the policy function and working with a secretary
like Bill Coleman. He is so exciting as far as policy making goes and
he is so anxious to be personally involved in the major issues of the
Department that you tend to get very much involved in policy
yourself. In fact, I think he measures the performance of his political
executives relative to their role in a policy making function. On the
other hand, if you have a long run interest in management and in
strengthening your own organization within the time frame you
expect to have, you more or less have to use extra energies. You just
don't always have the time or the energy to really do the kind of
management function that is necessary, especially when it is unlikely
that you are going to be measured on performance of this function.
The management job is doubly difficult because most of us who have
had a private sector background are not accustomed to the restrictions
of the civil service. Trying to work through it is so frustrating that the
management function very often becomes secondary to the policy
making function, particularly in staff assistant secretary positions. It
seems to me there clearly is a conflict—I'm sure for all of us— between
policy making on the one hand, and making sure that the programs
are carried out on the other hand.

I think one other factor maybe hasn't been mentioned. It is
certainly one I have to get involved in and I know a number of other
people here also are impacted by it; namely, the requirement to work
with the Congress and sell policy. You have to sell it to the
congressmen and also sell it to various constituencies.

There are a whole host of other conflicts and ambiguities that are
not always recognized. There is the relationship between an assistant
secretary of a department and OMB with respect to policy in the
management function. In my case, in Transportation, the problem is
not only between assistant secretaries and OMB, but also with the
secretary, with the career people, and also with the heads of operating
administrations in the Department. Transportation was created in
1967. Some units like the Federal Aviation Administration, the Coast
Guard, and the Highway Administration were all well-established
administrations. Administrators of those organizations enjoy a
constituency of their own and very often are operating at cross
purposes. One of our jobs is to make sure that they are not operating
at as many cross purposes as they were prior to consolidating the

Department in 1967. I expect that that is also the case at HEW and in many other large departments.

Alm: There are also role conflicts that some assistant secretaries face in their jobs. For example, many have dual roles both as the inside cynic and critic on one hand, while on the other hand they often get involved with both policy development and policy advocacy. These kinds of roles can be disconcerting and somewhat schizophrenic. Some assistant secretaries have regulatory functions such as being in charge of a merit system within an agency, while on the other hand they are part of the top political management team. These kinds of conflicts are very difficult; for example, dealing with unions and employee groups and the like as an interpreter of the federal personnel system, while on the other hand representing management.

The final ambiguity we talked about was very appropriate for this time of the year since many of us have received our OMB budget pass back. The problem of having limited resources to deal with increasing demands is a real one; isn't it, Jack Young?

Young: We have an interesting thing that goes on in HEW. We don't have this problem of policy versus administration. My assistant secretary counterpart takes care of the policy and I take care of the rest and Dr. Cooper does what he wants to. I think that this has been one of the most destructive aspects of the last few years. The demands from society for services are expanding and yet fiscal policy makes it almost impossible to do these things. I predict now that this may be the one thing that may tear the next Administration apart, particularly if they try to go through the transition with a lot of bright people all stacking demands on top of demands. It just can't be done. Much of Dr. Cooper's frustration is in trying to reform the whole health delivery system without adequate resources. This is something that we are going to have to learn to live with.

Alm: Let me just summarize the discussion we had within the White Team. I think that we pretty much concluded that there are a number of roles that assistant secretaries must play, and that many of these roles are conflicting. The most difficult ones deal with the relationship of the assistant secretary with the career bureaucracy and with the boss. Some of the conflict comes from the outside in the form of constituency groups, some of it comes from structural conflicts in the job itself and, of course, some of it comes from resource constraints.

Conklin: The question the Blue Team had to wrestle with was: "What strategies and techniques have you found to be most effective to you in performing your roles?"

Blue Team Report

Clark: Notwithstanding that we didn't have a program assistant secretary assigned to our group, I think perhaps strategies and techniques don't vary that much whether one is a program assistant secretary or a housekeeping assistant secretary, as we refer to some administrators. It is also very difficult, I think, to be specific in defining strategies and techniques because they are going to vary as the individuals in the roles will vary in terms of backgrounds, disciplines, and so on.

One of the first things we concluded was that the strategies or techniques that an assistant secretary must of necessity develop depend to a large degree on the style of the boss, the secretary in this case, and the ability of that assistant secretary to learn that style as rapidly as possible and to be flexible enough to adjust to that style. If any change is necessary, it is the assistant secretary—not the secretary—who must change. Then it is very important to learn who the external groups are and what their interests are. It is important, too, to get to know the members of your congressional committee because, as we all know, much time is spent on interface with the Hill and with congressional committees. It is important to know where their interests lie and to strategize and develop techniques in dealing with not only the internal forces but also the external forces.

Another cardinal rule in any given relationship between subordinate and boss is to not let the boss be surprised by events. It is necessary to learn the things that the boss is going to be interested in and to be sure that he is kept informed on those items that are of importance to him. There is nothing worse than a surprised secretary when something falls apart.

Another generalization would be that, to the extent possible, it is important to bring subordinates into the decision-making process. I think if you do that as much as you can there is going to be a greater acceptance of the decision later as it is implemented down the line. It is also important to know your subordinates and the other people in your organization. It is important to know the organization, not only in an institutional sense, but also as an informal organization. Only then can you know who to go to and which button to push when it needs to be pushed to get the information, to get the action or the reaction that is necessary at any given time. In a crisis situation when you use the informal organization it is important to be sure that the institutional organization, the various echelons of supervision, are advised as to what happened and why it happened.

Finally, it is important to delegate authority, to assign the responsibility, and to fix accountability. But the most important factor of all of those items is to have follow-up, because if you don't have the follow-up and get the feedback you will really not be sure that it was done when it was supposed to be done and in the manner in which you wanted it done. Follow-up is a vital part of the whole area of getting your own results.

Bolduc: I would like to amplify a couple of things, especially concerning participatory management. I think that it is true—in order to secure commitment, in order to reach acceptable decisions— that you need to get people involved in that decision-making process. I think that participatory management is probably the key strategy to getting things done. If I were in industry today, I would perhaps not use participatory management as much as we need to in government. I find that if your time can be used to redirect a course of action, that if your time is to be used to make policy, that you will still not succeed if you don't know how to use that bureaucracy to work for you. It simply won't get done.

People who have been career executives for a number of years understand how the system works and they can cut you off at the end of an intersection very, very easily. Frequently, we see very aggressive, dynamic, capable managers come into the bureaucracy. The first morning you are sitting behind that desk you are expected to make ten decisions and try to carry them out. You have to know the system; you have to know how to operate or the system will do you in. We collectively talked about the people within the organizational structure and how you must be able to get them involved. I personally think that is absolutely the key.

I find all too frequently when we have large numbers of idealistic people, that they take a look at a given set of circumstances and they identify the pros, the cons, and the alternatives. Then they decide that this is what *ought* to be and that that's the way they will go. But, all too frequently we, the public administrators, fail in the bureaucracy because we strive to attain what *ought* to be rather than what *can* be. I think that if we concentrate a little more on what can be achieved and try to achieve that, rather than get carried away with what *ought* to be, we will have more success.

I have a case which is a classic example. I don't know how many of you have participated in attempting to procure computer hardware in this day and age as it relates to privacy matters, the Freedom of Information Act, with having to deal with computer frauds, the Brooks law, and all of those related factors. But, believe me, the thing can turn against you overnight if you don't strategize it properly, and if you don't know where the power structures are and how to capitalize on those power structures.

One other thing that comes to mind is that I find too few people in the bureaucracy willing to challenge the system. Too few people are willing to take that risk to make it better. I find that there are too many disincentives in the bureaucracy which keep people from trying to change it. You find so many people coming in with all kinds of energy and they want to change the system and restructure it. They try it once and they get "shot down"; they try it twice and they get "shot down"; and the third time they throw their hands up and say, "The hell with it, I'm not going to try it again. I draw the same salary, I have fewer problems, I can go home at 5:00 p.m. at night, and they won't call me on weekends. So, I'm not going to try anymore." But the system doesn't change if you don't try, and it won't respond if you don't challenge it. We need to encourage risk-taking.

I think that one of the greatest contributions from a personal strategy point of view is to try to bring into the institutionalized establishment that dynamism, that willingness to try to challenge the system—and to continue even if it fails the first few times. I think that career people look at an assistant secretary to see if he is willing to take that risk. You would be surprised at their response, and I am sure that some of you have learned that they will respond, they will stand behind you, they will support you. But if they find you retreating because you've analyzed it and found that there are so many disincentives, they will get the signal and they will not try to challenge things. I think it is particularly true in the management side of the shop.

Public administration is on a very critical threshold. For years the sexiness of public administration has been on the program side. Programs are executed and programs are carried out—but the management side has always been identified as the housekeeper and as a secondary function. Program decisions are made and the housekeepers have to find the dollars, and the people, and the system to control it and to follow up on it. I think we have somehow got to work that dichotomy on a more even basis so that decisions are made on the program side in concert with the management impact. I think that is the strategy that we have to employ if we are going to really make progress and effectuate improvement within our bureaucracy.

Blake: Our team had more commonality of interest from a functional point of view than the other two groups did, and I suspect because of that, we may have had a bit of a bias in putting together our thoughts and observations. We all represent management or administration.

The basic task was to comment on strategies or techniques which, if adopted, might lead to success in fulfilling those responsibilities. I would like to mention three that come to my mind. They are primarily associated with those who are performing a senior, managerial, or administrative role in life.

I think that if one bears in mind three principles, one has a fair chance at success. First, keep in mind that management and administration are not an end but a means to an end. Put the function in the proper perspective, both to yourselves and for those on the receiving end. I've seen many individuals both in my own organization and in others who sometimes get a little confused by whether administration is an end in itself or a means to an end. I think if he or she who administers bears in mind that it is a means to an end, the other individuals in the organization will also understand it. And, you will have a better acceptance for doing what you are doing.

Second, one must bear in mind that there is more than one solution to a problem. It is so easy in life to say "no," but it is somewhat difficult in life to try to think through that first no and see if there is another way to find a way to say "yes." Most of the time, if one continues to examine a problem and understand it, generally some kind of successful answer instead of an absolute, unequivocal "no" can be found.

Third, if there is no other answer but "no," it is much more acceptable if a reasonable statement goes with it as opposed to a flat negative response. I believe that most people in life are reasonable and fair, and if you can explain why the answer has to be negative, and if you can explain in a constructive manner that you've tried to take a step to solve the problem, but unfortunately couldn't find one, most people will accept it.

Dembling: You indicated that the group had no program assistant secretary and that is right from a title standpoint. But, I'm in a peculiar role as General Counsel of an agency (GAO) with a staff function, because we also have an operating function since we render decisions to guide all the other agencies in the government. In addition to that, we serve as a staff office within GAO, so we have both a program and a staff role. I agree that in order to motivate a group of people to get a job done, we can't operate totally on participative management. But feedback to the individuals is necessary, and I personally must have some communication with the individual staff attorney. Unless you have their confidence, and unless they feel there is integrity within the system and not just arbitrariness at the top policy level, and unless they feel that they really are involved, I don't think that you are going to succeed in getting the organization moving. I have been in the Executive Branch in similar positions and I don't think it makes that much difference whether you have a political head or a non-political head. The organization has to be motivated, and consequently, some of these techniques that we have explored and addressed ourselves to must be applied to the problem. One other comment. The question came up whether as lawyers we sought out problems and got into policy problems and management functions and that kind of thing. I just said facetiously that I point out, whenever I'm criticized for doing that, that my title is not *legal* counsel, it is *general* counsel.

Conklin: For a little deviation now from the way the program was originally arranged, I think it is appropriate for us to ask Brad Patterson to give a White House perspective of the three team presentations.

Patterson: I was impressed thinking and looking at the presentations of other teams, as well as my own group. I am thinking also of this current debate about the shape of the new White House. I want to reflect on some of the ambiguities and points that have been made as they affect this question of White House relationships with the cabinet and the assistant secretaries. It seems to me that the ambiguities about the strategies of the assistant secretary level people throughout the Administration have contributed to an ambiguity about the role of the White House and the White House staff. I can give some specific examples. For instance, in the role of the assistant secretaries in policy development, you have mentioned yourself that this is a somewhat uncertain role and for a number of reasons you cannot put your finger on the source. This seems to me partly a result of the ambiguities that you face.

What has the White House staff done over the last twenty years in the area of policy development? And what have our presidents done? The answer is that they have piled on White House machinery for policy development, sometimes including, but often on top of or along side of, the role of assistant secretaries. White House staff members individually get deeply into policy development. For example, it was Leonard Garment, rather than the attorney general or the secretary of HEW, who, back in 1970, personally spent three months writing a paper on school busing and the problems of school busing. He spent all three months doing nothing else. And the president didn't turn to any of the assistant secretaries or even secretaries, but instead turned to his White House staff for this policy development role.

The growth of the Domestic Council is another case in the same area of policy development. Assistant secretaries have their dilemmas, but the president has certain responsibilties and direct concerns as well. The Domestic Council comprises fifty people in the White House who are involved in cross-departmental policy matters.

I don't know whether any of our groups touched on the problems of assistant secretaries as long-range policy planners—trying to look ahead. Judith Connor, I imagine that this is something that your office is trying to do. But the White House at one point tried experimenting with long-range policy development. The president created in the White House a National Goals Research Staff to try to fill this function, but it simply was not very successful.

The area of policy coordination is a real problem for assistant secretaries. Can he look beyond his department? The answer is that in most cases he can, but with great difficulty, because most program problems slop over the boundaries of agencies. The Bureau of Indian Affairs, for instance, has been notably unsuccessful in trying to coordinate Indian policy development, which is scattered in fifty two offices in eighteen agencies. So what has happened? Partly because of the president's own central role in policy coordination, the White House again has established a staff in the policy coordination area. The same thing happens outside domestic policy. The National Security Council (NSC) staff is an example. NSC hardly ever meets as a Council, but it has a staff of 150 people which is mostly engaged in the policy coordination role and also in policy development—one hundred and fifty people in the White House.

We talked about the role of assistant secretaries vis-à-vis the outside groups as well as the liaison and linkage role they play with outside client groups. Well, the White House evidently must consider that this is not good enough, because the White House has set up an office which at recent count had about thirty-five people—professional and support staff—in an office called the Office of Public Liaison. That office has two or three special officers for liaison with women, two officers for liaison with Spanish-speaking groups, one with Indians, several with blacks, business, veterans, and so forth. These are some of the same client groups that you work with. I am not saying that it is because you can't work with them, or don't, or haven't, that the White House fills in behind you. But, for one reason or another the President feels that he has to have that function in the White House.

Now, another function of the White House staff that has burgeoned in recent years is that of the political advance people. I'm not sure that assistant secretaries will feel that this is part of their role, although you could expect a very savvy political assistant secretary to do a little advance work for the president who appointed him or her. But it doesn't happen, and so the White House builds its own advance team, which at last count was about twenty-five people.

And of course, there has been some brief mention about the role of assistant secretaries vis-à-vis the Congress. As Bill Kolberg mentioned, you obviously are on the front line in terms of testimony before Congress. But the White House staff, beginning a long time ago, certainly with Eisenhower if not before, has had its own congressional relations staff numbering now about fifteen professional and support staff. This is a special congressional relations responsibility.

I can think of one other function—the relationship with state and local governments. Again, practically all the programs over which you as assistant secretaries have important line responsibility affect state and local governments. Yet the White House staff also has built into it a special office, as far back as Eisenhower's time and continuing right up until now, for liaison with state and local governments.

It is not any reflection on assistant secretaries, but I think it is partly out of the ambiguities and question marks surrounding the role of cabinet officers and their assistant secretaries, among other reasons, that presidents have felt impelled to pile on machinery in the White House to do some of those tasks. Now the interesting question, as the new White House is talked about, is that these very offices that I have mentioned are the targets, so to speak, for elimination. *Maybe* the new president is going to be able to cut off his Office of Public Liaison, and cut off the Domestic Council, slice down the NSC, eliminate the Goals staff (that was done before), slice back the advance team, and cut down on congressional relations staff. Maybe he will say in effect to his new cabinet—"Ladies, gentlemen, you take these new functions, you and your new assistant secretaries, and we won't do them here." But we shall see. . . .

3

The Political-Career Interface in Government

The success of this Government, and thus the success of our Nation, depend in the last analysis upon the quality of our career service. The legislation enacted by the Congress, as well as the decisions made by me and the Department and Agency heads, must be implemented by the career men and women in the Federal service. . . . We are all dependent on their sense of loyalty and responsibility as well as their competence and energy.
—John F. Kennedy

Governments require two levels of expertise in order to provide acceptable services: the professional level, which is concerned primarily with carrying out policy, and the political level, where the primary responsibility rests for formulating the goals and priorities of government—i.e., making policy. Between these two levels exists inevitable tension. This is true for communist societies as well as democratic, parliamentary as well as presidential systems of government. The reasons for this adversary relationship are similar in most societies. Professionals are oriented toward their bureaucratic organizations and functions, while political leaders want to meet objectives of parties and pressure groups. Professionals are usually experts in specific areas or disciplines, while political representatives are mostly generalists who pride themselves on "looking at the big picture." Professionals in most societies have long tenure, while political appointees come and go with different administrations. Professionals usually earn their rank through education, ability, and dedicated service, while political appointees usually are drawn from the elite groups of society. These and other differences in their backgrounds, perspectives, and goals create tensions and occasionally antagonism between the professionals (usually called bureaucrats) in government and the politicians who set goals and try to reflect the priorities of the party in power.

The American presidential system of government experiences more problems with this relationship than do the British and Canadian system (and probably parliamentary systems in general) because the presidential system requires far more political appointees in the executive branch of the U.S. government than are necessary in other western systems. One result is that the American system, unlike others, does not give career civil servants opportunities to rise to the top of their departments and agencies. Put another way, an outstanding career official in a U.S. department or agency (except the Department of State) cannot aspire to assistant secretary–level jobs, or to the deputy secretary level, because those key posts are reserved for political appointees. Indeed, in many U.S. departments and agencies, even the deputy assistant secretary jobs are in this category. It is not surprising, therefore, that in the American bureaucracy, considerable suspicion and envy exist among career executives who believe (often correctly) that they are smarter and more competent than their political superiors and ought to be making policy themselves, rather than simply implementing programs which they had little voice in shaping.

But this fundamental problem remains in modern societies such as the United States: how can government bring about necessary change in our increasingly complex society if the professional level of government (in the eyes of elected officials) is not sufficiently responsive to the needs of that society? In essence, is not a large number of political appointees (those the president and his departmental secretaries may choose without regard to the constraints of a career system) necessary in a new administration that wishes to change the programs and directions of government to meet the needs of the people? The answer is one of judgment, and scholars and public administrators will continue to debate how many political appointees a new administration needs to carry out its mandate. What concerns us, however, is the relationship between the political level and the professional level in the U.S. executive branch, and what might be done to improve that relationship.

It is an old cliché that appointed political executives arrive in Washington thinking that government bureaucrats are poorly motivated, not very intelligent, and unresponsive to the needs of the nation; and that six months later they tell their audiences that career government executives are smart, dedicated to the public interest, and indispensable to getting the job done. Why the poor image of the career executives in the first place? And why should political appointees be surprised that they can't do their jobs without the cooperation of good career personnel?

To the extent that the cliché is an accurate reflection of the conventional wisdom, it probably tells us more about the ignorance of many political executives than it does about the aptitude and motivation of career officials. Careerists often put new appointees through a crash course on government procedures to help them avoid disasters in the jungle of Washington's bureaucratic politics. The exchange of ideas on this subject among the twenty-four political executives gathered at the Federal Executive Institute in December 1976 quickly dismissed this stereotype of a federal executive for two good reasons: all of the participants had been in government long enough to know that most of the stereotypes are myths, and many had previously been career executives and were well aware that most civil servants who make it to the supergrade level are of high quality. Therefore, discussion at the conference quickly got down to more fundamental issues regarding relationships between career and political officials.

Under Secretary of HUD John Rhinelander, keynote speaker in this session, addressed the matter of the interface bluntly: "Very clearly, 99 percent of the people in the Federal government are in the career service. If you cannot work with the people in the career service, you're not going to be effective in government, and you should either not come in or you had better get out fast."* William Morrill, Assistant Secretary of HEW, put it another way: "My own axiom would run something like the following: You could afford to know nothing about the policies of the administration, *or* you could afford to know nothing of the culture of government agencies; but you are going to have a damn rough time if you know nothing about *either* of them." Indeed, fundamental issues discussed by these seasoned political appointees included whether it is becoming almost impossible to manage the federal government because of ever-increasing constraints on management; the declining attractiveness of an assistant secretary position; the difficulty of recruiting political appointees who know how to motivate career civil servants; and the necessity of accomplishing objectives through the system rather than fighting the system.

Several bothersome questions remained long after the conference had ended. First, if it is true that the federal government is becoming increasingly difficult to manage and that frustrations of political executives are growing, will it continue to be possible to recruit competent and dedicated people from outside government to take on these assistant secretary jobs? Second, if the government personnel system is as rigid and frustrating to operate within as these

---

*All quoted material in this chapter, unless otherwise noted, is from Thomas P. Murphy, Donald E. Nuechterlein, and Ronald J. Stupak, eds., *The President's Program Directors: The Assistant Secretaries* (Charlottesville, Va.: Federal Executive Institute, 1977).

experienced appointees say it is, why should it be so difficult to persuade the Congress, the bureaucracy, and the interest groups that it must be changed? Third, if the tenure of political executives is so short (eighteen to twenty months prior to the Carter administration) that their effectiveness is reduced, would it not be better to reduce the total number of political jobs or promote more top career executives into existing positions? An alternative might be to recruit political appointees who will remain in their jobs at least three years, as the Carter administration has sought to do. Fourth, is there a better way to create a climate of trust and mutual dependence between political appointees and career executives, to increase the willingness of the bureaucracy to change directions when a new administration comes into office?

In the final analysis, democratic government will not survive unless the society that supports it is willing to change priorities—and even beliefs—when the political, economic, and social environment clearly requires it. The United States faced such a decision in 1932-1933 when it became clear that the role of the federal government had to change if democracy was to survive. We may face an equally serious challenge as a result of public cynicism about government in the late 1970s, and if government does not respond in equally significant ways, the prospect exists that our democratic system will be pushed aside when a crisis hits and the public demands decisive action.

Listening as these key political appointees shared their experiences and anxieties caused one to be somewhat apprehensive. Is the federal government now so preoccupied with providing "safeguards" and security for so many diverse groups of federal employees that it has stifled creativity, innovativeness, and a willingness to change? And could government therefore be stalemated in the face of a new crisis? Although there was no consensus about this issue, enough pessimism was voiced to cause one to wonder whether in the future effective people will want to serve in government as assistant secretaries.

Is the Federal Bureaucracy Becoming Unmanageable?

William Morrill and John Rhinelander led off discussion on this subject, and other participants made numerous comments. Morrill observed that "having come out of a career system and having been in it for twenty years, over time and out of a series of individualized events—most particularly since Watergate—there has been an effort to create a system and a process to prevent managers from doing it wrong; and cumulatively, we are getting close to the point where you're preventing managers from doing it at all. You have insulated the system in a way where you almost can't move, or if you can move, it takes you so long to get it done that it may outlast the average life of an assistant secretary." Here an experienced career executive turned political executive questions whether rules for hiring and firing personnel have become so rigid that management has little operating room. Rhinelander was no less negative: "I think when you combine the merit staffing system with all the rules which have grown up on top of it, and couple that with the growing power of the unions and the rights groups, you have a system which is almost unworkable."

Rhinelander also talked about the equal employment opportunity (EEO) complaint system being a barrier to effective management: "I'm sympathetic to what you say because I have looked at it as an attorney, and I am concerned that the individual employee is provided a lawful process. On the other hand, we have built so many safeguards into dealing with the right of the individual to challenge the system, whether it's a grievance, an EEO complaint, or whether it's a lawsuit, that the deck has been stacked. For instance, under our EEO procedures right now, the individual in government who is alleged to have been the discriminator really has no rights until the process is through the first step and a decision has been made. I think that is simply an unacceptable way to conduct our business."

William Kolberg of the Labor Department joined the discussion with this comment: "It's not only the combination of those two systems. You mentioned earlier the EEO rules, and regulations on top of that, which today protect 90 percent of the work force in one way or another. They're either young, or old, or minority, or whatever it is, and they have rules and regulations. So you really have three systems, one on top of another." Fred Clark, also from the Labor Department, agreed with this pessimistic view of management's ability to perform in the current environment: "The few prerogatives that the management has left are fast disappearing as unions become stronger, and I think we're going to see the day when there is going to be legislation in the federal activity and that's going to make it more complicated."

If it is true that top management has been so hamstrung by rules and regulations that protect everyone and penalize practically no one in government, what is to be done? The Carter administration became aware of the problem during its first year and commissioned a task force on government reorganization to come up with recommendations for significant changes in federal personnel administration. By the beginning of 1978 this group had made its report and persuaded

President Carter to send recommendations to Congress that addressed management's needs but did not change the basic structure of the merit system of government employment. Whether Congress and the country at large will accept these changes in the federal personnel system remains to be seen.

The problem of getting changes accepted in this highly important area is highlighted by the response of one Washington columnist, who wrote under the headline "Firing Deadwood: A Mask for Bias." He stated:

> Government executives have long complained about the [Civil Service] Commission's impossibly slow personnel processes. It can take months to hire people whose credentials are impeccable. And it can take years to fire those whose incompetence is plain for all to see. . . . The prospect of easier firing, however, will not meet with universal acclaim. Nor is it only the marginally competent who are likely to be alarmed. Suppose you are a Black employee doing a reasonably good job for a boss you believe to be a racist. Or suppose you are a woman whose career is in the hands of a man who believes women really ought to be typists and fetchers of coffee. Or maybe you've got a "personality conflict" with the chief. Your career salvation may lie in the fact that you can't be fired arbitrarily and summarily, that there is a process, with built-in appeals right up to the Civil Service Commission itself. [William Raspberry, *The Washington Post,* December 21, 1977, p. A15]

Therein lies the dilemma. If changes cannot be made in the personnel system because someone might feel threatened by an unfair boss, will the entire bureaucratic system be responsive to the obvious need for change and to the demands of the American public for better performance from public officials? Congress began to debate this issue in 1978. It is becoming increasingly clear to political appointees in Washington that unless significant changes are made, the federal bureaucracy will become less rather than more responsive to the American public as time goes on.

Is It Worth Leaving the Private Sector
To Become an Assistant Secretary?

The growing inability of top officials to manage their organizations led into a broader discussion of whether it is worth it anymore to leave private life to become an assistant secretary. Again, Bill Kolberg had strong views: "I would say the job of assistant secretary isn't anywhere near as attractive a job as it used to be, and it's going down. I would describe it as follows: The pay is poor and we all know that, the perquisites have gradually gone away, especially those that have something to do with people's feelings about themselves, their responsibilities, and their importance. The coin of the president, although this president [Ford] has done better, has been depreciated a great deal. Twenty years ago assistant secretaries were invited to dinner at the White House, and were very big men or women in Washington. They are no longer."

Antonin Scalia of the Justice Department agreed with Kolberg, and observed that one of the most dissatisfying parts of his job "is the amount of my time that has been spent in what is ultimately . . . the nonproductive work of preparing for legislative testimony. I expect that about 40 percent, literally 40 percent, of my time has been spent on essentially responding to oversight requests and inquiries of the Congress. . . . It is enormously time-consuming on the part of those people who have to prepare the testimony, and it is not the kind of work that gives you a great deal of satisfaction because you are not really accomplishing anything. . . . And as that takes something like 40 percent of your time, you begin to wonder if you aren't in an army that is devoted to the care of its wounded."

Judith Connor of the Department of Transportation pointed to another impediment to leaving the private sector to become an assistant secretary: "It seems to me that we just are going in a direction where we find job appointments either from within the bureaucracy or the legal profession, because it is becoming increasingly difficult for anybody who doesn't have the flexibility of the legal profession to come into government. It is very difficult to get private sector companies, if you're not a lawyer, to permit you to go into government, or to get another potential employer to consider that you have picked up anything useful while you were in government service." But John Rhinelander felt that lawyers were inhibited by the same factors that prevent those from other professions from accepting positions in government service. He felt that economists would be in much greater demand in the future and that there were already too many lawyers in top positions. He agreed that the attractiveness of government service was declining: "Looking at the situation right now, I would say it is very difficult to get top flight people, whether their training is law or otherwise, from the private sector except perhaps for the educational institutions, to come in at less than the under secretary positions. To come to Washington now . . . as an assistant secretary, given the cost of homes and if you have young children to bring up, is going to be extraordinarily difficult."

The answer, according to several participants, was to promote more career civil servants into the ranks of political executives. But what would be the price in terms of "new blood" and creativity—and perhaps even energy—in the job? Alvin Alm of the EPA saw some advantages and some disadvantages: "I think there is no doubt that a career person coming up the ranks can grab the reins of an assistant secretary rather quickly, and since they've been tested in a bureaucratic atmosphere, probably the chances of at least not completely flopping are considerably less, and clearly, you gain time. What you lose is, obviously, outside perspectives and new ideas. Some have commented that just by having the luxury of leaving allows a person to do more. I question that notion. My personal feeling is that there probably ought to be a higher number of career people in assistant secretary jobs, assuming you had clearly political people in the top two jobs."

Kolberg thought that "it is going to be almost automatic that more career people are going to come into these jobs," because the job of assistant secretary had lost much of its attractiveness for people from the private sector. He regretted this even though he is a product of the career service: "you really do need the smart, young, interested, vigorous, innovative people from outside who have that sense of public purpose to come in and take on this tough job; and unless we change the pattern, we're going to have an increasingly tough job" recruiting bright people from the outside.

Assistant Secretary of the Army Donald Brotzman was not certain that promoting more careerists into these jobs was a good idea. "I am not impugning the ability of anyone that comes from the bureaucracy up through the ranks, but it gets down to this basic point, as far as the people are concerned. That is, if the president needs assistant secretaries from outside with a little creativity and innovativeness, perhaps sticking their necks out a bit, then I feel that this is the way the system should be."

John Richardson of the State Department pointed out that the foreign service officer in that department has the opportunity to rise to the position of ambassador (equivalent in many cases to the rank of assistant secretary), and that most assistant secretary jobs in his department are held by careerists. "So you have lots of opportunities for career people to come in, at the political level, in any case. And that's part of the routine of the service. So, it is easy to assimilate the Foreign Service person professionally at the assistant secretary level— there is no complication, and everybody understands it." Richardson did not say so, but it is also true that a number of presidents and secretaries of state have criticized the State Department for lack of responsiveness to changes in foreign policy mandated from the White House. One reason given for this alleged intransigence is that the Foreign Service, long entrenched in key policymaking bureaus of the department, changes very slowly. The Carter administration, in fact, reduced the number of foreign service officers in top jobs during 1977.

Some participants in the discussion made the candid admission—not strongly refuted by others—that being an official appointed by the president does not carry the same prestige and rewards that it once did. This, combined with the headaches entailed in these jobs—not least the growing lack of authority to get the right people in the right jobs to accomplish presidential objectives—means that many excellent people from the private sector can no longer be recruited into government. The trend, therefore, is to fill more assistant secretary positions with career executives who are fully competent, in most cases, but who often lack the broad perspective and willingness to take risks—the special contribution of people coming from outside.

This tendency to promote from within will increase as the Carter administration continues to insist that outside recruits remain in their jobs three or four years and as background investigations become more rigorous. There are definite advantages to having such continuity at the policymaking level, but the trade-off will likely be that fewer outstanding people from the private sector will be willing to stay away from their firms that long and thus lose opportunities for promotion. If Rhinelander is correct in asserting that it will also be harder to recruit good lawyers, it may well be that academic institutions will be the primary source for recruiting political leaders; and the question might then be asked whether the philosophical environment of the university is the most desirable place to find people who can grapple effectively with the hard—sometimes brutal—operational requirements of most federal bureaucracies.

How Can Political Appointees Influence the Direction of Their Bureaucracies?

The primary subject for discussion during the second day of the symposium, this was pursued in detail only after three teams had met separately. Many good ideas came out of the exchange of experiences, and participants took much pride in recalling how they had dealt with this question in their own organizations. John Rhinelander set the stage with this observation: "I guess in the final analysis, the most important thing at the assistant secretary level is to be able to work well with people and to improvise on your feet. If you cannot do that, if you bring rigid approaches into a system, I just do not think you can be effective."

Hugh Heclo, in his excellent recent book on political appointees (*A Government of Strangers*), lists four kinds of government careerists who must be dealt with by a political executive:

- *Opponents,* "who see vital interests harmed by change and who are unalterably opposed to the efforts of political executives";
- *Reluctants,* "who may be opposed to change but who are not immune to persuasion that there are some hitherto unrecognized advantages: they will at least listen";
- *Critics,* "who feel they have views to contribute and are willing to be supportive as long as what they have to say is seriously considered"; and
- *Forgotten,* "those whose failure to support political executives stems from their failure to hear what is wanted, or to hear correctly."

The symposium dealt primarily with the second and third categories: the career civil servants who can be won over by creating mutual respect and by persuasive argumentation.

Most participants in the symposium seemed to believe that an assistant secretary not willing to make a real effort to reach these two kinds of careerists would not be successful in government. Several felt there was no real substitute for having previous government experience at a lower level—perhaps as an aide to a political appointee or as a lower-ranking official who then left government and spent time in the private sector. This early introduction to the "culture of government" gives a new assistant secretary knowledge that saves time and prevents mistakes.

David Macdonald of the Navy Department and his team agreed that an assistant secretary "should start his job as an intense learning experience" and should take the time to "eyeball the operation" out in the field, not just in the Washington office. He felt that a political executive can learn much from his peers and that competition among assistant secretaries "is a myth which is quite exaggerated." Macdonald described the interface between political appointees and career executives this way: "The career employee [is] valuable for his expertise, his continuity and what you might call his governmental memory." The value of the political appointee, on the other hand, "lies in his approach, his ability to question the entire purpose of the function of some of the bureaucracy, and his independence, which really depends on his ability to lead. Since political appointees have no security, his security lies in his ability to walk out."

Control mechanisms over careerists that were mentioned in the team reports included control of the budget submission to the Office of Management and Budget and to Congress, approval of international travel, and concurrence on career promotions down to the middle-grade ranks. John Richardson argued, however, that showing an interest in the organization is a control device of sorts and an indispensable asset: "If a new assistant secretary is going to get along with the career people, the easiest way is to evidence from the beginning an enthusiasm for the functions they are performing and an interest in the overall purpose of the organization." Jack Young of HEW was convinced that open communication with the bureaucracy was essential, and he said "if you're going to survive successfully as a political officer, depending on your style and your background, you must find some ways to co-opt the bureaucracy." He also thought that political executives should focus on a few important things they want to work on, passing other projects down to the bureaucracy for action. Again, this was necessary because of the short tenure of most political executives. Young implied that most appointees would not have time to get to know the whole organization well, and his advice to an assistant secretary was to "limit your agenda."

William Morrill, observing that careerists should be given good feedback from meetings they do not attend, said it "must be passed on to them so that they know what happened—even though that might risk leaks and other things in an effort to achieve a cohesive organization." He cautioned that an assistant secretary, as a buffer between career civil servants and higher administration officials making tough political decisions, must be able to explain fully and not apologize when a recommendation from the career bureaucracy is not accepted. Morrill said his group felt strongly that a new assistant secretary must quickly learn his or her job: "if you don't know what you are doing, then it is very unlikely that you are going to gain the respect of your subordinates."

Paul Dembling of the Government Accounting Office emphasized the importance of getting career employees to accept direction from the White House. He argued that "it is important for assistant secretaries coming into government to recognize . . . that you can get the career service to respond even though it is necessary to shift them from what they have been doing previously into a new direction."

The group discussed a procedure in the Defense Department which John Rhinelander thought was an excellent way for assistant secretaries to learn their jobs quickly and become familiar with their organizations. This is the program of assigning military assistants, usually promising young officers, to be the political appointee's "eyes and ears." Rhinelander described it this way: "Through the military aide the bureaucracy understands what the assistant secretary, the under secretary, and the secretary are thinking about, and through him it really is a two-way system. . . . The Pentagon really works through the network of assistants to the secretaries. And one of the most important decisions early on is the person you select for that position." Kolberg seconded this idea, saying it was a tradition in the Bureau of the Budget to pick people from the career ranks and rotate them through the organization as executive assistants or staff assistants to the director. The information flow in these cases is excellent, he said, and the system provides good training for younger career officers destined for higher positions in their organizations.

The symposium then took up the desirability of increasing mobility for career executives in order to get teams of people willing to work toward objectives desired by assistant secretaries. Rhinelander agreed with Macdonald's suggestion that career supergrade personnel should have job protection but not position protection. He had found it very useful as a general counsel to have Schedule A slots for his lawyers, so he could move them easily without regard to normal Civil Service requirements. "I think you've got to be able to move them around, and one of the things I could do in the General Counsel's office was move a lot of people laterally. In fact, I think I've left behind a really superb legal office because I did have the flexibility."

Paul Bolduc of the Agriculture Department was less sure of the advantages, however: "I think that we have to balance it, because if we're not careful, we'll find ourselves just moving people around and creating jobs which do not really contribute in a meaningful way to achieving what we want to achieve, and then we end up with a bunch of disgruntled employees." Rhinelander maintained that the present system simply is not flexible enough to help the political executive have any impact on the organization: "I think one of the great problems and one of the great frustrations that people feel when they come into government is the problem which we've been focusing on: the personnel rules, the lack of flexibility, . . . the lack of the ability to either move them laterally or out if they're not performing. Part of the problem, of course, is the short tenure."

Brad Patterson from the White House Personnel Office took some credit for the process of selecting assistant secretaries, which caused some laughter from the audience. He also argued that assistant secretaries, soon after they have taken on the job, should get together with career supergrades to discuss mutual problems and concerns. He thought such an orientation program would go a long way to improve the relationship between political appointee and career executive. Patterson also observed that assistant secretaries needed to deal with the president more often in order to increase their effectiveness with the bureaucracy. He felt the Ford administration had been more accessible, which had proved worthwhile when assistant secretaries explained presidential decisions to the career employees.

Heclo, in the study cited above, makes this wise observation about the objective of the career-political interface (p. 210): "Mutual advantage produces institutionalized change. As the desires of the political executive become connected with the interests of at least some of the officials who will remain behind, the chances of an enduring impact grow." The assistant and under secretaries discussed the question of how to establish this "mutual advantage," but found no answer. Clearly, it cannot be done if the tenure of the assistant secretary is less than two years, especially if he or she is new to government. But it also cannot be accomplished if the political executive believes he is God's gift to Washington and that career bureaucrats are there to carry out his wishes. Several participants alluded to the need for mutual respect; and respect is *earned* by the political appointee. It is not conferred on him simply by his certificate of presidential appointment.

Thus, the dilemma reappears: the White House is responsible for appointing persons from outside the government who can work well with the career service, but the price to be paid by the appointees is becoming too high to attract the best talent. How the Carter administration and successive administrations resolve this dilemma will determine to a large degree the kind of top political leadership of United States departments and agencies during the next decade.

Do Political Appointees "Conceptualize" Objectives Better Than Bureaucrats?

In any discussion of relationships between federal executives and political appointees, the argument recurs that the U.S. presidential system, unlike the parliamentary system, allows for a large number of jobs at the top which the president can fill, if he wishes, to bring new ideas and programs to government. Jack Young, reporting on his team's deliberations, said that they took up the "critical question in this business"—should there be more or fewer noncareer jobs? "What we came to, in conclusion, was that the mix is just about right." Al Alm compared the U.S. system, in which about 2,000 jobs change hands, to that of the British government, where only 200 to 300 jobs change hands when a new political party takes control. Tony Scalia felt that such comparisons were not productive, however: "I am wary of analogies to the British system, or to any other one which is a parliamentary system. I just don't think it is comparable. Yes, our transitions are rougher and it is also rougher to have an independently elected executive who bumps heads with the Congress on occasion during his entire tenure. I think that's part of our system."

A political appointee in the Carter adminstration recently told a group of career executives from the Federal Executive Institute that his major contribution to government was to "conceptualize" policy options because the "bureaucracy does not do a good job at the conceptual level." When pressed for his definition of "conceptualize," he described it as defining the hard choices the president has to make and taking a rational, nonbureaucratic look at those choices with broad national policy in mind. The career executives disagreed that they were less capable of providing such advice to a president or to a department secretary; in fact, some felt they could provide better advice and judgment than many political appointees because they knew the realities of government and what could and could not reasonably be accomplished. The political appointee believed, however, that most careerists have a vested interest in their particular agency or function, and that therefore they are not as willing as are noncareerists to adjust to changing national needs and priorities. To him, a political appointee is less biased in his thinking—at least on questions involving important programs and large resources.

The question seems to come down to the matter of whether all policymaking political appointees contribute significantly to a new administration's objectives of bringing in new ideas and taking risks to effect change; or whether many are so inexperienced, and stay such a short time, that their contribution is marginal and mostly symbolic. If the latter view is closer to the truth, does this mean that career executives might be more effective if they are well selected and have enough mobility in assignments to afford them a broader view of government?

Another way of stating the problem is this: can the federal government afford to "carry" many political appointees in top positions simply because they wish to spend a year or two in Washington and have the necessary political connections? Probably not; at least not at the assistant secretary level. Perhaps government would be better served if the best of the career service were given the option of moving into these jobs, and the political appointees—particularly the bright young people—were given noncareer jobs at the GS-15 and GS-16 level. Such a mix would relieve some of the present tension between the assistant secretary level and the top of the career level (GS-18s who have know-how and experience but who too often are not brought into the key decision-making or "conceptualizing" discussions). It would provide for aspiring young politicians the opportunity to gain the experience that later in their careers will qualify them to be a department under secretary or deputy under secretary. In sum, government is now becoming so complex and so large that greater experience is now required of incumbents to perform most assistant secretary jobs.

The new Federal Executive Service proposed by the Carter administration contains the possibility of doing this, because it would include not only supergrade levels of the career civil service, but also one or two grades at the executive pay level as well—jobs that are almost exclusively appointees of the president. If this proposal is adopted, it may go a long way toward breaking down the barriers that currently exist between the career service and political appointees—a highly desirable objective. In the meantime, the tensions will continue.

Should Political Appointees Receive Training for Their Jobs?

In his introductory remarks on the political-career interface, Donald Nuechterlein of the Federal Executive Institute questioned whether training of new political appointees is desirable. "It seems to me that if this system of ours is going to work better than it has in the past, we have got somehow to create a better community between your level—the political level—and the career level—the people who are going to carry out government functions. . . . I think what Tom Murphy is trying to do at the FEI—and your program is the first piece of it—is to open up the communications process and get a team spirit going between the political level and the career level."

John Rhinelander was skeptical. "I would like to start with the premise that we really cannot do what I think the FEI hopes we could do, which is to pass on (at a level of generality) a body of experience which would apply across government, and which would better prepare people as they come into government at the assistant secretary level." He felt that problems faced by an assistant secretary who has previously served in government are quite different from those of somebody walking in " 'naked from the outside,' from the private world into a government. They don't understand your language, which is foreign, and they have little feeling for a career system which they've never dealt with before." Rhinelander did not deny the need for training of the completely new political appointee, however.

Reporting on his team's discussion, Macdonald took a different view. "The question was raised whether the FEI really could give an effective program for new assistant secretaries and sub-cabinet officers. The consensus of our group was that indeed they could, but it would be best that it be scheduled about three months after they came into office rather than when they are just entering or coming into office. Because it takes that time before they have some feel of what it is that the course would be all about."

Paul Bolduc thought "three months is far too long" to wait before a new assistant secretary is put in a training or orientation program. "They are going to get involved with what they are doing, they are going to be very excited, thus you will never get them, they won't find the time. I think the key thing is to get them either shortly before they come on board, or during their first week, and have a follow-up session three months later." Bolduc's team suggested that the initial orientation session should not last longer than three days and, preferably, should be held on a weekend. In addition, he said, "All agreed that it would have to be a presidential decision to get it done at all." Brad Patterson agreed with this view, saying that in order to work, any orientation program "has to have a White House component. I don't think it can be just the Civil Service Commission at a semi-technical level. For this level of appointee, you would have to have the White House family involved."

It would be highly desirable to have both experienced and inexperienced political appointees take two or three days away from their jobs early in their assignments to talk frankly among themselves and with key career subordinates about objectives, operating procedures, and methods of measuring progress. FEI's view is that these planning sessions are far more effective away from the office: the Federal Executive Institute has ten years' experience to prove it. The problem does not lie with the career executives; most of them would welcome an opportunity to get to know their new political bosses in a setting of "mutuality of interest." The problem lies with the political appointees, who believe that time from the office cannot be spared for this kind of team-building. In addition, some may fear that displaying their ignorance of government to career subordinates would be threatening to themselves. Many assistant secretaries prefer to work on a one-to-one basis with subordinates as a way of maintaining control, and the idea of a team effort is not their idea of managing. That is why, in this view, team-building among careerists and political executives should take place during the first month of the assistant secretary's tenure, on the theory that new appointees will be more receptive at that time to accepting new ideas and proposals.

As desirable as team-building at this level might be, Brad Patterson is probably correct in advising that there is little likelihood for it without a White House commitment to the idea of training political executives to be fully effective in their jobs. Few successful people are willing to admit that they need formal training to perform new functions; but having the idea sanctioned by higher authority relieves one of the responsibility for proposing it. Many said after the two-day session at FEI that it had been a productive session and that they had learned some new things. How much greater would the learning be for a group of *new* political executives with greater need to understand their organizations and learn where the human resources may be found?

Conclusion

Jack Young stated that his group finally came around "to the real problem. That this is a tension-ridden system; that these interfaces with some truly political officers versus the career service contained one hell of a lot of disgust, a lot of distress. We talked about how does one cope sometimes with the rebel leaders—those in the bureaucracy who are so dedicated . . . that when they took their oath of office in the career service, they took their oath of office in terms of those ideas and ideals. How do you deal with those kinds of individuals? How do you get to know who they are? How do you get to know what their ideas are about? And at that point we stopped and never got into coming up with advice as to how do you 'steal' the rebel leaders." There is, of course, no simple answer to Young's question. Kolberg argued that from a management point of view, "it is going to take years in order to change institutions and build them to do the managerial job that I think must be done at the assistant secretary level."

But one place where the effort can begin is at the communications level. There is no question that communication between the career service and new political appointees is generally strained and that mutual suspicion persists even a year later. To a large extent this results from the difference in their roles—the careerists usually protecting the system of which they are a product, and the political executives supporting a president whose vision usually does not extend beyond four years. But this is no excuse for either side refusing to enter into a dialogue that would reduce barriers and try to build that "mutuality of interest" Heclo talks about. The truth of the matter is that each side needs the other: the political appointee cannot accomplish his or her objectives without the cooperation of career civil servants, and the careerists are not going to find fulfillment in their jobs without the continuing interest and support of their political superiors, including the president. Thus, it is absolutely necessary that the two sides realize they are in it together and begin the process of "reasoning together"—of trying to find accomodations rather than continuing confrontations.

In sum, a climate of cooperation and learning between assistant secretaries and their career executives should be established to break down the barriers that obviously exist between these two levels. The gap is becoming too wide and costly for the federal government to sustain as it undertakes ever more functions and responsibilities in American society. Narrowing this gap should, therefore, be a high priority of any new administration.

Appendix: Excerpts from FEI Symposium Discussion on the Political-Career Interface*

Explanation of Themes for the Day

Nuechterlein: The subject for discussion this morning deals with the

---

*From Thomas P. Murphy, Donald E. Nuechterlein, and Ronald J. Stupak, eds., *The President's Program Directors: The Assistant Secretaries* (Charlottesville, Va.: The Federal Executive Institute, 1977).

political-career interface. We'll be addressing that first in a presentation followed by a discussion, and then we'll break into three teams for small group discussion. This afternoon we'll be talking about the role of the assistant secretary in policy formulation and implementation, and Ralph Bledsoe will lead the discussion.

I would like to say a few words about what we heard last night that leads into our discussion this morning. It seems to me that the point made by Fred Clark and others—that it is essential for any new assistant secretary coming into that role to get the career executives on board, to get them into your confidence—is a very crucial part of the process of government at your level. Here at the FEI we train the people who are just below you; those who have to respond to your policy direction, to your guidance. I've been here since the beginning of this Institute and we've gone through about 2,500 federal executives at the supergrade level. One of the things that is very clear to me in talking with these people over the years is that many feel there is a barrier between them and you.

In the discussion last night, the point was made that the most essential factor for an assistant secretary to keep in mind in adjusting to his situation is the personality and style and directions taken by his boss, presumably the secretary himself. That made me recall what I hear federal executives coming to FEI often saying, when we get into these discussions: "The most important thing for me is to know what that man above me is thinking, where he wants to go, and for me to adjust to him." Let me suggest to you that it may be almost as important for you, for the secretaries, and also for career executives to look downward with equal interest, because there are hundreds and hundreds of people that are depending on you for guidance. The way you treat them, the way you relate to them in your daily work will make a large difference in the way they respond to your leadership. I refer again to Fred Clark, who reported that every Thursday afternoon, without fail and regardless of what else comes up, he spends two hours with an "open door," when 750 people who want to can make an appointment and come and see him without any agenda. I just leave that idea with you.

It seems to me that if this system of ours is going to work better than it has in the past, we have got somehow to create a better community between your level—the political level—and the career level—the people who are going to carry out government functions. Maybe now is the time to start, when we have another transition coming up, when a lot of new people will be coming into top positions of government. They're going to be asking the same question that has been asked for a hundred years: "How do I get this job done with all these bureaucrats who really don't want to move?" "How do I break down those barriers?" I think what Tom Murphy is trying to do at the FEI—and your program is the first piece of it—is to open up the communications process and get a team spirit going between the political level and the career level. I'm absolutely convinced that the FEI has the intellectual and operational capabilities to accomplish this task. The question is: "Will the next administration take advantage of it?" I hope so.

Now let me introduce our speaker for this morning. John Rhinelander, under secretary of Housing and Urban Development, and former general counsel of the Department of Health, Education, and Welfare.

Presentation on "Political-Career Interface"

Rhinelander: I would think to start with the premise that we really cannot do what I think the FEI hopes we could do, which is to pass on (at a level of generality) a body of experience which would apply across government, and which would better prepare people as they come into government at the assistant secretary level. I think it's probably true that 75 percent of the people in this room were in the federal government before they got to the level of assistant secretary, and that the problems they face are entirely different from those of somebody walking in "naked from the outside," from the private world into a government. They don't understand your language, which is foreign, and they have little feeling for a career system which they've never dealt with before. I say that, having now been in six of the departments; and if I had to come to HUD or HEW, where I have been at the presidential appointee level, without having been in government for years before that, I do not think I could have handled the job. Having come there from my wanderings around the federal government, the problems I faced in the early days and the way I went about them were, I think, entirely different from someone who had not been in the government before.

Just by way of illustration, before I took my job as general counsel at HEW in the summer of 1973, I had resisted taking it for a number of months. I was in the private sector. When I finally decided I would do it, I asked a great many of my friends around the government about the office and I found out from almost everybody that they had a superb staff, that I would have a magnificent deputy, and that at the peer level of the assistant secretary group I would have a very fine group of people to work with. I am also certainly sure that when my name began to surface through the information mill, the same kind of cross-checking was going on about me that I was doing about the department, so that by the time I arrived physically on the spot, both those with whom I would work and those with whom I would interact had a pretty good feeling for who I was. Now you can do that if you have been in government, but you cannot do that when you are on the outside.

When I landed at HEW, two of the immediate problems were: one, that we had 35 suits against us for accounting funds illegally (Paul Dembling remembers that very well as does Jack Young); two, we were faced with the fact that in the litigation field affecting HEW, we were literally being run by the courts. We had something like 3,000 Social Security cases against us. It had been doubling in the course of the years, now up to something like 14,000 cases a year, and there wasn't a single major decision the secretary would make that would not be challenged in the courts.

My problem was to try to get a very large general counsel's office, which had something like 250 attorneys at the time and which was still woefully understaffed in light of the nature of the problems, to get them best placed to provide the kind of legal advice that I thought was necessary to the assistant secretary, to the secretary, and to the under secretary. I could do this, having worked in the federal service for a number of years, having almost made a career but never having been in the career service myself. I could get right down to the business of tackling the problems of the Department. I would also say that being in the general counsel's office, we were not constrained on the professional side by all the Civil Service rules in terms of hiring and firing people, which made my life a great deal easier than those in other parts of the government.

Again, if we're looking at the breadth of people at the assistant secretary level, I would suggest that those who are general counsels, or who are in the equivalent role of the legal advisor in the State Department, or an equivalent position in Justice, would face very different problems from those that others would face. However, a lot of it depends on the age of the agency.

One of my earlier jobs that wasn't at the assistant secretary level, but was in an almost independent agency, was to deal with an emergency balance of payments program that LBJ announced on January 1, 1968. It was originally staffed by people detailed from other agencies of the government; and, as everybody who has been in government awhile knows, in offices which are set up by detail, you end up with employees that offices would like to get rid of; therefore, one of the immediate problems was to get an absolutely top flight staff. One of the best illustrations I have of that is when I arrived at the Commerce Department. We were on the sixth floor (most people don't know that there is a sixth floor at Commerce; it is the attic). The secretary who was assigned to me the first day literally spent the whole day typing one letter. She never got it typed correctly the first day, and when the second day started, she started right back again. So, when you have to deal with a new agency starting up, the nature of the problem is very different from those you have to deal with otherwise. Again, I am just not certain that we can meaningfully pass on to new people coming in the kind of information they can really make use of. I think others in the audience agree with me because we talked about this ahead of time.

Very clearly, 99 percent of the people in the federal government are in the career service. If you cannot work with the people in the career service, you're not going to be effective in government, and you should either not come in or you had better get out fast. I think it's true there are something like 3,000 political appointments which are being discussed in terms of the transition. The number at the policy level is much smaller than that if you look across departments; for instance, at HUD I think we may have 30 or 40 people who will be moving in from the outside to the political levels, out of 15,000 employees. At HEW, I think there are probably even less than that, in terms of the changeover. The fact of the matter is, 98 percent or 99 percent of the government *is* the career service, and those are the people you have to work with. You have to work with them within the constraints of the Civil Service rules and regulations, and I think so much of it depends on your ability to work with people, as well as on the problems of the moment. If you land in a crisis situation, for instance with Jack Young at NASA, where you're building a field of high technology, the problems you deal with are very different from HEW, the State Department, or the Defense Department. It is also very true that the style of the person you work with is absolutely critical. The difference between Cap Weinberger and Frank Carlucci, who were the secretary and under secretary when I was at HEW, Carla Hills at HUD, and Henry Kissinger at State, is so varied that anyone who would suggest that you ought to work with Cap and Frank the same way you ought to work with Henry or with Carla would be misleading somebody else.

Finally, in terms of the barrier between the career service and the political appointee, I think it's very true that the average tenure now of political appointees is something like eighteen months. I'm not sure that I've ever hit that average in my career around the government. One of the great fears, of course, of the career service is: Who is going to come in to be on top of them? In fact, I think it's always better from their point of view to have somebody from inside because the threat of the unknown is probably worse than whomever they already have. There is the problem of educating them, and then the problem that just when the assistant secretary or under secretary really is on top of the job, the likelihood is that there is going to be a change.

I guess one of the general statements which is important for anybody coming into the government at this level to recognize is that we move on a train that is already under way. You inherit a group of problems, you inherit a group of issues which have been left for you by your predecessor. You will be there for a relatively short period of time and then when you leave you will be leaving, hopefully, a different set of issues and a different set of problems for your successor, although that's not always the case. But you have a limited time in which to deal with things that you don't really control. When you come in, you have to deal, nine-tenths of the time, with problems which are already there—rather than pick up and go in new directions.

Again, looking at the domestic side of government rather than the foreign affairs side for a moment, at HEW I think we had something like 350 separate grant programs; all with a statutory base. Over the course of the last six or seven years there have been enormous numbers of efforts made to seek the necessary legislation to consolidate them, to phase some out; but Congress has not been willing to do that with very rare exceptions, so the focus of the work of the assistant secretaries has been with statutory programs which were created before they got there and, to a large degree, have not been changed much since they left.

This set of generalizations is not, I think, very satisfactory from the point of view of the FEI in trying to give guidance to those who come into the government. I do think perhaps, in my case, the most valuable experience I had was coming into the government in the Pentagon as a special assistant. Those of you who work for the Pentagon know that when assistant secretaries come into the Pentagon there are one, two, or three military aides all ready to take them under their wing, hopefully to keep them from doing dangerous things which they shouldn't get into, and instead keep them busy christening ships, and saluting, and everything else. When I came into the Pentagon, I came in as a special assistant to the secretary and was taken under the wing of some very able people in the Navy and Marine Corps. Through other contacts in ISA [Office of International Security Affairs] and with the other services, I think they probably taught me more about how a bureaucratic system works than I could have learned anywhere else.

I say that, particularly having been trained as a lawyer and having worked in a very large law firm in New York. I know you all have to work with lawyers from time to time, and an important thing to recognize is that legal training basically prepares an individual to work on a problem alone. I think as a general rule, it is probably fair to say that lawyers are bad managers. The whole nature of the legal discipline is not to work within large organizations or in terms of managing a business organization. My experience in having come from a big law firm was enhanced, in terms of working effectively in the government, by my year, if you will, of training at the Pentagon. If I had come directly to HEW, if I had come directly from the private practice of law, I do not think I could have dealt effectively with the system. I say that also looking at friends of mine who have come down from New York, Chicago, and other cities, straight into government at the assistant secretary level from law firms, corporations, and even from the academic world, although I think people who come from the academic world have lived in an institutional system which, while not similar, is akin to that in the government. I think many of the striking failures I have seen in government have been people who are incredibly able as individuals, but who were not able to walk or swim in the kind of highly ambiguous bureaucratic situation which is the government.

If anything is important to pass on, it is that when you come from the private sector, from the world of business, the world of law or something like that where things are relatively clear, you discover there is nothing very clear in government. The roles are not clear, the roles differ from moment to moment. What may be important for my predecessor may not be at all important to me because the problems have moved on. And individuals change. We used to have daily staff meetings at HEW. I would say we had probably twenty or twenty-five people in the secretary's office and every month I think there was a new face. This kind of change affects relationships up and down the ladder within a department, with sister agencies and departments, and in light of that, it is always necessary to be adjusting to the personalities, the changing focuses, and the changing priorities of the times.

I guess in the final analysis, the most important thing at the assistant secretary level is to be able to work well with people and to improvise on your feet. If you cannot do that, if you bring rigid approaches into a system, I just do not think you can be effective. I would like to stop here with those generalities because I do think anything I'd lay down in terms of general rules would apply well to those who came into a few positions. But the generalities would be highly misleading to others who came into different positions. Would anybody like to make any comments on that?

Discussion Following Rhinelander's Presentation

Morrill: John, when you talked about your "moving train" it reminded me of a vignette that occurred between then assistant secretary of Defense, Alain Enthoven, and a senior career bureaucrat at the Bureau of the Budget. Alain was kind of musing about his job and said, "You know this job that I've got is kind of like trying to paint a moving train;" and the career bureaucrat said, "Yes, and with a one-inch brush."

Rhinelander: I think it becomes clearer if we just use some particular examples from my case. When I was the general counsel at the assistant secretary level at HEW, which is certainly one of the most fascinating departments, there was an enormous variety of "moving train" situations. We had the impoundment lawsuits; we had half of our Civil Rights offices being run by the district court judges. We had Social Security with its problems with the computer and which gave us such legal problems that today over 10 percent of the cases in the federal courts now come from the Social Security Administration. If I didn't focus my attention on those problems at the very beginning, I would have been remiss. Jack Young and I spent about three months at the very beginning on the impoundment cases. Jack and I were sworn in at the same time, as I recall, working first of all to get Secretary Weinberger to agree that we would no longer impound the funds in the education and the health fields; in the end, he agreed that he would remain neutral. Then we won the agreement from the Department of Justice and OMB. Consequently, about three months after we were there, we successfully got the funds released. I felt in terms of moving into HEW—this was right in the middle of Watergate—that this was probably one of the most divisive single issues that we'd had before the department. As a lawyer, I thought we had a case that we could not possibly win (bringing in a political judgment) because of the fact that our relationships with the Congress would be continually soured from then on. They suffered for a long time thereafter from the fact that the Congress felt, with a fair degree of merit, that we were not implementing the programs which Congress had mandated be carried out, when we had a legal obligation to do so. It was my judgment at the time that it was necessary to focus on those cases. That kind of situation won't arise again, now that we have the new Budget Act. However, that kind of crisis situation may well arise in any department at any time, and it will simply have to be handled in the best way possible.

I would say, in terms of looking at the federal service and the private sector, that my general counsel's office at HEW was an excellent office. It was certainly large and it had first-rate people. Compared with the private sector, I would say one of the big law firms in New York or Washington, D.C., would probably be a little bit better, but in terms of a government office, it was absolutely superb. If you come into an area in government where you have a staff of the quality I had at HEW, the kinds of problems you have to deal with are of a very different ilk from those situations where you have to build up a staff from scratch. Again, if you're fortunate enough to be a lawyer and in charge of a general counsel's office, you have the flexibility to bring people on board, as well as flexibility to transfer them, which you do not have in the classified service.

I think if there's any frustration which will shock anyone coming into the government for the first time, it is the time delays involved in filling positions in the classified service. I forget the average time now, but at HEW I think it was something like six to nine months for some of the higher positions. We had at one point something like nine out of the top twelve positions at Social Security unfilled, and you simply cannot expect the government to perform well with those kinds of vacancies in that big an organization. Social Security has something like $85 billion going through it in a year, and it has something like 85,000 employees. That clearly has to be one of the great frustrations, equalled only by the difficulty, real or apparent, in removing people who are not doing their jobs well.

My own experience is that you can in fact remove people; you can dismiss them from the federal service if you do it in the right way, particularly if the people to whom you have delegated authority do it in the right way. It takes time. It means you've got to prepare a record over a period of time, and you simply cannot make up your mind one day and expect it to happen. You do have to accept the fact that, given the new rights which have been articulated by the courts and through the administrative process, you walk through a minefield where it is very easy for an employee to bring in a grievance, or a complaint, or a lawsuit, or perhaps all three at the same time in order to slow down the process, and in fact to derail it, if things have been done improperly. It's not impossible to move people out, but it certainly is not the easiest thing in the world to accomplish. And I guess in terms of a common element in talking to people in government, the problems they perceive, rightly or wrongly, in dealing with the personnel system is probably one of the most frustrating parts of the whole experience.

Morrill: My sense about the last point that you made is that having come out of a career system and having been in it for twenty years, over time and out of a series of individualized events—most particularly since Watergate—there has been an effort to create a system and a process to prevent managers from doing it wrong; and cumulatively, we are getting close to the point where you're preventing managers from doing it at all. You have insulated the system in a way where you almost can't move, or if you can move, it takes you so long to get it done that it may outlast the average life of an assistant secretary. One of the things that probably needs to be done is to reexamine the structures and the hypotheses that we've got in the personnel business—not in a way that deters or detracts from a merit concept, but in a way which reinstills a notion that I think got badly battered in the Watergate period—the notion of trust. People in charge have got to be given enough flexibility, including to do it occasionally wrong and pay a penalty of removal, rather than a penalty of a process that keeps them from managing at all.

Rhinelander: I would agree with your basic premise that we have now either designed or implemented a system with so many safeguards and such great time delays that when you look at that and the average tenure of the presidential appointee, what you have in many cases are two governments: You have the official one, which is on all the charts, and you have the one which is the way it really works. Something I haven't mentioned, and I think one thing which we might be interested in discussing here in light of this, is that one way in which the political system responds to this situation is through the use of task forces or special assistants, which are ways around the formal organization chart and around the formal personnel system. At HUD we make much greater use of special assistants than we did, and probably could have, at HEW. Carla Hills probably has five or six special assistants (I have two) and her technique of managing is basically through a whole series of ad hoc task forces. What she really does is that when an important matter comes up, she simply pulls a different group of people together; and the fact that she hasn't filled "x" number of jobs is not that material. That's fine in terms of designing a program; but you cannot do it when you have to turn around and implement a program.

I'm sympathetic to what you say because I have looked at it as an attorney, and I am concerned that the individual employee is provided a lawful process. On the other hand, we have built so many safeguards into dealing with the right of the individual to challenge the system, whether it's a grievance, an EEO complaint, or whether it's a lawsuit, that the deck has been stacked. For instance, under our EEO procedures right now, the individual in government who is alleged to have been the discriminator really has no rights until the process is through the first step and a decision has been made. I think that is simply an unacceptable way to conduct our business. What we're finding at HUD, and what I suspect is true at other agencies, is that a decision is made internally that Mr. X has discriminated against Y. That really is the final agency action if the individual who brought the complaint wants to leave it there. But what we're seeing now is that individual lawsuits are being brought, and the employee is bringing an action against both the department and the office seeking damages—in both an official and personal capacity. What you have on the record is a finding of discrimination which may or may not be sound, and frequently these are not sound. But the process has built such a one-sided record into the case that it's very hard to go into court and tell the judge, "Look, this may have been the agency's determination, but it is not terribly well founded."

One of the great problems in government, and anybody at the assistant secretary level knows it, is the problem of coordination among peers. The general counsel's office is a good example. At times it tries to run everything, and at times it is also left out of the ball game, either to the betterment or sometimes to the detriment of the department. At State, I think it was more the case that the legal advisor was left out, to the chagrin of those in the legal advisor's office. I think it's probably fair to say in the domestic departments that if the balance is one way or the other, the General Counsel's office frequently assumes more than what others would perceive would be its proper role. As an attorney, I always felt it was critically important to try myself, and to train the attorneys working for me, to distinguish between giving legal advice and policy advice. I have no problem with any attorney giving policy advice, as long as it's very clear that it is separate and distinct from legal advice as to what are the permissible courses of action. But relationships among peers, between the General Counsel's office and the Programs Office, between the Policy Office and the Program Office, are probably some of the most difficult roles which have to be worked out, and it is very hard to generalize in advance how that should be done. A lot of it depends on personality, and again a lot of it depends on which are, if you will, the hot subjects of the moment.

I'd like to go back to one thing. In the personnel systems at Defense and State, the tradition is for career people in the Foreign Service and the military to be reassigned almost as fast as presidential appointees. At least in the Navy, I think the average tour as skipper of a ship was something like fourteen months when I was back at the Pentagon. That's a very different kind of personnel system, with all its own problems, from the career GS system in the domestic departments, where you really have people who have been in an area for sometimes five, ten, fifteen, twenty years, and even all the way up to the assistant secretary level.

Macdonald: What would you think of giving the career supergrade jobs protection, but not position protection along the lines that you're talking about?

Rhinelander: I would be much in favor of that. I think you've got to be able to move them around, and one of the things I could do in the general counsel's office was move a lot of people laterally. In fact, I think I've left behind a really superb legal office because I did have the flexibility. I think I probably filled or moved half of the assistant general counsels, which were the level below the deputy general counsel. These were "schedule A's" and we had the leeway to do it. I think that is critically important. I do think you have to strike a balance between protecting the individual who has given his career to the government and is vulnerable against the needs of people who come in trying to carry out the programs of the president. The present system doesn't do that very well. One reason, for instance, that the general counsel's office frequently assumes greater power than they probably should have is that you have a lot of flexibility in hiring the general counsel's staff. Lawyers by tradition either are, or think they are, great generalists; and you find out that people look to the general counsel to pick up a lot of things that ought to be handled elsewhere. The Defense Department is a classic case. The deputy there, I think, has been acting general counsel more than he's been deputy. The general counsel at DOD has frequently been the key special assistant to the secretary of defense, handling hot situations all over the place. I think what you're suggesting would give a great deal of needed flexibility to the policy-making level of government, as well as protecting the rights of individuals in the career service.

Bolduc: What is the danger of doing that?

Rhinelander: I agree that there are dangers.

Bolduc: I think that we have to balance it, because if we're not careful, we'll find ourselves just moving people around and creating jobs which do not really contribute in a meaningful way to achieving what we want to achieve, and then we end up with a bunch of disgruntled employees.

Rhinelander: But that's happening now. I think everybody in this room probably knows individuals who have been effectively shunted aside. Every office usually has one area which is sometimes referred to as the "dumping ground," or whatever you will. That leads, of course, to a whole other set of unfortunate circumstances.

Bolduc: The point is that if we were to move in that direction, I think we'd have to guard against making the present situation worse.

Patterson: John, I'd like to hear Fred Clark comment on this, particularly with Bill's point: What about the growth of the employee unions? And now there's talk about military unions.

Rhinelander: I think when you combine the merit staffing system with all the rules which have grown up on top of it, and couple that with the growing power of the unions and the rights groups, you have a system which is almost unworkable.

Clark: The few prerogatives that management has left are fast disappearing as unions become stronger, and I think we're going to see the day when there is going to be legislation in the federal activity and that's going to make it more complicated. I don't see any improvement of a return of the prerogatives to management that used to be a right.

Rhinelander: What has happened is that you have combined two systems: (1) the merit system from the government side, which began

I think at the end of the nineteenth century and has evolved since then, and protects individuals, through an elaborate series of rules; and (2) collective bargaining from the private sector where again you have an old tradition and system of protecting the rights of the individuals. When you marry them both together, what frequently happens is that you go to the lower common demoninator, and I think it is coming to a point where it is getting unworkable. Again I would go back to the office of the general counsel. I don't know of any general counsel's office which is unionized. While the rules vary in some of the general counsel's offices, individuals have significantly less rights than there is in the general merit system. In other cases, they have been given almost the equivalent of these rights, but even so there is greater flexibility in dealing with the general counsel's office than you do in the general merit system.

I think one of the great problems and one of the great frustrations that people feel when they come into government is the problem which we've been focusing on: the personnel rules, the lack of flexibility, the lack of ability to get people on when you need them, and the lack of the ability to either move them laterally or out if they're not performing. Part of the problem, of course, is the short tenure. People don't wish to spend the time to build the record needed to remove from the service those who are not performing. You'll simply leave it to your successor, and your successor leaves it to his successor, and then this builds up. This is one of the consequences of the short tenure.

Kolberg: I'd add several things. It's not only the combination of those two systems. You mentioned earlier the EEO rules, and regulations on top of that which today protect 90 percent of the work force in one way or another. They're either young, or old, or minority, or whatever it is, and they have rules and regulations. So you really have three systems, one on top of another.

Rhinelander: I can say I lost two EEO complaints in my last six months at HEW. One was where I purportedly discriminated in favor of males and in the second I supposedly discriminated in favor of females.

Kolberg: In addition to that, in the government (which you don't have any place else, I think), you always have the political system, which gives an appeal point for anyone who wants to use it; and anyone who has been in Washington long enough knows how to use it. If that doesn't work, on top of that you have the press which is looking for things of this kind; and when you add those five or six things together you have major problems. And then I would go back to the point you were relating it to; I would say that Mr. Carter is doing it right by at least saying and setting a tradition openly, "I want to get people here for three or four years instead of one or two." It's going to take that long, it seems to me, as the system has become more complicated especially in a managerial sense. Perhaps in a policy sense (if you aren't worried about managing), it isn't so important; but in a managerial sense, it is going to take years in order to change institutions and build them to do the managerial job that I think must be done at the assistant secretary level.

Rhinelander: I think you may even be optimistic in saying "years," because one thing which is frequently overlooked or referred to too lightly in looking at our whole system of government is the role the courts now play in the process. In the film we saw yesterday [the American Society for Public Administration film on cabinet secretaries], there were references to this when the cabinet secretaries were recalling their experiences of the two branches of government: the legislative branch and the executive branch. The courts now have an enormous role to play in the way that: (a) you manage the federal establishment, (b) you reach policy decisions, and (c) you allocate your money. Federal court judges now are experts in Jack Young's old art of apportioning funds and the whole budget process. They've got in their files draft orders against practically every department. Now this is an extraordinary situation. When I looked at it from one point at HEW, I think every member of the District of Columbia district court bench had three major cases involving HEW. They're just being parcelled out. When you got more cases than judges, they had to begin to double it up. But this is a significant factor.

   In some areas of foreign affairs, it is, or at least it was to a degree, still possible to ignore the advice of counsel because a lot of things are not likely to end up in the courts. While it is true now that a case has been brought seeking an injunction against negotiating with Panama before a judge in the Panama Canal Zone, by and large a lot of decisions made in the foreign affairs world are not likely to end up before the courts and be subject to an injunction. When you move to the domestic side of government, that's just not the case. I had been forewarned before I took my job as general counsel. I was persuaded before I assumed office that it was the case; and I then spent a lot of time convincing Secretary Weinberger, and it didn't take long to convince him because he was a defendant, I think, in more lawsuits than any other federal official. But the pervasive role of the law and the oversight function of the court really matches that of the Congress now. I think it's often ignored and is often understated; but I think it is a very important factor to keep in mind, particularly when you're on the domestic side of the big grant agencies of the government.

Connor: With regard to your comment about the classified positions, it seems to me that we just are going in a direction where we find job appointments either from within the bureaucracy or the legal profession, because it is becoming increasingly difficult for anybody who doesn't have the flexibility of the legal profession to come into government. It is very difficult to get private sector companies, if you're not a lawyer, to permit you to go into government, or to get another potential employer to consider that you have picked up anything useful while you were in government service. I just think that the difficulty of being associated with any special interests, the low salaries and all, we've just got to go in the direction where more and more of the top people come from the legal profession.

Rhinelander: You are making one false assumption; that lawyers from the outside don't earn very much money, and therefore they will be happy to step into it.

Connor: You can always go back to your profession, whereas others of us who do not have that profession scramble when we come out. My point is that I think that it is going to have something to do with management style, especially in relation to the comments about the way lawyers are trained and the way you describe Carter's style of picking his people. I think that it is going to have serious implications with respect to the degree to which so-called professional management is conducted in government, and by whom. I think a different style of management is needed in the bureaucracy. The orthodox one, which we have been talking about when we referred to classic management techniques, just won't work the way it once did.

Rhinelander: First of all, in this country lawyers have always had a very significant role in government, going back to George Washington's administration. My impression, and it may be wrong, is that those trained in economics, in the quantitative field, are perhaps gaining on the lawyers. I would have said that they are now at least number two—a discipline which is becoming more and more important in government. It is very true that in the government we deal basically with laws established by statutes, and basically implemented by elaborate regulations either controlling the internal process or the external process. The lawyers have a very heavy (if not disproportionately heavy) hand. The courts are heavily involved. I'm not sure I would say that this results from the entry-reentry problem.

Looking at the situation right now, I would say it is very difficult to get top flight people, whether their training is law or otherwise, from the private sector except perhaps for the educational institutions, to come in at less than the under secretary positions. To come to Washington now at about the $40,000 level as an assistant secretary, given the cost of homes and if you have young children to bring up, is going to be extraordinarily difficult. I don't think it's as much the conflict of interest rules because lawyers are affected as much by the conflict of interest rules as most others. I think lawyers face really the same kinds of problems that you do in the private sector. In my case, when I left my New York law firm in 1966, I talked with each one of the partners, thirty-five of them, and thirty-three told me not to go and two suggested I go. I don't think that's very different from what you would get in the private sector. Now it is true that lawyers have a greater mobility, at least they think they do, than others. But I'm not sure even that's the case anymore. If you look at industry, there is an enormous movement of people from one institution to another. I think it's true that in terms of history, lawyers have always been perceived as having greater mobility than many others; but I'm not sure that's still the case. I think a lot of it is the fact that many institutions have rules now, where if you go, you can't come back; or if you go, we will not assure that you can come back, and many people are unwilling to take that chance. I guess I faced that one early, and I've never been back anywhere yet; and I still have a few more institutions I haven't touched. As long as that is a concern, it's going to apply to lawyers as well as it is to others.

Now it's true that from the investment banking world, the law firms, and the accounting firms, the likelihood of a partner not coming back if he wants to come back could be pretty remote; but that is different from private industry. I'm not sure that the conflict of interest rules make that much difference. I think you've got questions of pay, you've got questions of ambiguity or role, and you've got problems of frustration. I think those who have been in the career service by and large enjoy immensely government at the assistant secretary level. I think to those who come in from the outside it's a very mixed bag. Some come in and do very well. Others come in and are a total flop.

ELT Reports on Political-Career Interface

Nuechterlein: Well, ladies and gentlemen, let's all, if we can, make this discussion a bit more informal. Maybe the reports could be a little shorter, and perhaps we could get more "give and take" among the different groups. The Blue Team and the Red Team spokesmen, I believe, will speak for about five minutes or so. The White Team wants to vary its presentation a bit. Let's start with the Blue Team.

Blue Team Report

Macdonald: The Blue Team had a very productive and interesting discussion about the interface between the political appointees and the career appointees. We noted that the assistant secretary should start his job as an intense learning experience, and in that connection it was pointed out that he should "eyeball the operation" out in the field as much as he could in that regard. The question was raised: Where do you learn what you're supposed to know as an assistant secretary? I think that there was some consensus that we learn from our peers to a great degree, and that the competition among assistant secretaries is a myth which is quite exaggerated. There is nevertheless a verticalism. Most of our contacts are either upward or downward, and I agree with Paul Dembling who pointed out that when you are an assistant secretary it seems as if you never sign a letter that you write and you never write a letter that you sign.

Staff meetings were thought to be quite important. John Richardson, in particular, pointed out that informal staff meetings are just informal access channels to all of the career people around us and under us, and therefore they are extremely good for developing relationships and managing the system. It was noted that in connection with those assistant secretaries who supervise bureaus, that to get something done you had to do it slowly. Fred Clark made the point that you just can't take a bureau and decide that they are going to go in one direction. It is a constant sort of pressure—a carrot and stick interaction process. But eventually results can be obtained.

The characteristics of the career employee and the political appointee were compared: The career employee being valuable for his expertise, his continuity, and what you might call his governmental memory; whereas the value of the political appointee lies in his approach, his ability to question the entire purpose of the function of some of the bureaucracy, and his independence which really depends upon his ability to lead. Since political appointees have no security, his security lies in his ability to walk out.

We also discussed some control mechanisms that are used in bureaucracy, and I think the budget was the most important of those. The fact is, the assistant secretary has to dig into and really understand the budget—both the original budget submission and the reprogramming. It was pointed out that one assistant secretary controlled the international travel of his career employees and that some things like that—just the fact that they are approved at the assistant secretary level—lend a great deal of control in and of itself. Also promotions are a control device. I found out that in both the Department of Agriculture and the Treasury Department the assistant secretary reviewed career promotions for Grade 14 and up. That is a very tender thing to do since a political appointee reviewing a career appointment does require care. Yet, I think it certainly can and will be done.

Finally, the question was raised whether the FEI really could give an effective program for new assistant secretaries and sub-cabinet officers. The consensus of our group was that indeed they could, but it would be best that it be scheduled about three months after they came into office rather than when they are just entering or coming into office. Because it takes that time before they have some feel of what it is that the course would be all about.

Feltner: The point about learning from peers is that you *can* learn from your peers and I would encourage new assistant secretaries to do that. I think that sometimes there is a reluctance on the part of new assistant secretaries to ask their peers for advice. I would suggest that they not be reluctant to do that.

Richardson: An obvious point, but one that bears emphasizing. If a new assistant secretary is going to get along with the career people, the easiest way is to evidence from the beginning an enthusiasm for the functions they are performing and an interest in the overall purpose of the organization. That will go a long way to overcome other kinds of suspicions—I've seen it happen.

Dembling: This wasn't a point that I made—Dick Feltner made it, I think—but the question was asked concerning how a political appointee gets the career group to respond to political requests that may originate in the White House, or from purely political requests. And his comment was that he had no real problem in getting the career service to respond to that, even when they had to shift gears in responding to such a request. And I think that that is important for assistant secretaries coming into government to recognize, that you can get the career service to respond even though it is necessary to shift them from what they have been doing previously into a new direction.

Nuechterlein: Thank you Blue Team. Let's move on to the White Team. Jack Young, I guess you've got the ball.

White Team Report

Young: We started out with a question that was not assigned to us. And that's because Brad Patterson said, "Listen to the conversations this morning about how fouled up the personnel situation is" (and he meant in terms of selecting non-career people for these political jobs) "haven't we sort of done a good job?" That was the end of that. By the time the group had calmed down somewhat—all having told their own experiences of how it took nineteen months before we got through this and how we blamed the FBI, and so forth—what turned out is that wherever you look on the civilian side of the personnel system something happens, even to the White House system. That led us into an old question in the field, and that is, "Should there be more, or less, non-career jobs?" Which is a critical question in this business. What we came to, in conclusion, was that the mix is just about right. We talked about the regional officers—should they be career or non-career—and came to the conclusion they should be non-career.

Then, I think we proved that it is very difficult to generalize in this field because we saw everybody's different style as we saw each person talk about his own situation. And much of this is situational, much of it relates to the kind of background you bring to the job, and so forth. But what we really felt was important was the whole field of communications. We spent a lot of time talking about how you communicate to the bureaucracy as a new political officer. This ran the whole field from, be sure you attend the birthday parties, the Christmas parties, and actually even stressing that it is essential to talk to these people. I don't think we discovered anything new in the communications field since almost all of you knew this before we got here.

Then we moved on quickly into the field of advice. And here we went back to some ideas that we talked about yesterday—that if you're going to survive successfully as a political officer, depending on your style and your background, you must find some ways to co-opt the bureaucracy.

Further, you must limit your agenda and pass down into the bureaucracy as many things as you can so that you can concentrate on the items to which you have assigned top priority. And I suggested you might ask for ninety days. Well, John Rhinelander straightened me out again, since he made it clear that sometimes you don't have that choice to wait ninety days. But often political officers, particularly if they have come from a background where they have not worked in complex organizations, come in and they don't know the territory—they begin to move too quickly and blow themselves out of the water. And sometimes, if they really want to get things done, it is better to wait a little bit. And I say that old song from the *Music Man* hits the nail right on the head—"If you are going to be a drummer in this business you got to know the territory."

Then at the end we got to the real problem. That this is a tension-ridden system; that those interfaces with some truly political officers versus the career service contained one hell of a lot of disgust, a lot of distress. We talked about how does one cope sometimes with the rebel leaders—those in the bureaucracy who are so dedicated (as Brad Patterson brought up, there are such things as "Indian rights" and "Indian treaties") that when they took their oath of office in the career service, they took their oath of office in terms of those ideas and ideals. How do you deal with those kinds of individuals? How do you get to know who they are? How do you get to know what their ideas are about? And at that point we stopped and never got into coming up with advice as to how do you "steal" the rebel leaders.

Nuechterlein: Who would like to add to what Jack said? Brad, were you satisfied with the discussion around whether the political appointees had been a well-selected lot?

Patterson: I must respectfully dissent from Jack's phraseology on the opening question. I was not trying to attract any praise to the non-career personnel system, but it turned out I did attract some criticism which there is no use reporting back now. I'd like to make one comment on the Blue Team's suggestion of the FEI and the overall orientation program. I think you know, and some of the rest of us here know, we have had an orientation program jointly among Civil Service, OMB and the White House. I think it has to have a White House component. I don't think it can be just the Civil Service Commission at a semi-technical level. For this level of appointee, you would have to have the White House family involved.

Nuechterlein: I was merely asking Brad if he could briefly comment on what that program consisted of because the Blue Team had commented this morning on FEI's desire to do that kind of work.

Patterson: Very briefly, it was a program involving first of all some written materials for new assistant secretaries. The idea was to catch new senior non-career appointees, including senior supergrades, early. Maybe the three-month idea is also a good idea, but catch them early, give them some written materials such as the rules on lobbying, the rules on handling the press, the rules on conflict of interest, and other general rules that the absolute newcomer (of which there are very few in this room) could run afoul of. Second, we set up an informal dinner session in the evening with some senior people around government and about fifteen of the new people. Third, we arranged a two-day orientation seminar at the White House, with White House people such as Buchen and Nessen, the head of OMB, and the head of the Civil Service Commission appearing, and a dialogue with them back and forth. That is, the students had read the material and then were given a chance to ask questions. There was lots of opportunity for dialogue; a little VIP reception by the President—in the Jacqueline Kennedy Garden—is always a nice touch. The feeling was generated therefore that the President personally, and his senior staff, are interested in them because they are, in effect, his appointees. And, finally, a follow-up, which we never got to within the agency orientation part of the program.

Nuechterlein: That essentially is to bring the White House closer to the political level in the departments, isn't it?

Patterson: Well, it's to create this linkage and to try to give the new people a sense of what we are all talking about here from our experience.

Nuechterlein: But that wouldn't involve any interface at all with the career people?

Patterson: No.

Bolduc: I think timing is the key. I think that three months is far too long. They are going to get involved with what they are doing, they are going to be very excited, thus you will never get them, they won't find the time. I think the key thing is to get them either shortly before they come on board, or during their first week, and have a follow-up session three months later.

Two points: First, the initial session should not be the only session that would be held. Second, I think everyone agreed that it shouldn't be longer than three days and probably would have to be done over a weekend.

All agreed that it would have to be a presidential decision to get it done at all. Oh yes, you would have to have the cooperation of the White House as Brad points out.

Nuechterlein: Before we get into a detailed discussion, let's hear from the Red Team.

Red Team Report

Morrill: We spent at least a part of our time discussing the agenda question about ways in which one can work successfully with a career bureaucracy, and therefore we echoed some of the points that have already been made here—for instance, accessibility and contact in communication, both within the immediate office and with the field where that is appropriate.

Secondly, perhaps it has not been emphasized here because it comes under the general rubric of caring about the organization, but we discussed the dimension of what if a decision goes contrary to what the career bureaucracy may have recommended. Do they understand clearly why that was done and, if possible, can they be made to understand the wisdom of why that decision was made? An important point was made that feedback from meetings, which they might not attend, must be passed on to them so that they know what happened—even though that might risk leaks and other things in an effort to achieve a cohesive organization. And thirdly, a point that perhaps has been said, but not emphasized, was the need by the assistant secretary to get on top of the job substantively; that if you don't know what you are doing, then it is very unlikely that you are going to gain the respect of your subordinates.

We moved into what might be characterized as a series of discussions about short-term and long-term efforts toward improving management, particularly those kinds of things that might take a while to produce. There was a feeling which Jack Young noted that there should be focus on important thrusts that will be particular to a situation, with special emphasis on being selective. We also sensed that there should be a continuing effort on some hard management thrust, at least in the direction in getting people to be clear about what their jobs are, what is expected of them, and other dimensions of trying to improve the management structure.

Lastly, and really off the agenda, we came back to a question that I think may have been stimulated in part by the film last night about the role of the assistant secretary in advocacy and what did that mean? There seemed to be a feeling, perhaps not unanimously held among this group, that one thing that also must be imparted was a reflection to the bureaucracy of the policy thrust of the secretary and the president; and, however uncomfortable that might be, one had to be equally strong in dealing with that issue, as well as reflecting the interests and concerns of the career bureaucracy upward and outward. That balancing act some felt was done well, but others felt it tilted too heavily in the direction of advocacy from the bottom up, and *not* enough from the top down.

Nuechterlein: Would anybody like to add anything to that before we open it up? Any personal points?

Rhinelander: Let me just add one thing that we discussed this morning, pertaining to the staff assistant or personal assistant (however you describe him) within the office of the assistant secretary. We spent some time talking about the Pentagon, where the tradition is that there is a military assistant to the assistant secretary. There is one or more of them and, in fact, that is one of the most valuable positions. It offers to the assistant secretary ready information into the bureaucracy. In the military, in particular, there is a tradition that those who have been military assistants (a navy assistant, an air force assistant) to assistant secretaries or secretaries in fact move up the chain themselves. And they are one of the most valuable resources to provide information, and early information, to an assistant secretary. It frequently serves to get information early so you can deflect things, so you can get them coming up through the system in a way in which they can be handled. Someone commented that a lot of people make mistakes in bringing in, as a special assistant, somebody from the outside who doesn't know the system. And I think that there is much to be said for the tradition, which is very strong at the Pentagon and not as strong in other departments, of having as at least one of your assistants somebody who is a part of and a comer in the organization. It really gives you the information which you need to know. When you come into an assistant secretary position, you have an enormous briefing book with many more issues than you can ever hope to handle; but you really need that sensitive information. It's through a qualified personal office staff that you can really get it.

Morrill: John Rhinelander, what about the mutuality of that transaction in the Pentagon where the career military people find out what you funny politicians are really up to?

Rhinelander: I think that is absolutely right. It is a two-way system. Through the military aide the bureaucracy understands what the assistant secretary, the under secretary, and the secretary are thinking about, and through him it really is a two-way system. This is why I remarked this morning that you've got to differentiate between the organization on the books and the way the building *really* works. The Pentagon really works through the network of assistants to the secretaries. And one of the most important decisions early on is the person you select for that position.

    Now when I went to HUD as under secretary we didn't have a career person in the office, so I brought with me somebody from HEW who had been a career official. And while it wasn't the Pentagon system of bringing him up from HUD, at least I had somebody who in fact knew how the government worked and was very attuned to getting information. If you don't have current information, you are just dead in the water.

Kolberg: John, I can testify to the same point. I really picked up on a tradition that the Budget Bureau had for years of picking people from the career ranks and rotating them as executive assistants or staff assistants to the director. I also thought that was good for the director, and it was good for the staff. And I've done the same thing, and I'm on my third one now over the past three and a half years. And I can say that as a technique for accomplishing what you suggested, I think it worked admirably. I've never been worried about good career people talking to congressmen or senators, or handling that kind of thing—they can handle that just fine. The most important things are the substantive knowledge and the information communication back through the institution; that really makes a systematic approach a very desirable thing.

Patterson: Bill Morrill had a very perceptive point about advocacy in both directions, which makes me think about a question I would like to throw out for a minute. In order to be an effective advocate of the president's programs back to the bureaucracy—that reverse flow—an assistant secretary has to speak credibly about those programs. Question: How many of the assistant secretaries here have had enough personal contact with the president in order to fill that role credibly? A comment first, before I throw it open: For instance in the Eisenhower cabinet meetings, Bob Gray and I would always try to include or encourage the inclusion of assistant secretaries with their bosses at a cabinet meeting, when the cabinet member was going to make a presentation. Sometimes we got them in under the guise of flipping the charts, or running the slide projector, or the motion picture machines, or whatever—since we used them often—or just plain sitting there in a chair. But for some reason, some way we got those assistant secretaries as well as the secretary in there at the meeting to listen, and to hear it, and to be able to help us report back. So, question: How many of the assistant secretaries here have had satisfactory personal contact with the president to play the role that Bill was talking about?

Morrill: With President Ford, yes—with President Nixon, no.

Kolberg: Likewise, same experience.

Nuechterlien: Why don't we just have a show of hands—how many of you had adequate contact with the president to know how to carry out his wishes?

Orlebeke: I don't think that an assistant secretary ought to expect regular access to the president. The assistant secretary's representative to the president is normally the secretary. If there are occasions when substantive matters are discussed where an assistant secretary has a great deal of background, then it is helpful, of course, to be included. My own experience is that I've been in perhaps two meetings with President Ford; but I don't feel deprived on that account. I feel that my boss, Secretary Hills, has had good access to the president.

Morrill: Let me supplement a minute: I think the question of how much is adequate has been well described, but there are some limits. On the other hand, to take an issue, particularly in a large department like HEW, if there are some very tough budget decisions to be made, it is often well if there is a face-to-face discussion of that matter led by the chief operating official who has an opportunity to explain his best case. And if he loses, he is a little inclined to be saying, "Well, at least I got the information that I thought important before the president, and from his perspective he decided something different and I can accept that." When it is done *ex cathedra* that acceptance may not be there.

Young: I support that, and I think that President Ford has done outstandingly well in this area. If I went along with the secretary, or if the secretary went alone to see the president about the HEW budget, we were both in deep trouble. So, we will take *all* of our assistant secretaries for an hour and a half with the president where they will talk face to face about why, on the recommendations of OMB, did he cut this part of the health program, and so forth. In terms of communicating what this president wants, that hour and a half is so well spent. Then I'm not caught in the crossfire—and OMB is not the bad bunch, because he did seek their advice, and so on and so forth. Just absolutely great!

Nuechterlein: In other words, there is no substitute for personal contact at any level: Is that really what you are saying?

Connor: I think also that on the issues we are really talking about, most of them are important enough for the president to know about. They are important enough to have been in the system for a long, long time. So if we are talking about being able to communicate back down to the bureaucracy, usually involvement in the issue has been extensive for a very long period of time. And direct association with the president is not necessary, for the most part, in order to be literate about the issues. I ran into that, for example, in urban mass transportation, when we were going for a budget which the constituency on the Hill, and everybody except the president, wanted $24 billion over a six-year period. The administration's position was $11.8 billion over a six-year period. Therefore, we had to explain to the Mass Transportation Administration bureaucracy why we were fighting for $11.8 billion in the face of an obvious need for transit facilities. I think that you arrive at a figure over a period of time in such a contorted fashion that you are prepared to explain it. The times that you get caught off base are when "deals" have been made at the last minute, when you have been very much involved and things are going along very fine, and then all of a sudden the answer comes back and it is something that was just never there. It wasn't there through the whole process, and all of a sudden it just pops up; that's when it is very difficult. Under those circumstances, I think the cabinet officer's responsibility is to communicate back, or the assistant secretary for congressional affairs to communicate back, to the program assistant secretary what happened, and why.

Nuechterlein: Do you feel you were successful in explaining to your mass transportation people the reason that they didn't get what they so obviously felt was needed?

Connor: Well, everyone always wants more money and more people. So you can explain, and yet not end up being successful in terms of making them happy. But I think we did make a very persuasive case. Of course, the president's budget was a major factor. But even beyond that we had severe reservations about the ability of the cities to actually be able to absorb much more money than that over a six-year period in a responsible way, and I think that the bureaucracy comprehends that.

Nuechterlein: We haven't heard from the Blue Team for a few minutes. Go ahead, Roger.

Hooker: I was just going to say that I think that the jam in President Ford's case (he's been very credible in this respect with the whole bureaucracy) is because he's obviously taken such a personal interest in the budget. And that has been publicized; and people are aware that there has been an appeal, and a very real appeal, on the part of all the secretaries as an important factor in the budgetary process. That, I think, is a very visible phenomenon and relatively easy to translate.

I was thinking earlier in our discussion that there are some presidential political decisions that are made that are virtually impossible to explain to the bureaucracy. I think John Rhinelander touched on it this morning when he talked about the impoundment question. (Thank God I wasn't around when it occurred.) I'm just glad I didn't have to explain that to the people that were managing programs in the field. I just think that President Ford by opening himself up to cabinet members and by taking such an interest in the budget—even if you disagree with where he comes out—has at least opened up the process so that it can be understood. In effect, everybody felt that they had their day in court.

Feltner: This should almost go without saying, I think, but it is extremely important in explaining an action to subordinates, especially one which is clearly a political action so that you do *not* have to apologize for it. You know there is a temptation sometimes to say, "I wouldn't have decided it that way, but I have to do this." I've seen it happen on down the line. I've seen agency administrators, who, when passing the information on down to the people below them, apologize for it and make it very clear that they wouldn't have done it that way, but the assistant secretaries said such and such, so therefore, we have to do it. It is a tempting thing to do but it puts you in a very weak position.

Bolduc: The point you made about making presentations before the president for an hour and a half—that's the model you are referring to?

Young: I think the point that the team brought out is that it isn't so much the outcome as it is the way you were dealt with. Of course, this president [Ford] does have one big advantage, because for those who were unfortunate enough to be close to the other one [Nixon], the contrast is just so great, and also genuine. You can't put on a process to sort of fake out the bureaucracy, or your fellow political officers; it's got to have integrity in it, and that's what I think is very important. For example, when the secretary and I came back with a decision after seeing Nixon, many civil servants didn't trust us, or they said, "Well, that's Mathews and Young again." And it wouldn't carry because the civil servants got too many turndowns; of that there is no question. For example, if I can come back and say (like I could under Ford), "When the secretary and I were talking to the president, this is what we said, this is how I tried to protect the program and this is the answer, and I got due process," they would say, "Thanks." I just think that presidents get credibility out of a process based on trust, candidness, and fair negotiations in dealing with the bureaucrats and their political leaders.

Bolduc: The reason I raised the question is that I think OMB in terms of the budgetary process, at its high level, has an opportunity to articulate its position before the president while these same opportunities are not always afforded each department.

Nuechterlein: Would anybody like to raise another type of question, or can we continue with this one?

Rhinelander: Let me make one final comment. Part of the question is the willingness of the president to meet with larger groups than just the secretaries. President Nixon didn't meet with the secretaries for a long period of time. President Ford is open to relatively large meetings, but the other side of the equation is whether the secretaries want to go and meet with the president alone (and some do) or whether the secretaries want to take with them assistant secretaries. I think that is equally important. With President Ford, he is willing to have relatively frequent meetings with assistant secretaries. And then the question is whether the cabinet officer wants to go with assistant secretaries, or handle it one on one? I think you will find that in the present cabinet, it is handled differently—not from the president's point of view—but by each cabinet officer.

Morrill: Just a brief note and then moving on to another area: Our experiences, not only with respect to the budgetary process but indeed with other important policy issues where President Ford has made himself open to approach, indicate that if the president can tolerate it, the process is better for it than the closed system. The other point I was making was that there was some discussion about constituencies, and how to deal with those external forces. It strikes me that when you come into an assistant secretaryship in any given department, there is a set of forces that comes to bear on the career bureaucracy and the external constituencies that are automatically triggered because they have some stake in the program and are involved in one way or another. A question that we've spent much time on over the last year is, "What are our responsibilities as assistant secretaries, or non-career people, for expanding and altering that external constituency?" It is easy enough to visualize on a health problem a clear list of people that have something at stake, be it the private community, or what have you. But we are aware that that is not the only point of view in the society. There are folks paying health bills, for example, who are getting increasingly restless about all of that, and one says, "Well, how do I engage that broader constituency in that dialogue?" And what responsibilities does an assistant secretary have for expanding the universe of that constituency?" (which may in fact have something to do with his ability to effectively communicate the policies from the top down).

Nuechterlein: If I may, I'd like to throw out a question that we started with in our group, one having to do with the career executives, with the fact that a great many of you in this group moved up from the bureaucracy into your present positions. In my team there were only four people who came in as assistant secretaries from the outside. The question I'd like to pose to you is: Do you think that in our system the interface would work better if more career people were promoted, or willing to take the risk of moving out of the career service into the political level? Would the system work better if you had more of that kind of movement, or do you feel a new president coming in ought to, more or less, clean out at your level and bring in people who can reflect different ideas than the ones that have come up through the bureaucracy? I'd like to hear a few people address the question since we got started on it.

Morrill: It seems to me that much of what we've said here in some ways goes more to the question of *who* is selected as an assistant secretary, versus *what* they do after they get there. And my own axiom would run something like the following: You could afford to know nothing about the policies of the administration, *or* you could afford to know nothing of the culture of government agencies; but you are going to have a damn rough time if you know nothing about *either* of them.

Blake: In our group, an interesting example came up which I think is sort of unique in government, and it bears on your point. (I believe it was John Richardson who brought it up.) In the Department of State the system there, as I understand it today, is that with the exception of two assistant secretaries all the other assistant secretaries are foreign service officers who have been presidentially appointed and Senate confirmed; but if they are removed, they revert again to Foreign Service duty. In one sense, it appears to be the best of all worlds.

Richardson: I think it is a pretty good rule. Since I've been there, it's been done both ways—mostly political, now mostly career, and it is different than in other agencies because the Foreign Service, as established, makes it possible for an officer to be able to rise to the ambassadorial level, which is similar to an assistant secretary. So you have lots of opportunities for career people to come in, at the political level, in any case. And that's part of the routine of the service. So, it is easy to assimilate the Foreign Service person professionally at the assistant secretary level; there is no complication, and everybody understands it.

Alm: I guess understanding your question depends partly on where you sit. I think there is no doubt that a career person coming up the ranks can grab the reins of an assistant secretary rather quickly and since they've been tested in a bureaucratic atmosphere probably the chances of at least not completely flopping are considerably less, and clearly, you gain time. What you lose is, obviously, outside perspectives and new ideas. Some have commented that just by having the luxury of leaving allows a person to do more. I question that notion.

My personal feeling is that there probably ought to be a higher number of career people in assistant secretary jobs, assuming you had clearly political people in the top two jobs. I read Harold Wilson's biography [former Prime Minister of Great Britain] and any of you who have a chance will find it interesting to read the first chapter because he talks about the first time he assumed power. As we go through this transition with 135 people writing issue papers, it is amazing to read about the British transition—creating new departments, new ministries, filling new jobs from the civil service almost overnight compared to the rather protracted transitions we have.

Scalia: First, on the general question, I am of the firm view that there is no answer to it. I've known superb assistant secretaries who were career people and superb assistant secretaries who were not career, and the opposite in both categories. So, I don't think there is a generalized answer; it depends, of course, partly on the individual. I suspect it also depends partly on the agency you are talking about. There are a number of agencies whose business is much less policy-charged than others, whose business over the years has become more routine—there are policy decisions to be made, but not policy decisions that have to be made in a new agency like EPA, for example. I suppose that the way it would break out is that in a new mission-oriented agency, other things being equal, some fresh blood is more effective than laterally transferring somebody from an agency that used to be part of this function in the past. I think there is no categorical answer. I am wary of analogies to the British system, or to any other one which is a parliamentary system. I just don't think it is comparable. Yes, our transitions are rougher and it is also rougher to have an independently elected executive who bumps heads with the Congress on occasion during his entire tenure. I think that's part of our system. If it is part of our system, and there has to be some meaning to it, I think it means that there has to be a change in the executive when there is an election. And I think this means much more in our system than it means in the British system—that there has to be a change at the policy-making level of the executive branch.

Henry: Let me suggest what I think would be a fruitful line of discussion if you only had two or three more hours. It pertains both to the proposition of how do you find more effective potential assistant secretaries in the career service, and the question of how you really can push as many operations down into the career service as possible. I think it would be useful for a group of this kind to ask: "What are the things which the career service as it is now constituted can be trusted to handle for itself, and what are the significant limitations thereof; and then, how do we go about institutionalizing and developing that career service so it can be a more effective, potentially self-contained corps and a potentially promotable corps into the assistant secretaryship positions?" That question has no precise answer, but if we are talking about improving the political-career interface over the long run, I suggest that the political officers have a responsibility to address themselves to the institutional capabilities, and incapabilities, of the career service.

Richardson: There is one response from one small corner of the Foreign Service area. My observation is that one of the functions that ought to be well performed by the career service is the management function, broadly defined. Much of the management function ought to have continuity as one of its features. In fact, however, that doesn't work at all because the career service is so structured as to first of all give preference to political affairs officers who are not, at any time in their career, told that it is important to learn anything about management, nor are they given much encouragement to do so. And secondly, the top levels above the assistant secretaries, which are political, come in and out about every year or two (in my observation); thus, there is no continuity, especially with regard to the top management functions—that is, the patterns and structures which ought to provide continuing shape to the environment in which everything is done. But there isn't continuing shape because it changes about every year and a half, and some new foreign service officer or new political appointee comes in. And in neither case does the structure, either at my level or the level above, clearly provide the continuing capacity to pursue any single line of approach to the management of the whole enterprise. I think that this is a very serious failing in the particular little corner of the government that I have been in.

Kolberg: I would say the job of assistant secretary isn't anywhere near as attractive a job as it used to be, and it's going down. I would describe it as follows: The pay is poor and we all know that, the perquisites have gradually gone away, especially those that have something to do with people's feelings about themselves, their responsibilities, and their importance. The coin of the president, although this president has done better, has been depreciated a great deal. Twenty years ago assistant secretaries were invited to dinner at the White House, and were very big men or women in Washington. They are no longer. That has gone down rapidly, in my experience, and in that sense in most of our experiences as we talked about the problems. As each succeeding administration makes it tougher on conflict of interest, it will no longer be possible for lawyers to come and get experience that they can merchandise on the outside. So, lawyers are going to have a harder time seeing it in their career advantage to come in, because there won't be that transferability. This whole session has been dealing with the emotional, managerial pressures that come to play in a job of this kind both from above and below; and as the government gets bigger and more complicated, with more problems to solve, the outside public interest groups and the pressure of the media will surely make it tougher and tougher in that day-to-day sense. It's harder for people to come out of private companies now, and go back. The rewards just aren't there anymore.

And I could go on, and that's why I think these are far less attractive jobs than they used to be, and that worries me a great deal. I think it is going to be almost automatic that more career people are going to come into these jobs, and I would say, at some point, you've gone past that point. You really do need the smart, young, interested, vigorous, innovative people from outside who have that sense of public purpose to come in and take on this tough job; and unless we change the pattern, we're going to have an increasingly tough job. And I would say at some stage along the way, if we don't change that, the assistant secretaries will typically be people like Bill Morrill, and Jack Young, and I, and a few others in the room who come from the career ranks to do the job. This is not to depreciate what we can do, but I really believe strongly in a mix.

Scalia: I think one of the recently dissatisfying features about the assistant secretaries jobs—at least in my experience and many that I know—is the amount of my time that has been spent in what is ultimately (assuming that we are doing things right) the nonproductive work of preparing for legislative testimony. I expect that about 40 percent, literally 40 percent, of my time has been spent on essentially responding to oversight requests and inquiries of the Congress. It is hard to tell how typical that is, not only in the government, but how typical these past few years have been because of Watergate, because of the division politically between the two branches of government. I expect, however, it isn't mostly Watergate and it isn't mostly political divisions, but that we are into a new era of much closer congressional oversight of the executive branch. It is enormously time-consuming on the part of those people who have to prepare the testimony, and it is not the kind of work that gives you a great deal of satisfaction because you are not really accomplishing anything. You are trying to defend what has been accomplished, or explain what has been accomplished, or what has been done. And as that takes something like 40 percent of your time, you begin to wonder if you aren't in an army that is devoted to the care of its wounded.

Nuechterlein: We are into a subject that I am sure could go on for quite a while, but we are about at the end of our time.

Brotzman: The question you asked raises the issue of our basic political system and the pinning of political responsibility. I think the people that we all work for would like to be sure, or at least 51 percent would like to be sure, that the person they elected for president was going to have a fair shot at carrying out some of his policies for this country. If this requires that the president have the opportunity to appoint down to assistant secretaries, then I think he deserves to have this opportunity. I am not impugning the ability of anyone that comes from the bureaucracy up through the ranks, but it gets down to this basic point, as far as the people are concerned. That is, if the president needs assistant secretaries from outside with a little creativity and innovativeness, perhaps sticking their necks out a bit, then I feel that this is the way the system should be.

Nuechterlein: One final question that I would like you to think about is this: If Mr. Carter were to ask you what you would recommend to the upcoming group of assistant secretaries, and above, concerning what they could do to break down the barriers between the political level and the career level, what would you say? The suspicion exists. This tendency of the new crowd coming in to say that the people who have been there don't count for much and are drawing big fat salaries and not producing is damaging to the system.

Therefore, think about this a little bit, and perhaps this afternoon we can come back to this question. I suspect that the people who are going to replace many of you are in for some shocks, both positively and negatively. They will find that the people they have got under them are a whole lot smarter than they thought they were going to be, and that the careerist can help them if they want to be helped. But they are going to be in for some big shocks in terms of the problems that they must deal with since many of the problems are not like the ones they have been dealing with down in Georgia.

4

The Assistant Secretaries: Policy Formulation and Implementation

---

There is nothing wrong with public officials repeating their mistakes, but it's not mandatory.

—Abba Eban

The Assistant Secretary and the Policy Process

In order to better understand the decision-making, policymaking process, and in order to put some flesh on the policymaking framework, we are going to analyze the assistant secretaries' role in policy formulation and implementation. We all know that an assistant secretary does not operate in a vacuum—nobody does in the policymaking process. We also know that the assistant secretary is not necessarily the bellwether in the policy process. Nonetheless, he or she is an interface very important to any administration's policy design. Frank Sherwood once wrote that the concept of hierarchy puts great emphasis on an organizationally defined leader.[1] He says that people take on leadership positions in order to influence not only policy and program decisions, but the values behind them.

The role of assistant secretary, who is the link between the career bureaucrat and the political appointee and the president's program director on the line, is an intriguing one to investigate. The fact that most assistant secretaries are appointed because they are compatible with the overall political and administrative philosophies of a particular president puts them in key positions. They perform as key policy people in two ways:

- They are boundary role players.[2] That is, they often reflect in speeches to interest groups and political constituencies exactly what the message of the administration is.
- They play important linkage roles. Many times they are the main contact a career bureaucrat has with the president's overall political design. Therefore, how they operate is important to how enthusiastically and expertly career

bureaucrats perform their day-to-day functions.

The manner in which the assistant secretary copes with the complexities of the policy process in contemporary times may serve as a microcosm of an administration's policymaking style. The role has changed dramatically in its importance during the last twenty-five years because of the growth of the White House staff.

Furthermore, it has become much more complex because of quantity and quality of performance demanded. And because assistant secretaries are in an interface position, in studying them we can zero in on the realities of the methodological, conceptual, abstract analyses of the policy process that academics have constructed during the past several decades. Academics and policymakers can thus draw some practical conclusions about the real world of the policy process as seen through the actors' eyes.

The Policy Role as Seen by the Assistant Secretaries

The brand of rational, all-encompassing strategic planning that most academics tend to discuss when they consider the generic problems of policymaking and the policy process is not what the assistant secretary is concerned with. Most of the assistant secretaries who participated in the FEI symposium made it very clear that they are involved in day-to-day crises and, consequently, they have very little time to think about—let alone deal with—the "big picture." On the day-to-day level, the tangibles drive out the intangibles of the policymaking process; most assistant secretaries deal with short-term needs rather than long-term needs or strategic analyses.

But it can be demonstrated that the most neglected area in the American policymaking process is strategic analysis; the problem is not limited to assistant secretaries. It is a special problem in the federal government, where all the incentives work in the opposite direction. The political realities are the short time available to political appointees, the need for quick political credit, short congressional terms, recurring presidential elections, and constituency group pressure. The problem of conducting rational strategic analysis is related to many roles in government. At the same time, it has dramatic impact on the role of the assistant secretary. Judith Connor, assistant secretary for environment, safety, and consumer affairs in the Department of Transportation, confirms this observation: "It is my firm belief that we are not going to plan, that there is nothing in our system of government which at the present time constitutes pressure towards the development of the long range planning processes."*

Brad Patterson, formerly assistant director of operations in the White House Personnel Office (now associated with the Brookings Institution), makes this observation on the role of assistant secretaries and other policymakers at the lower interface levels of the policy process:

> One footnote about planning is that if we don't do it ourselves in the federal Executive Branch, it sure is going to be done for us. In fact, it is *being* done for us all over the country by the different interest groups which are very well organized and which have very definite ideas which lead them to go right ahead on their merry way charting the future for themselves.

The absence of long-range planning time for the assistant secretary underscores several important operating techniques: first, he or she must stay in tune with current thinking on administration policy. This does not mean necessarily being involved constantly with the "big picture"; but in order to make sense out of a specific program or a particular aspect of a policy, the assistant secretary must be attuned to what is influencing the larger picture in order to stay up to date on the administration's plans. Otherwise, time and motion will be wasted pursuing programs or policies that are not consistent with the current policy of the top leaders.

Second, for an assistant secretary to remain effective, he or she should be able to spot those close to the president who have a personal impact on him and who speak for his larger plans. The president cannot be involved in all kinds of decisions; in fact, most of the time only major decisions grab his attention. But he is surrounded by advisors who act as "filters," monitoring the overall administration policy plan. If an assistant secretary knows who those people are, his or her ideas, plans, and programs are likely to be transmitted to the president.

Third, an assistant secretary should have a similar notion of who the president's special governmentwide advisors are, because they often make statements and take actions that hint where the power is

---

*All quoted material in this chapter, unless otherwise noted, is from Thomas P. Murphy, Donald E. Nuechterlein, and Ronald J. Stupak, eds., *The President's Program Directors: The Assistant Secretaries* (Charlottesville, Va.: Federal Executive Institute, 1977).

gravitating in the policy process and which way the president is leaning on certain issues. Thus an assistant secretary will acquire some feel as to when to push programs, when to hesitate, and when to attempt something novel. Like most organizational leaders, the president depends on his advisors to explain his conceptual design downward to the "troops"; therefore alert assistant secretaries constantly listen to those advisors.

Fourth, an assistant secretary performs a linking-pin role for his or her bosses, institution, and subordinates. Research on this role shows that the better the relationships among leaders (assistant secretaries and their bosses), the higher the quality of output from an organizational unit.[3] In addition, the higher the quality of linking relationships upward, the more effectively the policy process flows downward (the assistant secretary and the career bureaucrats in his or her unit). In essence, the more an assistant secretary can fit together the micro needs of his organization with the macro demands of the president, the more sophisticated he or she will be in timing and in his or her relationship with the overall presidential administrative plan.

And fifth, an assistant secretary must attend to the real political demands of the policy process while at the same time understanding and remaining attuned to the larger philosophical and normative dimensions of operating in a policy process where the rule of law, limited government, and separation of powers are also realities. If an assistant secretary grasps the complexities of the larger picture of the democratic process, he or she will understand more fully what specific capabilities are essential for changing the system, will have a sense of proper timing in bringing leverage to bear in a situation, and will waste less energy pursuing policies that will probably not be implemented. In addition, he or she will become more sophisticated in negotiating laterally, vertically, and interdepartmentally for a program, for his or her "troops," and for the public interest. For, as Donald Brotzman, assistant secretary for the army for manpower and reserve affairs said at the symposium, "We think one of the principal responsibilities of the assistant secretary, since he sees issues going up and also sees them coming down, is to help our bosses to determine if a policy is necessary to deal with the real problem."

It was evident from the symposium discussion on formulation and implementation that the American system generally operates in an incremental way. Most new assistant secretaries have to pick up the pieces from policies their predecessors have left behind. Mike

Moskow, an under secretary in the Department of Labor, said in his formal presentation at the symposium that when he first became an assistant secretary he spent most of his time on his predecessor's agenda. An assistant secretary often must be satisfied with very small policy changes, and even they may take a couple of years.

But assistant secretaries need not become disenchanted with their limited role as policymakers. They simply must orchestrate the role in relation to the kinds of leadership or operational styles that are most effective in an incremental political system. They must be excellent negotiators on many levels:

1. The assistant secretary must negotiate with outside clients—with their constant feedback and ideas for programs they would like to see implemented—and with the professional careerists, who have longer tenures and thus a different perspective about timing, and who often distrust the political appointee called the assistant secretary. The assistant secretary must gain these people's trust, support, and enthusiasm.

2. He or she must negotiate between departments. There is an increasing need, as Harland Cleveland says, for lateral negotiation and systemwide sensitivities within the governmental arena as more and more problems become interdependently complex and as the vertical capabilities of leading an organization become subordinate to, or at least equal to, lateral relationships in terms of the policymaking process.[4]

3. And finally, this surely means acquiring upward negotiating capabilities, because interpersonal relationships with an administration's high-level officials (under secretaries, secretaries, and even the president) are important to the assistant secretary who wishes to have an impact on the policy process.

It was evident from the dialogue at the symposium that those officials' trust in an assistant secretary's character, expertise, and management capabilities has a direct impact on his or her policymaking status. Thus, assistant secretaries must convince their bosses that they are leading an effective team that can be trusted to champion the administration's policy proposals. They must perform more like a coach than like a star player. Mike Moskow explains the need for a comprehensive negotiating style:

> The assistant secretary has to be what I would call a "base-toucher" in the policy formulation role. I think the old saying is, "There's no sense hitting a home-run if you don't touch the bases along the way" and I think that's a very appropriate slogan to follow in the policy formulation area. He must be touching bases with his constituency,

other groups in the administration, the White House, OMB, and
Congress to make sure that there is support for the new proposals that
he is thinking of and for major changes in existing policies. He cannot
go it alone. Just touching base can be extremely important, because
very often people are terribly offended if they aren't consulted on
something ahead of time. Even if their advice isn't taken, the act of
consultation—the act of touching base—can be extremely important.

In summary, negotiating in a democratic environment where the
emphasis is on incrementalism demands a leadership style steeped in
patience, verbal expertise, and listening skills. For, at base, the
epitome of job satisfaction for an executive is to accomplish tasks
through other people and through the implementation of policy
proposals that often contribute to the success of the larger policy
goals of the president.

The assistant secretaries' symposium made one thing very clear
regarding the implementation stage of the policymaking process:
namely, that it is an ambiguous, amorphous, interdependent
phenomenon—not at all clear. Everyone involved in the policy
process makes policy. Assistant secretaries make policy by setting
standards of performance for their colleagues and for their programs,
by using discretionary judgment when interpreting proposals, and by
interpreting the law. Congress tends to give a broad generalized
format within which specific laws have to be carried out, therefore the
interpretation of law by an assistant secretary surely can be defined as
the making of policy. Furthermore, the assistant secretary's
discretionary power of deciding whom to contact above and below is a
form of policymaking. But policy is made all the way up and down
the line. Paul Bolduc, assistant secretary for Administration (USDA),
made it clear that policy does not come only from those at the very top
when he said: "In fact, a point was made that policy is really
enunciated at all organizational levels. Even the Xerox operator
participates—if he makes a decision and enunciates a policy that no
one will in fact make any more than ten copies per day on a specific
Xerox machine, he is articulating policy."

An assistant secretary's policymaking design should take into
consideration the fact not only that the policy process is complex, but
that policy comes from many different sources. This policymaking
design should include the following factors:

1. An assistant secretary must be sensitive to the policy process as
well as to the sources of policy up and down the line. The more
sensitive assistant secretaries can be to the flow of information, ideas,
and interests in an organization, the more they will be able to

determine the direction of policy, as well as its source. Since the position is an interface position, an assistant secretary with an accurate antennae will be able to coordinate and manage the different policy options that pass through his or her agency.

2. An assistant secretary needs a structure within which to effectuate policy. As Paul Bolduc said, "An assistant secretary has to develop a structure to assure that he will receive the type of input he needs to have in order for him to make policy." This suggests an outside structure that facilitates communication and dialogue with the clientele. The assistant secretary must think ahead to anticipate problems related to policymaking and deal with them dynamically. And finally, the assistant secretary must constantly monitor his or her organization in order to develop with subordinates an administrative structure that will help in the formulation and implementation of policy on a practical day-to-day basis.

3. Assistant secretaries must manage their time more effectively. This is important to their policymaking design because they are better able to set organizational priorities and emphasize policies that are essential or deserve attention based on the priorities of the administration. And finally, by using time efficiently the assistant secretary will not waste time on outdated priorities or on demands that promise little operational impact. An assistant secretary who goes around the country making speeches at academic institutions or service agencies while neglecting to manage his organization certainly may obtain visibility with certain external groups, but this may negate some of his "real" effectiveness in his organization. As Dean Acheson once said, "It is important that a person in a leadership position of an organization take care of day-to-day things so that when it comes to effectuating policy people will follow him."[5]

Bill Morrill, assistant secretary for planning and evaluation at HEW, underscored Acheson's concern when he said:

> My view of the situation is that policy planning drives out management and implementation because it is more fun. The president, the secretary, and Congress are much more involved in policy planning, and one gets more . . . gratification from policy planning, thus whatever time is left over too often is too little and too weak for the implementation process or the hard management procedures.

Mike Moskow took Acheson and Morrill one step further when he said, "I think it is a result of our whole political system. People get political points for the initiation of new ideas that they generate; they don't get political points for doing a job well or for implementing a policy well. I think that's the whole structure of our system."

If Acheson, Morrill, and Moskow are right, assistant secretaries who spend their time looking at the big picture and trying to make dramatic changes more than likely will end up with nothing tangible. On the other hand, those who spend more time managing their organization may be more effective in bringing about change and getting programs implemented. In other words, time management demands that an executive such as an assistant secretary do a sophisticated analysis of his or her role and identify factors important to having an impact in policymaking. High visibility may be a waste of time in this respect.

4. It is also critical that an assistant secretary have a working knowledge of the budgetary process. Too often policymakers talk in high-level, declarative terms while ignoring the practical budgetary realities of government policy. To have a real impact on policymaking, one must have direct or indirect authority in the budgetary process. For as Paul Bolduc (Department of Agriculture) said:

> The assessment of priorities, the assessment of results of program evaluations, zero base budgeting, or whatever the case might be, when you get down to the bottom line, it means budget. If the policy that has reached [the assistant secretary's] level requires "x" number of dollars, and that cannot be accommodated by the financial constraints and resources available, then that bottom line must stand and by so doing it is enunciating policy.

An assistant secretary must have more than a superficial understanding of the budgetary process so that he or she can dovetail declarative policy with operational realities.

5. An assistant secretary must know what is happening out in the field. In fact, it is absolutely critical that he or she physically go out into the field. For as David Taylor, assistant secretary of defense for manpower and reserve affairs, said: "Too often we sit in Washington and make global decisions on personnel policy and on resource allocation among the services and within the services from one area to another." He meant that too often decisions are made in a cosmic framework that has little or nothing to do with reality. This was probably brought home most dramatically in the assistant secretaries' dialogue by a story Brad Patterson told about his former colleague, John Ehrlichman, who had called him in an attempt to obtain an off-the-road ambulance service for a Navajo reservation. Ehrlichman was emphasizing White House staff, but what he said

can be applied to policymakers in general who spend their time in Washington at the center of the policymaking process. In his statement, he said:

> If I ever had this to do over again, when I was appointing somebody to the White House staff with my left hand, I'd say, "Here's your certificate to the White House staff," and then with my right hand I'd say, "Here's an airplane ticket. Get your tail out of Washington and spend six months out at the farthest possible end of the service delivery system to find out how it's working and what's happening way the hell out there with the population that the system is designed to serve. And after six months you can come back.

Assistant secretaries must have a systemic understanding of their organization, but they must also have an idea of what is happening out in Iowa, Arizona, New Mexico—at the end of the line. To choose among alternatives is only one segment of the policymaking process. To implement policy wisely is as important, if not more important, to the clientele being served. It thus is absolutely critical for assistant secretaries to keep in touch with people in the field so they can be aware of necessary changes in the implementation of a program or project.

6. And finally, in terms of his or her policymaking design, an assistant secretary must ensure the respect of the career bureaucrats for his or her managerial expertise. Much was said in the previous chapter about the political/career interface. Assistant secretaries who neglect their careerists and who do not very quickly learn the environment of the professional bureaucrat will be at a major disadvantage. Maybe this point can be made most clearly in terms of General Andrew Jackson's comment to his troops at the Battle of New Orleans during the War of 1812: "Elevate them guns a little lower." An assistant secretary who "knows the turf" on which he or she operates is likely to be effective. To have a respectful, meaningful, and productive interface with the career bureaucrats, an assistant secretary must "tend the store," work on the development of a management team, and direct his or her immediate subordinates in a professional manner. In fact, this may be the most important step in the right direction to effectuating a successful policymaking role.

The symposium certainly substantiated the tenets of the bureaucratic politics approach to policy analysis.[6] In fact, after analyzing the dialogue on implementation and formulation, it can be said that:

• Where one stands is surely dependent upon where one sits.

- Where one sits has a tremendous impact on what one perceives.
- Where one operates has an impact on how one operates.

Different agencies have different styles and different operational needs, and this has an impact on individuals associated with the agencies. It should not suprise anyone that assistant secretaries in HEW have different styles than do assistant secretaries in the Department of Defense. This is part of the "turf dimension" of the policymaking process. And it surely substantiates the fact that in the American democratic system, policymaking is a political process whether it occurs at the polls, in the bureaucracies, or in interdepartmental dialogues.

The reality is that policy is made in an environment of "power striking power" and consensus building, which many times means settling for less than the best. This reality sometimes gets lost in the abstract wishes of social science designers. And nowhere is this dimension of bureaucratic politics made more definite that in the comments of Charles Orlebeke, HUD's assistant secretary for policy development and research:

> We tend, both as assistant secretaries and as departmental officials, to define problems in terms of our own departments, and therefore we are not very receptive to how that problem might be defined by another department or even by the White House. An example I gave was the problem of neighborhood deterioration or abandonment. This is a HUD type problem, but we also know that the tools we have to deal with that problem are very limited. We realize that we have to go to Treasury on tax policy affecting neighborhoods, but that agency may say, well, neighborhood deterioration is not a problem as far as we see it. We see it in completely different terms—as the normal working of the market. And HEW may see it as a problem of lack of social services or school desegregation. And if you're from HEW, you can say, "By the way, HUD, while we are talking about school desegregation, we wish you'd stop pouring all that subsidized housing into those neighborhoods where there are schools that we are trying to desegregate." These interdepartmental differences in perspective and goals present a very difficult challenge for the administration and the White House in dealing with its departments. Also, I think it creates problems within departments themselves as political appointees seek honestly to get beyond their particular programs and into the really generic problems—however they may be defined. So the problem with the primary question, I guess, is that as we talked about policy direction to

career officials, words like "clear" and "exactly" do not sound like the environment in which I operated.

A bureaucratic politics perspective is supported and substantiated by the parochial and personal interests of agencies and the people within them. In addition, it accentuates the problem of the different perspectives of massive organizations.

The Assistant Secretary's Policymaking Commandments

Ten commandments issued from the assistant secretaries' dialogue on being successful in the formulation and implementation of policy:

First, an assistant secretary must know the turf on which he or she is operating. In addition to being cognitively and substantively capable in the role, the individual must understand the organization's processes and how they lead to results.

Second, to be an effective assistant secretary and to maintain the motivation and élan of the careerists in the organization, one must win a few key policy contests.

Third, an assistant secretary must know the difference between an advocacy role and an implementation role in the policy process. Nothing is wrong with advocating certain positions, but the individual must know when to stop when his or her position has been overruled or incorporated into another policy. This is important— presidential appointees must sometimes implement policies that are not exactly the ones they favor. Mike Moskow said he saw very little problem with assistant secretaries who sabotaged presidential policy designs or had major problems implementing them. An assistant secretary who cannot implement a presidential order as effectively and honestly as possible should resign.

Fourth, an effective assistant secretary must have a policymaking design. But the key to that design is to have the options of making his or her case to those who are the "deciders-in-chief" for policy pronouncements. That is, the assistant secretary must have access to the bosses, whether under secretaries, secretaries, or sometimes even the president. An effective assistant secretary must have the latitude to make his or her case at different levels, in different forms, and at different times. For even luck favors the prepared mind.[7]

Fifth, assistant secretaries must pay attention to constituencies outside the department. They must not become a captive of the constituencies, but they must be able to get feedback from constituencies to learn how well the organization is doing, to broaden their information base, and to see if those supposedly being served think the delivery system is operating efficiently.

Sixth, an assistant secretary should learn how the people around the president, the White House staff, and the major presidential executive agencies such as OMB, CSC, and GSA operate within an administration.

Seventh, an assistant secretary must have a good feel for interpersonal relationships and must know the leadership style of superiors. This allows one to determine when to make decisions independently and when to take issues to superiors for a decision. Development of this skill can lead to positions of influence with superiors and to additional respect from subordinates.

Eighth, even though it is true that in the bureaucracy most relationships tend to be with either subordinates or superiors, an assistant secretary would be wise to nurture and develop a lateral perspective, especially as the growing interdependency of governmental programs coincides with the collapsing of the traditional boundaries between the private and public sectors. An assistant secretary who learns consulting, negotiating, and conflict management techniques can operate more smoothly in an interdepartmental-interdependency framework.

Ninth, an assistant secretary should be aware of the short tenure of the job. This awareness may prevent amateurish attempts to do things too quickly or haphazardly. At the same time, the individual who is aware of how the short tenure affects his or her relationship with the professional bureaucrats and the bureaucracy itself can gain policymaking strength. This was vividly explained by David Macdonald, under secretary of the navy:

> One of the things that the political appointee, and particularly the assistant secretary, can do is to utilize his own expendability. The fact that he doesn't have to stay around, and in fact won't stay around, is an asset which permits him to be an advocate for his own Bureau where advocacy is appropriate; and to protect his people, and be the politically expendable appointee when the Bureau is attacked by Congress or by individual congressmen or women. . . . I think it is essential for the political appointee to stand up and defend his agency if that is, in fact, his judgment.

Tenth, an assistant secretary has to be aware of the major differences between public and private executive problems. Government does make a difference in executive life. A public executive must consider numerous underlying normative, legal, ethical, philosophical, and democratic values when formulating and implementing policy. The instrumental values can never override and/or diminish the inherent values that are the essence of the democratic way of life. In sum, ethical, moral, and philosophical aspects of a democracy are not just abstract principles. They are the very essence of what can be defined as effective and meaningful in the democratic policy process.

Notes

1. Frank P. Sherwood, "The American Public Executive in the Third Century," *Public Administration Review* (September-October 1976), p. 587.

2. Michael L. Tushman, "Special Boundary Roles in the Innovation Process," *Administrative Science Quarterly* (December 1977), pp. 587-605.

3. George Graen, James F. Cashman, Steven Ginsburg, and Williams Schiemann, "Effects of Linking-Pin Quality on the Quality of Working Life of Lower Participants," *Administrative Science Quarterly* (September 1977), pp. 491-504.

4. Harlan Cleveland, *The Future Executive* (New York: Harper & Row, 1972), pp. 30-47.

5. Interview with Dean Acheson at his Georgetown home on April 6, 1966.

6. For example, see Graham T. Allison, *Essence of Decision* (Boston: Little, Brown & Co., 1971).

7. Allen Wheelis, *The Quest for Identity* (New York: W. W. Norton & Co., 1958), p. 74.

Appendix: Excerpts from FEI Symposium Discussion on the Policymaking Process*

Introduction of Michael H. Moskow

Bledsoe: Having been a student and observer and part-time participant in both organizations on the private side and now in

---

*Thomas P. Murphy, Donald E. Nuechterlein, and Ronald J. Stupak, eds., *The President's Program Directors: The Assistant Secretaries* (Charlottesville, Va.: The Federal Executive Institute, 1977).

government, I would like to make an observation about the subject that we are going to be taking up this afternoon dealing with the assistant secretary's role in policy formulation and policy implementation. It seems that what we've built into our organizational society as we have created it in this country, is a different contextual world in which people at the executive level have to operate. I call this world a vertical world, which means that 80 to 90 percent of one's time is spent in a vertical pattern of relationships. That is, one is either dealing with subordinates or one is dealing with superiors in the day to day kinds of work activities.

When dealing upward and dealing downward, one is certainly playing a different kind of role than one perhaps is able to play when he is dealing with peers around certain issues or certain problems that he faces in everyday work. The FEI, I think, is devoted to trying to assist executives in looking at things more from the standpoint of a peer operation than from a vertical kind of a context. I am hoping that that's what some of you assistant secretaries may be getting out of this session that we've had in the past two days. Certainly, that's what the FEI has dedicated itself to as far as the career executives are concerned. The Institute is dedicated to assisting executives to share interchanges by addressing some of their organizational issues on a peer basis as opposed to the vertical kind of world within which they are normally used to operating.

The subject that we are going to cover this afternoon, namely, Policy Formulation and Policy Implementation, I think, is best characterized by some of the conflict phenomena that the White Team elaborated on in their report of yesterday. That is, the conflict which was noted between the role that an assistant secretary may have on the one hand in advocating certain policy positions, but then, on the other hand, perhaps having to reverse one's role, and indeed maybe even having to implement some sort of policy which may not have been consistent with that assistant secretary's own line of thinking at the time he was playing the advocacy role. So it means that frequently we all find ourselves in conflicts, as we transition from the role of formulators to implementors of the policy process. I am hoping that you will address these kinds of issues when you go into your smaller discussion groups.

But first, I would like to introduce to you our guest speaker, Under Secretary of Labor Mike Moskow. As under secretary, he is responsible for administering laws and programs to protect and improve the welfare of American workers.

Presentation on "Role of Assistant Secretaries in Policy Formulation and Implementation"

Moskow: To get a group like this together to talk about policy formulation and policy implementation over a period of two days, I think, is a real first in the history of American government. It is obviously something that should be done on a regular basis. But since it is a first, I think it has a special importance to all of us who are fortunate enough to be here.

The subject of the roles of the assistant secretary in policy formulation and policy implementation is really a difficult subject to talk about. Difficult for a number of reasons. First of all, the definitions cause me great problems—the words "policy," "formulation," "implementation," and "assistant secretary" are all ambiguous, since I think all can mean different things to different people. In fact, there is no common unambiguous usage for any of these terms. But let me start by at least talking about the definitions; then I'll deal with some broad generalizations which obviously are not based on any hard, empirical research. The extrapolations are based on my own observations, and I'm not sure that my observations in this area are any better than any of yours, except for the fact that I probably hold the record in this administration for the most presidential appointments and Senate confirmations, a total of four in two different agencies, as well as serving in four different agencies. I don't think there is anyone else in the Executive Branch now who can match me in that respect. But still my generalizations are based on working as an assistant secretary in two agencies, and as I start to think about all the areas of government that I have not been involved in—the defense area, the State Department, the Justice Department— I soon began to realize how little I know about the subject.

As far as policy formulation is concerned, most people automatically assume that policy is formulated by the congressional branch and implemented by the executive branch. I think that in reality that that's a very simplistic definition, and I think all of us here know that policy is formulated not only by the Congress, but that the executive branch formulates policy also in the way it implements laws. Also, the courts formulate policy as well. In fact, I've always thought that an assistant secretary who sets a standard for an acceptable level of implementation in his organization is making policy just as much as the Congress did when they passed the law which gave the assistant secretary the authority to set that particular standard.

The assistant secretary who determines the formula for distributing manpower training funds or public employment funds is making policy just as much as Congress did when they gave him the authority to do that. As far as the courts in our agency, we've seen in at least one aspect of the equal employment area the courts taking on a larger and larger role in making public policy. That is something that concerns me personally, because the courts make their decisions based on the facts of an individual case. And this means that they can't take into account all the various public policy considerations that should be examined in making a decision in the equal employment arena. So clearly, the courts make policy also.

As far as the term *assistant secretary* goes, obviously the functions vary depending on the agency. And they vary within the agencies as well. For as I start to think about this, some very striking examples of differences come to the fore in the Defense Department and the Transportation Department. In addition, there are administrators who are presidential appointees confirmed by the Senate who report directly to the secretary with line operating authority. For example, Bob Patricelli operates the Urban Mass Transit Program and reports directly to the secretary and deputy secretary. In the Labor Department, we have line assistant secretaries who operate programs, and we have staff assistant secretaries. We have an assistant secretary for policy, an assistant secretary for evaluation and research, and an assistant secretary for administration and management. Some of the other agencies have similar structures. And yet, others have a unique set of functions performed by their assistant secretaries. Another way assistant secretaries differ is of course by their personalities, and their own personal goals. Some are managerial and more oriented towards management and, therefore, spend most of their time working very closely with their staff on the day-to-day management of their individual programs in their agencies. Others are more of the "mister outside" type, who will spend most of their time making speeches outside the organization, and thus delegate to someone else (usually a deputy) the day-to-day ongoing responsibilities to run their agency. I would add some assistant secretaries do use the position as a visible stepping off point for other career objectives that they might have.

Let's talk for just a minute about what an assistant secretary is: First of all, he is a presidential appointee confirmed by the Senate. He is supposed to reflect the president's views and operate within the broad philosophy of the president. He has a special personal obligation to the president, because it is the president who put him in that job. And the president can take him out of that job any time he wants to, in most cases. Furthermore, the assistant secretary deals on a daily basis with the career civil service. And finally, he often has a constituency of his own (grantees, regulatees, or others) that he deals with on a daily basis.

In terms of the assistant secretary's effectiveness in the policy formulation and the policy implementation role, there are several characteristics that are important for him. First of all, in terms of his dealings with the career civil service, he's got to be able to motivate the people working for him. Any manager, to be effective, has to be able to motivate the people working for him. In this case, it is a somewhat more difficult job in some respects, because he is there for a short period of time, and additionally, he doesn't have the institutional knowledge that the people in the career civil service have. The motivation of his staff, I think, speaking of my own personal experience, is something that truly can be done. It requires some attention to motivating people, but I think that most people, when the chips are down, want to do a good job. They have pride in what they do and they want to think that they are making an important contribution to the work of the agency. And if he is skillful in dealing with them, he can be extremely successful in bringing them along, while, at the same time, getting great support from them. He also, of course, has to try to infuse some new talent into the organization as well, since that is part of the job of any good manager.

He additionally has to be very substantively involved in the program. He—if he is to convince the people working for him of the soundness of his position—must get to know enough about the programs to convince them of the soundness and merits of his positions. I mean, just telling people to do something to change their program or to change their policy in a certain way is not going to be nearly as effective or have nearly the same lasting effect as it would if he could convince them of the soundness of his proposals and/or of his decisions.

Again, one of the key reasons for doing one's substantive homework is that, in most cases, the career people are going to be there longer than an assistant secretary is going to be there. The average assistant secretary is only in office about two years, and with that rate of turnover, obviously the career people who are working for him have much more longevity. In policy formulation and implementation he's got to learn to deal with his constituency. He can't be a captive of the constituency, therefore he's frequently walking a tightrope. Some times that tightrope gets narrower and other times it is a little wider, but it is clearly a tightrope that he is walking. The constituency can be a very important source of information to him concerning his policies and his agency's policies, as well as the way he and his agency are implementing them. It can be a very effective source of feedback, because obviously he should not limit his sources of information about what he is doing and what his agency is doing to just internal agency channels. He's got to get information from the outside. And just a simple phone call from one of the groups that he is dealing with, telling him about a problem in a regional office, say somewhere in Chicago, can be a very effective signal to him that there is a problem with which he has to deal. If things aren't beng implemented the way he said they would be implemented, clientele feedback can be very effective in rectifying such situations. Furthermore, if the constituency turns against him completely, he's probably going to be ineffective in his job—and that's why I say you've got to learn to deal with them. An assistant secretary can't be captive on the one hand, but on the other hand, he can't have his constituencies turn completely against him.

If he has any legislative proposals, obviously his constituent group can have considerable impact with the Congress and even within the Executive Branch. So he has to at least be able to deal with them on a regular basis; and they have to view him or her as someone that they can deal with in a compatible manner. The problem he runs into with the tightrope is that he is running a specific program area which is just a piece of the president's overall program. However, to him and to his constituents there is nothing more important than that single program, so everything he can do to improve that program or get more resources for the program (funds or people) is going to be to his credit in the eyes of his constituents and in the eyes of his staff.

On the other hand, the secretary and his agency are looking at an agency-wide picture and the president is looking at a government-wide picture. Therefore, the more resources that are allocated to this particular program, the less that can be allocated to others within that agency-wide or government-wide situation. This is exacerbated by the fact that the president and secretary have to view his proposals on a comparative merits basis. So, it is a tightrope that he is walking and it gets narrower or wider depending on the circumstances of the time. He's got to be able to deal effectively with his boss or his bosses, his secretary, his under secretary, and all manner of people that he's reporting to. He has to make some important decisions as to what issues, what problems, what decisions he should bring to the attention of the secretary or under secretary in his agency. What's important enough to bring to the secretary's attention must be brought to his attention. If the assistant secretary has a policy issue to decide under his own delegated authority, he must decide which of those issues are amenable enough within his delegated authority to make the decision himself, as well as the issues which are important enough for him to decide to bring to the attention of the secretary or under secretary.

Under the delegated authority to an assistant secretary, sometimes there are some very important, even crucial, decisions that he is responsible for; for example, signing off on regulations for his particular agency, or making a decision about the allocation of funds, many times are completely within his official delegated authority in that agency. But, on the other hand, if he goes off and makes a very important policy decision that is not in line with the policy of the secretary or under secretary, his tightrope gets a lot narrower because the confidence of the secretary or under secretary in him is reduced in such a way that he becomes unsure about whether he's in line with policy thinking. But again, some of the decisions in certain agencies are routinely his even if they include signing off on the allocation of funds in the billion dollar category. So, many times, it's his judgment as to whether he should bring a policy decision to the attention of the secretary or under secretary. He also has to learn to deal effectively with the groups outside his agency—the White House, OMB, Congress, and, in many cases, the press as well. These actors are very important in policy formulation and in policy implementation, since these processes take place over a period of time.

Since the priorities of an administration, of a president, and of a secretary can change during any given period of time, it becomes important that an assistant secretary be in tune with the current thinking and the current priorities of the administration. I think that the classic example is in welfare reform. Back in the Nixon administration, President Nixon proposed a Family Assistance Plan as one of his major proposals. After a couple of go-arounds with the Congress, a bill passed the House of Representatives (HR-1) which was a major step forward for the administration. It was a compromise, but it was clearly the administration's policy. Nixon supported it; Secretary Richardson and Under Secretary Vennemen at HEW were also strong supporters of that policy. The only problem at that point was to get the bill passed by the Senate; and of course everyone assumed that the bill would pass the Senate easily. In fact, we were so certain of it in the Labor Department that we were gearing for major administrative responsibilities. We set up a planning staff of eighty people who were working full time on planning for the implementation of HR-1 when it was passed. Over at HEW they had a planning staff which Dick Nathan headed up spending full-time planning for the implementation of that bill when it was enacted. Major changes were anticipated in our policy toward welfare recipients.

However, somewhere in the course of that year of 1972, after the bill had passed the House of Representatives, President Nixon's policies changed. He moved away from his initial proposal of welfare reform. The people at HEW who were still fighting very hard to get this bill passed in the Senate were running in different directions from President Nixon at that point and the result was, as we all know now, that the bill did not pass the Senate, and planning staffs were abolished, and that was the end of HR-1. But, this process went on over a period of months, and I think it was clear that Nixon, while going down one road, made a slight turn that resulted in that bill not passing the Senate. Thus, many adjustments had to be made by those agencies which had anticipated a different outcome.

The assistant secretary has to be what I would call a "base-toucher" in the policy formulation role. I think the old saying is, "There's no sense hitting a home-run if you don't touch the bases along the way"; and I think that's a very appropriate slogan to follow in the policy formulation area. He must be touching bases with his constituency, other groups in the administration, the White House, OMB, and Congress to make sure that there is support for the new proposals that he is thinking of and for major changes in existing policies. He cannot go it alone. Just touching base can be extremely important, because very often people are terribly offended if they aren't consulted on something ahead of time. Even if their advice isn't taken, the act of consultation—the act of touching base can be extremely important.

The assistant secretary also comes in with a legacy. His predecessor has made some decisions which carry forward, and he, in some cases, has to pick up the pieces from policies that his predecessor left behind. In fact, I think that very often the initial period is spent on your predecessor's agenda, and certainly in the jobs that I have had that is so; during the first six months at HUD I spent three-fourths of my time working on things that my predecessor had started. The time frame is so long for some things that I'm still spending the bulk of my time on items that my predecessor initiated or was deeply involved in. This means that an assistant secretary sometimes has to be satisfied with very small changes that take a long time, sometimes a couple of years. Large changes take a long time because of the enormous amount of consultation and the tremendous amount of convincing that has to be done. So he's got to learn to be satisfied many times with changes in degree, and not necessarily major transformations in program structure or program design.

The assistant secretary rarely has much time to think about the big picture. Questions such as: "Where is my program going?" "What is its goal?" "Is the goal desirable at this point in time?" "What other ways are there of achieving that goal?" Surely these are questions that he rarely has very much time to focus on or to devote attention to. He gets caught up in the day-to-day crises and the day-to-day decisions that just eat up the vast bulk of his time. Things like calls from congressmen, calls from important constituents, working with his staff on regulations or guidelines to the field, speeches he's giving, testimony in Congress, plus all the normal functions of a manager like hiring and firing, planning, directing, checking up on people afterwards, take up the bulk of his time; therefore, he rarely has the extra time needed to really think about his overall program and where it's going. And where his overall program is going is a very crucial part of policy formulation.

Consequently, the role of the assistant secretary for policy and evaluation (whatever he's to be called in an agency) is a crucial one, and I think one that is extremely important for policy formulation and policy implementation, since that particular role doesn't have those same day-to-day responsibilities of other assistant secretaries. He doesn't have the crises to solve on a daily basis and he has a broader view of the agency, and hopefully, a broader presidential view that encompasses the entire administration. So it is essential that we spend some time with the staff focusing on those evaluation issues. Now the trade-off is, of course, that the assistant secretary in charge of evaluation doesn't know as much about a program as the line assistant secretary who is operating it. But, though that is true, I think it's also just as important that someone be spending some time focusing on overall issues and broader policy questions; in effect, the responsibility should be assigned to someone else in the agency. I think that that person can be more objective in his views because he doesn't have the line responsibility and the operating responsibility for a specific program.

Well, as I said, these are some broad generalizations based on my own experiences. I would be happy at this point to entertain some questions and discussions in order to find where you agree and where you disagree with the types of insights that I've been talking about. Therefore, I'll stop here and answer any questions that you might have.

Murphy: How about the impact of different leadership styles of secretaries and the function of the assistant secretary and the under secretary in relation to the phenomenon of style?

Moskow: That's very important. Of course some secretaries run the agency very carefully and very closely and they will want to make sure that they let it be known that every decision over a certain level must be brought to their attention. Some will delegate broad authority to assistant secretaries and it will be sort of a "management by exception" principle. The assistant secretary will then be able to decide on his own which issues to bring to the attention of the secretary.

The relationship between the secretary and the under secretary is one that is very important. The under secretary's role varies depending on the agency. In some cases, the secretary does not want to run the agency on a daily basis and he assigns that to his under secretary; thus the under secretary is in constant touch with the secretary so that he can reflect the secretary's views on a daily basis as he deals with the assistant secretaries. Consequently, in this model, the assistant secretary always has the right to appeal decisions of the under secretary to the secretary.

In other cases, the under secretary performs special assignments of special functions that the secretary has assigned to him, meaning that he does not have that line responsibility for operating the agency on a daily basis. So, I think that this is really more a question of personalities of the secretary and under secretary than anything else, as well as a question of the type of management style that those two— usually the secretary—wants to set for the agency.

Bolduc: I wonder if you would comment on the policy-setting mode of GSA and OMB and the impact that these institutions have upon the assistant secretaries and the execution of the policy in their departments?

Moskow: One, I think that the most important of the two that you mentioned would be OMB's role. OMB obviously has a vested interest in spending as little money as possible, and that's the direction they come from—and they make no bones about it either. Therefore, I think there is a danger there, for if all policy issues were to go through just the funnel of OMB before going to the president, he would be getting a distorted view on those policy issues as they came to him. I think that is why it is essential that there be a White House staff of some sort that also provides some input to the president as issues arise, because they would not have the same bias toward spending as little as possible as the OMB staff would have. I think, based on my own experience, that it is important to work closely with OMB just as it is with the White House staff, but I think it is important to recognize the different perspectives from which they are coming. In effect, it is essential to remember that OMB gets credit for cutting the budget or keeping the budget as low as possible—and they have to earn their salary just as anyone else does.

Patterson: Are there limits on the size, function, initiatives, and interference capabilities of the White House staff? And if so, where are they?

Moskow: That's a tough question. By interference, I assume you mean interference with the agencies. Well, sure you can get into a situation where an agency is just flooded with calls from the White House. Now what does that mean? Sure the White House is calling, but there are five different offices in the White House, and someone at possibly a pretty low level may be calling to ask for some information; to ask for a report on something; to ask someone to see someone; or something of that sort. And that I think can go overboard. But I think that that can be controlled by proper management of the White House staff.

Hooker: I would have to say that I am a little skeptical about the White House staff function. I guess one of the reasons for the Domestic Council having been set up in respect to domestic programs was to act as a buffer basically to OMB, or at least to be coming at a problem from a different direction. In fact, at least in my tenure, it certainly was different under different directors of the Domestic Council. But when "push comes to shove" with the Domestic Council and OMB, there is no match. OMB clearly has the manpower and staff and everything else at its disposal. The question in my mind is: Should the White House staff try to serve that role or should it be served by direct access to the president by the cabinet?

Moskow: I've seen two Domestic Councils and I think the two have differed. I think the first was much stronger than the Domestic Council is now, and I think that I would disagree that when push came to shove the Domestic Council was no match for OMB. I saw a number of cases where the former Domestic Council would win the day on a policy issue with OMB. In terms of the analytical staff, obviously OMB has the upper hand. And the Domestic Council, at least in my experience, relies on that very heavily and draws upon that. But in terms of the recommendations to the president as to what policy he should follow on a certain area, at least in my experience, the president did not always "shoot down" the Domestic Council to go with OMB when the two differed on an issue. Given the size of our government today, I guess I don't think it is realistic to expect the president to be able to deal as closely with the agencies as you seem to be implying in your question. I think he is always going to want to have some people who are going to be a filter, as well as some people upon whom he can rely to reflect his government-wide view. At least it seems important for some confidants to present their views to him on certain issues before they come to him for a final decision.

Bledsoe: I wonder if you would comment on the dilemma I mentioned a minute ago, about where the formulation stage of the assistant secretary really is, when he is on one side of an issue and the decision goes in another direction, leaving that person to take the responsibility for implementation? What do you see arising out of that kind of a dilemma? And what kinds of behavioral patterns have you observed on the part of people under those conditions?

Moskow: I haven't found that to be a great problem. I've seen that happen in a number of cases, and I haven't found it to be a major problem because I think that the way most people enter assistant secretary positions, at least initially, is that they want to have the option; that is, they want to be assured that they will be able to present their views to the person that is making the final decision on a certain policy issue. Obviously they want to be able to lay out the options. They want to be able to present their view or their recommendation to the policy maker. But obviously the final policy maker—the president or the secretary—is the one making the authoritative decision on the issue.

Now, the option is that an assistant secretary has the ability to present his view to the policy maker; but if the policy maker decides against an assistant secretary, then that person has to fall in line and accept the decision of the policy maker in that particular case. Now that's worked out very well in the situations that I've seen. Obviously, if an assistant secretary goes forward with a very strong proposal that his staff has worked on for a long time, and he's ginned everyone up with his confidence that he is going to get it accepted, I think that before he gets to that point, he has to do the base touching that I talked about earlier, otherwise he gets too far out on a limb. In effect, an assistant secretary has problems if he has not performed the intermediate steps that he should have performed. But if he does get to that point, and he gets that far along, and then has to come back with a negative decision, he's going to have the primary problem of convincing his own staff of his wisdom and/or efforts. If it gets to the point where he feels that he disagrees so strongly with the president or the secretary on an issue, obviously he has to leave his job.

Morrill: About implementation, let me put forth a premise and ask you to comment on it. My view of the situation is that policy planning drives out management and implementation because it is more fun. The president, the secretary, and the Congress are much more involved in policy planning, and one gets more "brownie points," more gratification from policy planning; thus whatever time is left over too often is too little and too weak for the implementation process or the hard management procedures we talked about earlier in this conference. I would like you to comment.

Moskow: I think I agree with that. I think it is a result of our whole political system. People get political points for the initiation of new ideas that they generate; they don't get political points for doing a job well or for implementing a policy well. I think that's the whole structure of our system. It starts with the Congress and continues in the Executive Branch from the president right on down. When someone goes out to get elected, he says, I introduced this bill, or this piece of legislation was passed, or we had a problem and I dealt with it. I agree with you that it is a very serious problem. And I think that the short time frame of the electoral process adds to that problem.

Kolberg: Could I ask you a follow-up question? What should we do about it? Because in my view we shouldn't leave it where it is. It must have something to do with the way we organize. You've been in two different departments with two totally different organizational structures; at least, that's what I've noticed in the way political executives are used at HUD as compared to how they are used in Labor. What would you say about those two modes? Perhaps, for instance, we ought to take assistant secretaries out of line jobs and essentially make them policy planners, or assign them more directly to a full-time job in the actual administration, leaving a different mix on the implementation side than the policy side. In effect, I think there is a problem here and that we aren't dealing with it very well.

Moskow: I don't have any easy answers to that. Maybe that is something that would be good to discuss in the groups when they meet after this session.

Macdonald: In my estimation a lot of the best policy suggestions for new initiatives come out of the people who are really in the bowels of the administrative process for administering the program that's involved. What about combining the policy programmer and the administrator, thus forcing him to take responsibility for the implementation of the policy he is proposing. Might not that give a little bit more incentive on the one hand to the administrator, since he'd have the policy role; and on the other hand, even give more importance to the process of policy formulation?

Moskow: Well, I don't understand that fully. When you say the administrator, do you mean the political appointee?

Macdonald: Yes, the political appointee who is responsible for a particular administration of a particular program or bureau.

Moskow: Well, I've seen policy proposals made in many different ways; I've seen legislative proposals for changes in a program come from the people operating those programs, and I've seen them come from the people who were not operating the programs. The staff, or the general counsel, or the assistant secretary for policy, or some other group in an agency may come up with proposals. I've seen them come from all directions and all sides. I wouldn't just limit it to coming from the people who are operating those programs.

Bolduc: Mike, coming back to the point made a minute ago. I think some of that is changing. Late last spring the White House and OMB came forward with what we call the Presidential Management Initiatives Program, and after experimenting and exploring with that approach they now have formalized and institutionalized that process into what is called an Annual Management Plan. This plan will be developed simultaneously with the budget and submitted along with the budget, and it will call upon certain key factors in the area of personnel management, fiscal management, and data processing management to see how they will impact upon program delivery and the efficiency of the delivery of that service. I think it is a turning around—a general awareness—and I think that it is a movement in the right direction.

Moskow: It is a step in the right direction and the key to managerial success. I think the success of a presidential management initiative is linked to the president's own personal involvement in it, and his telling his Cabinet members that this is something that he wants to do since it is important to the American people. And if he doesn't do that on a regular basis—like about once every few months—by having a meeting with his Cabinet to discuss that, then that type of presidential management issue is going to be doomed to failure.

Before we finish, let me go back through a couple of the earlier questions. A question was asked about the reaction of people when a decision is made adverse to their policy recommendations. I would generally agree with you that people accept it if it is well explained; then they'll carry it out. I'd suggest two caveats to this conclusion; one is related to the clarity with which the decision is made, and second, it is affected by the importance of the subject matter at stake. And just to give one example—both of these aspects are combined in the decision-making context of the SALT talks. There we had presidential decisions each time the negotiating team would go off to Helsinki or Vienna or wherever we would go. Generally the delegation would be back to the president before the airplane ever landed in Europe because of the lack of clarity. Our negotiators were dealing with a hideously complex matter and everybody knew the written language was ambiguous. And when you have a lot of minds looking at it, ambiguity is going to creep up. And secondly, where you are dealing with a subject of that importance to so many groups, I would suggest that while people accepted SALT in theory, they came back time and time again because of the ambiguity in the situation. I think those are caveats which are important. I think welfare reform may be a parallel example on the domestic side. The issue is viewed to be of such an enormous importance to such a large number of groups in the government and outside the government, that you don't have the same kind of reaction as you do in many other areas.

Bledsoe: I think Mike has certainly given us a few new points to look at in our group discussions, as well as substantiating some of the points that we have already covered. I think our work is cut out for us.

ELT Reports on Policy Formulation and Implementation

Bledsoe: Our format this afternoon will be similar to the one used in the morning session in that we'll ask each group to give a very brief summary report on the dialogue held in their respective groups, and then we will open it for general discussion. So I'll ask the Red Team to give the first report. They had as their primary question the following: To what extent is it clear to responsible officials in your organization exactly what the policies are in your organization? How is clarity achieved? How are new officials/employees in responsible positions informed? And, how are incumbents kept current on what the policies are?

Red Team Report

Brotzman: We dealt in broader brush strokes. First of all, we started out trying to answer the question: Why a policy? What is the need for a policy? And with some semblance of agreement on this, we thought most of them emanated from the initiation of a problem someplace real or someplace perceived. Sometimes it comes from within an "eager beaver" on your staff; sometimes it is crisis-induced; and many times it comes from the top. Frequently, Congress gives us policies or guidance, but just as frequently we the Secretariat determine the reason to act because the Congress was ambiguous in its guidance.

I have pointed out to some of my former colleagues that I wish I could go back and reinvent some of the wheels that I had invented over there in Congress, because I didn't realize until I got into this position as an assistant secretary how often Congress failed to give specific directions in legislation.

The second question we talked about was: Who actually decides if there is a problem requiring a policy? We think one of the principal responsibilities of the assistant secretary, since he sees issues going up and also sees them coming down, is to help our bosses to determine if a policy is necessary to deal with the real problem. Now this brings up the area of jurisdictional conflicts.

Orlebeke: I made the point that frequently it is very difficult for career officials to discern exactly what policy is, and how to relate a particular departmental policy to other departments. We tend, both as assistant secretaries and as departmental officials, to define problems in terms of our own departments, and therefore we are not very receptive to how that problem might be defined by another department or even by the White House. An example I gave was the problem of neighborhood deterioration or abandonment. This is a HUD type problem, but we also know that the tools we have to deal with that problem are very limited. We realize that we have to go to

Treasury on tax policy affecting neighborhoods, but that agency may say, well, neighborhood deterioration is not a problem as far as we see it. We see it in completely different terms—as the normal working of the market. And HEW may see it as a problem of lack of social services or school desegregation. And if you're from HEW, you can say, "By the way, HUD, while we are talking about school desegregation, we wish you'd stop pouring all that subsidized housing into those neighborhoods where there are schools that we are trying to desegregate." These interdepartmental differences in perspective and goals present a very difficult challenge for the administration and the White House in dealing with its departments. Also, I think it creates problems within departments themselves as political appointees seek honestly to get beyond their particular programs and into the really generic problems—however they may be defined. So the problem with the primary question, I guess, is that as we talked about policy direction to career officials, words like "clear" and "exactly" do not sound like the environment in which I operated.

Brotzman: Nor me. We have a program at DOD called FYDP. (I don't know if you can talk in acronyms or not. Incidentally, I've organized a new group over at DOD called JAWS—Junk Acronyms When Speaking.) Anyway, we have FYDP, which means "Five-Year Defense Plan." This is a system of "program budget decisions," which means that we at the service level discuss the budget issues with those at the defense level. After much debate, differences boil down to a few "major issues" which are decided by the Secretary of Defense. Ultimately, the plan ends with the president. This is how we actually make policy that falls into the budget, on a five-year basis. The systems for arriving at policy determinations vary greatly in all the agencies represented in our discussion group.

Bledsoe: We will now have the report from the White Team. And the question that they addressed was: What are the most important dimensions and/or features of your policy involvement in your position?

White Team Report

Bolduc: Consistent with our earlier discussion yesterday and this morning I thought that I would very quickly summarize some of the high points of our discussion, and then turn it over to some of my colleagues so that they might comment on some of the more specific issues and specific points.

One of the first things we dealt with was trying to answer several preliminary questions: What is policy? Who makes it? At what organizational level? And how is it carried out? We took about thirty minutes to come up with what we think are half-way decent answers, but there still was not general agreement as to whether, in fact, the definitions we arrived at represented policy. We talked about objectives; we talked about how policy is in fact made; we noted that Congress participates in making policy; the president participates; administrators participate; we all participate. In fact, a point was made that policy is really enunciated at all organizational levels. Even the Xerox operator participates—if he makes a decision and enunciates a policy that no one will in fact make any more than ten copies per day on a specific Xerox machine, he is articulating policy. We talked about discretionary decisions that are made by the Department of Justice. In regard to an interpretation of the law, they are by reason of that interpretation and by reason of providing that opinion, in fact, enunciating policy. The end result was that we felt that policy was really "action that is articulated or enunciated indicating intent."

We chatted a little bit about our personal involvement with policy and it was rather interesting to see that Judith Connor at the Department of Transportation participates in a policy role very much different from each one of us. She participates in the policy formulation and policy execution stages within an operational agency.

We also talked about the environment within which each one of us works; for example, in the Department of Transportation, Secretary Coleman frequently makes policy determinations independent of input by the operational agencies. That was somewhat different from what happens at the Department of Defense where it was pointed out that frequently policies are decided upon through the process of participatory management or the suggestion type of approach.

We talked about one of the very key things that one ought to take a look at if he believes himself to be a policy official. And that is, that he can develop a type of structure that will give him the vehicle by which he can, in fact, effectuate policy. All of us think that in one way or another we participate in policy decision making. And yet, frequently, policy is being made around us and even much below us. In fact, we may sit up there thinking that we are making policy, while the policy is being made by a GS-15 or a GS-13. So really, an assistant secretary has to develop a structure to assure that he will receive the type of input he needs to have in order for him to make policy.

Another point that was made was that we all have to be particularly careful as it relates to policies that are made much below us. Let me cite an example. About a year ago we had a constraint with regard to our space situation in Washington, D.C. We had received objections to dealing with a space management program that called for trying to locate an office away from Washington that would occupy 150,000 square feet. I had issue and position papers prepared, and they were still in a discussion stage when a suggestion was made by one of our people that the Rural Electric Administration be transferred from downtown Washington to Hyattsville, Maryland. This was a Friday afternoon, and we were still talking about it.

By Tuesday afternoon legislation had been introduced and passed prohibiting us from relocating that agency from downtown Washington to Hyattsville. That is a form of policy. That was not made at our level. We never had a chance to make a decision. But they worked around the system and through Congress.

One last item in connection with policy making, and that is that I think all of us need to participate directly or indirectly in the budget process. In effect, the assessment of priorities, the assessment of results of program evaluations, zero base budgeting, or whatever the case might be, when you get down to the bottom line, it means budget. If the policy that has reached your level requires "x" number of dollars, and that cannot be accommodated by the financial constraints and resources available, then that bottom line must stand and by so doing it is enunciating policy.

I might say one other thing about what went on in our group. We touched very briefly on the judicial role in the policy making process. One of our members who had to leave early talked a little bit about the lawyer in this process. We also got into a discussion of how more and more decisions are being moved into the courts in various areas. Hence, when decisions are made in the courts they indeed become policy that must be followed.

Another subject that we touched on that I found interesting was the old myth that policy was made by political appointees, and that career people did not in fact make policy. I suggest that the myth really no longer holds, although it is still youthful. My own feeling was that I agreed the myth no longer holds. Policy is made at all levels and also in the program offices. There is still such a thing as political policy making (which is more of a presidential administration type) than just departmental policy making. But policy making dealing with urban areas, or transportation, or whatever, is a little bit different and it is neither totally within the purview of the appointee, nor totally in the purview of the career officer.

Bledsoe: We will now move to the Blue Team whose assigned question was the following: How are program goals and objectives related to, derived from, or injected into policy? How are the *results achieved* related to program goals and priorities? To policies? To policy formulation?

Blue Team Report

Hooker: We certainly had an unstructured discussion. I think it can be said that if we did touch on the question, it was strictly by accident and not by design. I was thinking as I was sitting here about a story that many of you may have heard about Abba Eban. I think it sort of sums up what all of us are thinking about today. He had this great quote that I heard which said, "There is nothing wrong with public officials repeating their mistakes, but it's not mandatory."

The first thing we addressed came up out of the blue as a result of a story that Brad Patterson told; therefore, I will turn the microphone over to him. The question arose as to what extent do we, as assistant secretaries, derive policy input from going out into the field and examining certain delivery systems in order to find out how they are working out there. I think that most of us would admit that we don't do enough of it, but let me turn the discussion over to Brad.

Patterson: It was just a poignant little story. I was at my desk a couple of months ago and got a phone call and the caller said, "I am calling from the most godforsaken area of the Navajo Reservation. I am way out here in the sticks, and there is a little Indian health clinic, but it can't operate very well because it needs three ambulances and one of them should have an off-the-road capability which would allow it to go out into the bush where the roads stop." He said, "Couldn't you possibly get GSA or Defense to find one more ambulance with an off-the-road capability? Because it makes all the difference in the world as to whether this little Indian health clinic is going to be able to do very much or not with the people it really needs to serve, way the hell off the road." The caller was John Ehrlichman, and there was some poignancy of course to his focus of interest. Later when he came to town, before he went to jail, we had lunch; and he said, "You know my experience out in the southwest has led me to say, if I ever had this to do over again, when I was appointing somebody to the White House staff with my left hand, I'd say, 'Here's your certificate to the White House staff,' and then with my right hand I'd say, 'Here's an airplane ticket. Get your tail out of Washington and spend six months out at the farthest possible end of the service delivery system to find out how it's working and what's happening way the hell out there with the population that the system is designed to serve. And after six months you can come back and be a member of the White House staff.' "

At the time, of course, I was working on a memorandum for the president on whether he should sign or veto the Indian health care improvement act. I thought to myself, what real difference does it make if the Navajo families might or might not be near this extra ambulance facility with an off-the-road capability? Is the president's signature on that bill going to make a difference? It seemed to us to be the epitome of policy development. Yet, how much difference would it make to the delivery system, unless you met some of these specific questions? How do we know what's happening way the hell out there in the system that is supposed to serve the needs of a designated population?

Hooker: I know that in my own case, the Department of Transportation administers a lot of grant-in-aid programs, and that my job is basically legislative and intergovernmental. Since I came into the department in December of 1975, I spent until September 1976 worrying about nothing but the legislative program. I had no time to do anything else. I finally spent about two months, from September to November of this year, travelling and just seeing how these delivery systems work. It was immensely valuable from my point of view and I suspect that maybe the legislative program of the department would have been slightly amended had I done it the other way around. But, in any case, that is another story which one of our team members wants to talk about.

Taylor: I've told some of you this story before. Earlier this week I was visiting an aircraft carrier. It is really astonishing the conditions under which the young men live on an aircraft carrier. They have an area about 100 feet square as a lounge for 110 young men with a little TV set and maybe six chairs. They sleep in bunks that are 14 inches apart going up against the bulkhead. It was a tremendous eye-opener for me, and I have made many of these trips before. But it is extremely important to get out in the field. Too often we sit in Washington and make global decisions on personnel policy and on resource allocation among the services and within the services from one area to another. On a number of trips I've come across misinterpretation of policy that we thought was perfectly clear when we put it out, and yet, on the line it was being totally incorrectly interpreted. This happened in the Air Force where it had to do with the allocation of housing by grade. We thought that the regulations were crystal clear when they went out. But as a result of some complaints by some senior NCOs, we discovered that the people at the local level misunderstood what we meant and were really penalizing the senior staff. We quickly got that rearranged when we got back. It was a real important eye-opener to me to get out and see what it was we were doing for our people.

Hooker: I'm not sure of the chronology, but I think we turned to the question of what kinds of intelligence systems any of us could think of that would help us find out what is really going wrong with delivery systems. Clearly, we all hear from our constituents in one way or another. We hear from Congress and so on, but are there other kinds of devices that might be used? I think that there wasn't any clear consensus on that, but certainly Brad Patterson again had an interesting idea which he attributed to Sargent Shriver.

Patterson: The Shriver technique consisted of hiring a bunch of newspaper men to go around and police the Peace Corps, watch the volunteers, travel with them, go abroad with them, sit in their training sessions with them, and then send him "eyes only" secret envelopes of their own impressions as newspaper men as to what was going on. It was a rather unsettling technique. Shriver institutionalized it and called it his inspector general's office. It highlighted problem areas, but at least the newspapermen dug into their task with the enthusiasm of an exorcist. It caused his line people some difficulty, but he insisted on it because he wanted to make sure that he knew what was happening at the bottom of his organization. He wanted to hear all the complaints before they appeared higher in his organization and before they appeared in the newspaper.

Bolduc: One of the things that we have in Agriculture is an internal auditing system which has about 550 professional auditors located throughout the country. In Agriculture we have approximately 16,000 field locations, and it is critical that we get on-going daily feedback in terms of the effectiveness of our delivery service and the problems that are associated with it. Our field auditors visit about 3,500 of those 16,000 locations annually. In addition to conducting fiscal examinations, program evaluations, and management assessments, they have a listing of items they can check against, in terms of program delivery, to provide us on-going feedback through the organizational structure. This is the type of intelligence upon which we can correct policy decisions or implement corrective measures to assure that we are providing an efficient and effective management program system in the field.

Hooker: Does anyone else have any insights?

Connor: I would like to take a different perspective. I remember a time a couple of years ago being in a car going to lunch; there were six of us in the car and we took a survey to find out which was the worst department among the federal agencies in terms of delivering its own service. There were six people and five people voted Agriculture as being the worst and one person said HEW. It just happens that my husband and I own a farm and Ag's farm management service is the one service that comes directly out of the federal government with which we had experience that really can't be faulted. When there is a local agent system in a small town of about 1,700 people, that local agent "walks on water" as far as the community is concerned, because he is a source of all information. He tells you what to plant, how to fertilize, how to take crop samplings, and he does everything you could possibly conceive of. I cite that example only because I found it very interesting that five people in the federal bureaucracy from different departments all made the same judgment about the Department of Agriculture—and they were all Washingtonians, all living in the Washington area. None of them were sampling any of the services. So it really is important to get out there and find out what's going on.

They were probably influenced by one program—food stamps. They probably don't like giveaway programs and they don't like food stamps—and obviously they weren't using food stamps.

Bolduc: I think about 72 percent of Agriculture's budget is what is called income security. Only about 8 percent of Agriculture's budget is directly spent for agriculture programs such as agriculture research and animal and plant health inspection services. Most of the adverse publicity that is generated impacts the food stamp program for which an assistant secretary in Agriculture is responsible. That's one of the several programs he has. And since that's what the public reads about in the newspapers, they draw conclusions from it about both the department and its leadership.

Feltner: I could defend the delivery system that's there. I think it actually works pretty well, even in food stamps. In fact, I know the delivery system actually works pretty well. Sure, it has had its problems, but the publicity has been almost totally negative, so I'm not really surprised, Judith, that you would get that kind of reaction from five people who have been reading *The Washington Post* and who have automatically associated food stamps with the Department of Agriculture.

Hooker: I guess the next topic we turned to and spent a little time with was the question that was raised about how any of us budget thinking time into our various schedules. How do we go about getting away from the pressures of the office or whatever, and just spend some time thinking? Obviously, as you might imagine, everybody had different techniques. A couple of us did it driving to work or commuting each way to work. Some people had sudden insights as they were shaving in the mirror. Other people stayed one night a week in the office where they just reserved two hours to sit and think and write down their thoughts. But that led into a much broader discussion dealing with the whole question of long range planning and to what extent any of us here really do that—a very interesting generic question for all of us in the public sector. Recognizing that the pace of history really is accelerating to the extent that problems crop up faster than our reaction time can cope with them, we spent some time relating what each of us is doing about this kind of a phenomenon.

There were various responses in our group. I think that certainly in Transportation we have now got a national transportation policy. We are about to get out a report that will indicate some of the major questions that will arise over the next twenty years, and how to deal with them. That's one side of the issue. In the defense field there is a lot that goes on in thinking about military weapons systems out into the future. In Agriculture they don't do as good a job as they should; it is very quixotic and episodic. Everybody gets hyped up about it for a period of time and then the interest wanes. And in EPA (which currently operates under a five-year plan), Al Alm had an interesting experience as a member of that agency at the Woodrow Wilson Center that I think he should tell us about.

Alm: About a year and a half ago a committee was set up to look at a long range planning mechanism for the federal government. A number of people participated in this, and John Sawhill was one of them. We were interested in strategic analysis of those kinds of issues or trends in the future that really impact policy decisions today. Most of the examples we came up with tended to be in the resources area— what future energy supplies would be; what kind of prices one could expect; what were the potential shortages of other materials? We looked at the long-term agricultural situation and then translated these back into programs now in operation—programs of research, agricultural policies, and the like. The group concluded that there was a need for this kind of strategic analysis; and second, that it really couldn't be done in the departments because the kinds of concerns overlapped any particular departmental jurisdiction; and finally, we concluded that there are too many rigidities in a department to do this kind of planning, since so many short-term needs just push long-term analysis out of the process. So our final conclusion was that an office of strategic planning ought to be set up, but the question was where?

The group was split between a separate office like CEA or CEQ, but we finally recommended OMB for a couple of reasons: One, if this institution were to really impact policy and resource allocations, OMB had the necessary focus and clout. Two, there was some hope that with a function like this, the OMB director could focus on issues where resource and policy decisions made now will affect the U.S. and the world in the 1980s and 1990s.

Bolduc: In the bureaucracy I think that planning is a very basic ingredient to management, and out of plans flow policies, and out of policies or vice versa flow objectives and targets. I think that not only don't we have an overall plan in Agriculture, I think that we could go around this room and probably find some very, very significant weaknesses in that most of us really don't plan where we are going to be five years from now, particularly in functional areas. For example, we could take housing—many of you may not be aware that Agriculture puts over $4.2 billion a year in the housing market. HUD also puts money in the housing market. What should our government-wide priorities and plans be? Should we attempt to take people who are currently residing in substandard housing, improve that housing to an acceptable level first, and then undertake new construction? Or should we move into new construction first, and then upgrade the standard of living in substandard housing later? We need direction, we need planning, and, in this case, it requires coordination between HUD and USDA. Then we get into community facilities—water and sewerage projects, school systems, etc. And though the whole thing locks in together, we don't do planning in that regard.

In our discussions we came to the conclusion that Congress is uniquely ill-situated to deal with some of these problems. For example in the energy field, I suspect most of you have seen that OMB "mess" chart showing that when the Federal Energy Independence Act went up to the Hill, the administration officials had to testify before a total of 108 standing and subcommittees on that single piece of legislation. As somebody pointed out, I didn't know there were that many Congressional units. That's remarkable! Obviously Congress isn't set up to plan the energy package, and from what we've seen happen, it's not clear that the Executive Branch is either. There are kinds of things that make long-term planning difficult and frustrating—but critical to our national needs.

Hooker: Some of the problems you mentioned about planning deal with constraints that are almost absolute. For example, when planning ahead for programs that have large future budget implications, you have a fairly sterile exercise. Even a five-year picture figures in the budget; therefore, I don't know if anybody takes those figures seriously; we certainly don't. Secondly, when you deal with policies that overlap a number of agencies, planning becomes extraordinarily difficult. The planning that can go on in government is the kind of planning that is more or less under the control of a particular agency that doesn't require significant budget impacts. For our basic regulatory programs we develop five-year plans—five-year strategies. We get a lot of public comment. We use the most current year as the year for our guidance to our regional offices and we set commitments against it.

Patterson: One footnote about planning is that if we don't do it ourselves in the federal Executive Branch, it sure is going to be done for us. In fact, it is *being* done for us all over the country by the different interest groups which are very well organized and which have very definite ideas which lead them to go right ahead on their merry way charting the future for themselves. This means that probably nobody is doing any planning about such things except as it is done by Indians themselves. And, of course, Indian people are beginning to organize and are telling us now in no uncertain terms hat they want reservation areas of the United States and their tribal governments to become "politically independent societal units, for he life of the nation." This is an interesting addition to the federal system in America. In addition, they want federal programs to go directly to them and not to the states anymore; they want to be treated as the equivalent of state and local governmental units. I don't know if in the long, long run that's a particularly brilliant idea, or a particularly pernicious idea, but the point is they are planning and I just wish I could find somewhere in the Executive Branch where senior governmental officials are thinking about this also.

Connor: I'd like to make a comment to that, Brad, especially since I was here at the FEI for an eight-week session about four years ago. The thing that perhaps frustrated me most was that my fellow students spent a tremendous amount of time worrying about the fact that there was no "planning." It was a concern dealing with both personal and national interests. In other words, the greatest frustration among the supergrades was that their own agencies had no idea where they were going to go, and an even greater frustration was the belief that we are not going to plan; that there is nothing in our system of government which at the present time constitutes pressure towards the development of long-range planning processes.

Patterson: I think you are quite right that there is no pressure. The secretary himself or herself has got to be an unusually conceptually oriented person to insist on this. And I can think of a couple of examples where this was attempted—one rather successful and one rather not successful. In the State Department there is a Policy Planning Staff and it has been in existence since the 1940s as a separate unit of twelve or fifteen officers who have no operational or cable writing responsibilities; who in a way second-guess a lot of the departmental operating people. Under a very sophisticated senior official they produce mature basic papers for the Secretary of State which are inserted in his level in the decision making process. I am quite sure that this successful unit is there now and has been there for thirty years. The other one that didn't do so well—as some of us may remember—was the National Goals Research Staff which we tried to undertake in the White House in 1970-71. It was under the supervision of Len Garment. There was a lot of bickering and conflict relating to staff, money, space, logistics, support, and so forth. The staff produced one report which was sort of a so-so document. Then Ehrlichman just wiped it out because he said, "We'll fold it into the Domestic Council's long-range planning function." I don't think they ever did because the Domestic Council's planning didn't work so well. So, there have been some successful and some unsuccessful attempts to institutionalize planning groups. It takes an initiative and thoughtfulness and a modest degree of institutionalization to resist all the pressures we identified as pressuring us not to do it.

Moskow: I think we have to be careful how we use the term planning, because I think we are using it in a different sense here. Some of us are talking about how an agency would plan for its programs in the future over a multi-year period, and I think most agencies now have a small policy planning staff for that function that doesn't have any direct program interest; it doesn't operate programs, and it doesn't have any immediate impact on those programs. But the type of analysis that Al Alm is talking about when he used the term "strategic analysis" I think is quite different. Al is really talking about how the environment is going to change in the future and about what factors there are going to be in the environment that will change and affect the role of government and government programs overall. That is very different, but no less important. That type of planning or strategic analysis is probably being done by most of the major corporations in the United States today. It's developed over the last five or ten years and it is being done on quite a large scale. Businesses have some of the same problems that we have in terms of trying to get program people involved in it and to go along with it. It is a very crucial function to be performed, but I don't think it can be done in an agency. I agree with it, but it's too big for an agency. No matter how strong-willed the secretary or Cabinet officer is, most agencies don't have the capability to perform this type of analysis. In fact, all the incentives in government are exactly in the opposite direction— toward the short time frame for political appointees, for political credit for new initiatives and new ideas. These factors all run counter to the type of strategic analysis that Al was talking about.

Hooker: I have often thought about that, too, particularly in terms of the Congress. Clearly many Congressmen are coming in from close elections back in their districts. If they asked their constituents to make substantial sacrifices to deal with a problem that is not even going to come into being for five years, they would be cutting their own throats. That's a damned difficult thing to ask of them. But that is an institutional problem that we have in this country that makes it very difficult.

Bolduc: However, if we don't do it, someone's going to do it for us, and let me give you an illustration. Environmentalists, various local interest groups, and the housing industry have made their concerns known to the Forest Service. They ask us to tell them where we're going to be five years from now, so that they could do some of the strategic planning that is needed in private industry. For a number of years the Forest Service didn't respond to their liking. Last year, and this represents to the best of my knowledge a first in the history of this government, the Congress enacted the Resources Planning Act requiring the Forest Service to develop a comprehensive five-year plan of action. It required the Forest Service to go public with the document. They held public conferences at ten geographical points throughout the country to seek local input to assure that the five-year plan and, more specifically, the one-year plan, was addressing in part views consistent with the local needs. That's what you find if your agency doesn't take the initiative.

Alm: I think what's happening is that there is a tremendous gap between the decisions that are being made for the future and the analytical framework for dealing with them. We are putting large amounts of money into energy systems that won't produce anything tangible until the 1990s. Many of our legislative requirements right now deal with actions and benefits that occur far in the future. So I tend to think that this kind of analysis is really critical just to deal with the decisions we're making right now. All of us would be able to develop better policies if we had a better understanding of what the future looked like.

Nuechterlein: I'd just like to add one thing. I was fascinated by the discussion on long-range planning or strategic analysis, because my field is international politics and American foreign policy, and I'm coming to the conclusion, and it worries me, that the only way this country really faces up to long-range planning is when there is an emergency. The kind of emergencies that we're looking at down the pike in foreign policy are going to be things that we will not be able to deal with in the short term. And yet, the public in this country doesn't see any foreign issues or policy problems that are going to mobilize them to do anything. It worries me to think that here we are talking about the inability of the Executive Branch of the government to provide any real leadership in long-range planning, while learning that the private sector is doing it. It is certainly needed in the international environment. We're still on this crucial question of energy three years after the initial crisis, sitting around thinking that we're going to go on driving for "60¢ a gallon gas" for the next ten years. We're kidding ourselves, and it worries me that as a society, as a government, as an Executive Branch, we simply cannot get ourselves together and face the public with the reality of what it's going to cost.

Macdonald: Let me just express a small dissent. One of the things we should probably plan for as a government is to enable the individual to do the maximum on his own account. At least this is what I always felt was the policy of the conservative portion of the Republican Party. But beyond that, I don't think I'm quite as concerned over what appears to be a lack of planning as I might have been before I came here. At the ratification of the Jay Treaty in 1795, a Congressman, Fisher Ames, stood up and said, "You know, the difference between a monarchy and a democracy is that in a monarchy, it's like a square rigger. It sails along before the wind, high and dry for quite a while, and then it hits some shoals, flounders and sinks. Whereas a democracy is like a raft. It never sinks, but you're always up to your knees in water." I think that generally this kind of a government of checks and balances, and mutual restraint, and special interests all pushing their own objectives within the conceptual design of a government made for the accommodation of those interests, really is always going to look as though it's up to its knees in water. But somehow we always survive and I think that we will for a lot longer than some of the elite minority governments that seem to be so expert at planning.

Bledsoe: Perhaps that's a good philosophical note on which to end. But I would like to give Mike Moskow maybe one more shot, if he would like to say a word or two, and then we'll wrap up this discussion.

Moskow: Well, maybe a note of dissent on the dissent. I believe as much as anyone else does in the importance of the individual being able to determine his own future and his own position. I believe in the market system and the private enterprise system. I believe that the market is going to make decisions a lot better than the government can in many cases. But both of those things are not inconsistent with government doing the type of strategic analysis that Al Alm was talking about, because I think that that is not the type of analysis that's going to be dictating to people, or to companies, or to labor unions, or to individuals about how they should behave in our society. It's the type of analysis in my view that's going to be helpful to government policy makers to help them make better, more informed decisions as they set policy in the future.

Macdonald: I really don't disagree with anything you say, Mike. And I hope you'll allow me to make one more point. I just think you can overplan. Of course, we've got to plan in the Defense Department and do so constantly years in advance. But, generally, the fact that we don't have an overall economic plan, an overall social plan, I think is a desirable thing.

Moskow: I do, too.

5

A Pracademic Approach to Policy: Some Conclusions

A reflection: academics are likely to be good at generalizations, even though they might not be much good for anything else. Practicing "political administrators" seem not to be inclined at all to generalizations. They think in terms of specific situations, personalities, and so forth rather than in terms of words and concepts. Specifically, what seemed to be real and important to them was "happenings," anecdotes from real life. Without discounting the value of these and without trying to make a comparison of values, I found myself wishing for a participant who could say: "From my experience, I offer these three generalizations (or propositions)."

—Dwight Waldo

A Methodological Discussion

Today one hears too much of commentators' views and not enough from the practitioners themselves. To remedy that, in this book we have used real people, real actors from the policy process, in order to analyze the decision-making, policymaking, and implementation stages of government.

This book has been concerned with the use of power as well as with the elaboration of its composition, manipulation, and interpretation in the policy process as seen by professionals. Though the search is for objectivity in the social sciences, this does not mean that one is required to become a cybernetic machine or to pursue the study of politics to the total exclusion of the subjective view. The development of this book as an analysis of a decision-making role as seen by those in that role will, we hope, add behavioral and operational dimensions to the existing journalistic, historical, and impressionistic literature on the bureaucracy and on political appointees in the policymaking process.

Too many models and conceptual frameworks in political science, public administration, and the management sciences have almost entirely ignored the individual personality, seeing it at best as an

Note: A "pracademic" is a person who enters and leaves the formal governmental organizations on a periodic basis. A considerable number of professors and other professionals serve the government for short tenures and then return to their academic or private practices better qualified to be citizen leaders outside the formal governmental structure.

instrument, voice, or symbol. In practice, though, the powers of an assistant secretary are neither self-executing nor exercised by a committee, but are predominantly dependent upon one person's qualities. As McGeorge Bundy has pointed out on numerous occasions: "The man must make the office more often than not." No one can claim for the office of the assistant secretary in any organization the peculiar dignity that invests the Supreme Court or the White House. In fact, the role is so variable that it tends to differ for each individual who holds it.

Throughout this book, we have tried to see from the assistant secretaries' point of view the complex interplay between career bureaucrats and political appointees, between external and internal constituencies, between the departmental assistant secretary and the special assistants in the White House, and among the agencies and institutions.

The symposium at the Federal Executive Institute in 1976 was invaluable, because the assistant secretaries who were invited could speak candidly, honestly, and openly about their jobs. Indeed, for many the session almost amounted to a group exit interview. In addition, when one extrapolates from their generalizations, many of the broader findings from historical, social science investigations into the assistant secretaries' role in the policy process are confirmed. For while different role incumbents are likely to differ in the way they interpret the requirements of their roles, the broad outlines of the role behavior will be noticeable along with the individual characteristics and functional expertise of the decisionmaker.[1]

An analysis of the policy process requires investigations into it from the viewpoints of the various actors themselves. In this way, a comparative analysis might be undertaken so that generalizations from a more reputable representative base could be formulated. The regularity and consistency of the variables identified in each study would give more credence to the generalizations noted in the more academic, traditional methodological texts. In addition, policymakers who are in "the line of fire"—those who are doing policymaking rather than academically analyzing it—offer more than generalizations. They help one to better appreciate the importance of personal idiosyncrasies, of luck, and of the bargaining and negotiating that occurs in interpersonal relationships, as well as the complexities of the bureaucratic/administrative policymaking process. Overarching theories and models, on the other hand, tend to sweep specific problems and situations under the rug.

We did not attempt to force our analysis of the role of the assistant secretary into a predetermined methodological framework. Rather, we let the assistant secretaries speak for themselves. Surely, there is some interpretation by the academics who were at the symposium, as well as by those who wrote the narrative accompanying the symposium in this book. But this is done with a conviction that mixing the theoretical, academic dimension with the practical, operational dimension is more meaningful. We hope that scholars will use this information as resource for future research into administrative policymaking and, more specifically, into the role of the assistant secretary.

Few issues about American government are more critical today than the matter of whether the federal government is capable of governing. Can the United States government translate intentions into outcomes? Any careful review of its outcomes over the past decade (for example, the War on Poverty) will make the point of this question painfully obvious. Some radical critics focus on the seeming inability of government to bring to bear even available, well-understood capabilities on problems that most Americans recognize and want solved (for example, hunger in the United States), and therefore they conclude that the system should be destroyed. Less radical observers are convinced that most people appointed to government positions are simply interested in their own egos and needs and in using the positions simply to catapult themselves into better jobs. Still other critics are convinced that those who secure top government positions are not of the highest quality available, whether in business, industry, or the universities. As this book indicates, nothing could be further from the truth.

As we reviewed and interpreted the dialogue of the assistant secretaries, we found that the radical despair is not unlike the frustration of many of the assistant secretaries as they reflected on the unfortunate fate of many of their best intentioned plans, ideas, and dreams. We also discovered that short-circuiting of the best laid plans and solutions is due more to the complexity of modern government and to its sheer size than to any machinations by evil individuals. Surely no critic who reads this book could conclude that government is a conspiracy to do second-rate work. Rather, it should be clear that so many people are operating in specific programs that it is often nearly impossible to synthesize all of the complex dimensions into any one overall programmatic, strategic plan of a president, no matter who he might be.

This book suggests that bureaucracy, in many ways, is the least understood source of unhappy outcomes produced by the United States government. Eliminating it, however, is not a solution. Large organizations that function according to routine, and politics among individuals who share power, are inevitable features of the exercise of public authority in modern society. Therefore, the key is to analyze the actual workings of the policy process in order to understand some of the major features of the bureaucratic political game. In this way, we can suggest creative and reasonable solutions for problems engendered by the bureaucratic system. Government officials will differ substantially over issues and solutions, but their various proposals can be dissected and inspected through the process of internal bureaucratic politics.[2]

Members of the bureaucracy, as well as external critics, are likely to find government processes embarrassingly slow in producing policies that lead to effective outcomes. But as we have seen in this book, the process is based on consensus-building efforts, bureaucratic politics, internal maneuverings, normative differences, and the realities of the American democratic environment, elements that dictate a rather slow process—and a slow process might be the price one has to pay to ensure democracy. Our analysis, then, is oriented not only toward practitioners in government but also toward academics who want to see how government really operates and what can and cannot be done. Our plea is that more academics get involved in operational policy roles so that they can write, analyze, and teach more effectively about the realities of the policy process.

Some Generalizations and Extrapolations

First, there are as many differences as similarities among the assistant secretaries whose discussions are included in this book. Assistant secretaries perform not just one but many roles, from administration, to management, to political advisor, to implementor, to policymaker. And the fact that they perform different roles in different agencies may mean that role theory in relation to the assistant secretary position has to accentuate the importance of the incumbent on the role rather than vice versa.

The second generalization is based on Hugh Heclo's comment that a simultaneous politicization of the bureaucrats and bureaucratization of political appointees is taking place in contemporary government.[3] This may mean that in today's corporate world (the post-industrial society identified by Daniel Bell and John Kenneth Galbraith), a different leadership style may be needed to cope with the problems endemic to large bureaucracies and the bureaucratic environment. Maybe we need leaders who can deal with lateral, horizontal relationships as effectively as they can with vertical chain-of-command relationships. The times may demand a different kind of political appointee, especially in the interface roles. We are not quite sure what specific kind of personality type and leadership style is needed, but we believe that we must understand the realities of bureaucratic government today. This will ensure that the bureaucratization of political leadership Heclo warned us about does not produce political appointees who become frozen in the bureaucracy in such a way that the president and the elected representatives cannot change the system when change is needed. The Senior Executive Service reform package that the Carter administration is proposing to more effectively mix the political and bureaucratic experts at the top of the federal organizational scale may be one way to make certain that we will get leaders who are interested in change, who are risk takers, and who will "take the bull by the horns" when it is absolutely essential.

Third, the tremendous growth of presidential power and the concomitant growth of White House staff during the past several decades has led to a plethora of special advisors, task forces, and experts. The trend has developed to the point that assistant secretaries today feel less valued than they once felt in the chain of command emanating from the president. Some believe that the White House staff has become the major protagonist that undercuts or avoids the assistant secretary. Brad Patterson said at the symposium that he believes the White House has grown stronger vis-à-vis the assistant secretary's role almost by default, that the departments did not grasp at certain roles that the president thought were essential. But at the same time, the assistant secretaries believe that pressures from the White House are so great and the power of the White House is so overwhelming that their traditional role as program directors for the president has been challenged and weakened during the past couple of decades.

Fourth, tremendous tension exists between political appointees and career bureaucrats (especially those bureaucrats at the supergrade level). Three major factors appear to contribute to the tension. (1) Political appointees have much shorter tenures than do career executives, and it is not generally understood that different tenures lead to different perspectives on time, responsiveness, and obligations. Political appointees seem to want to accomplish goals quickly while careerists opt to accomplish things carefully. This creates perceptions of haste or sluggishness by the respective sides. (2) Tensions among the political and career executives are exacerbated by the issue of loyalty. To whom does one owe his or her ultimate loyalty? Does obedience to authority imply mainly hierarchical obligations? Should anyone be astonished at the changing definitions of organizational loyalty in the post-Watergate environment? It is often stated very simply—political executives are loyal to the administration that gives them their jobs, while careerists are loyal to the institution that protects and nurtures them. Though simplistic, that explanation is surely part of the picture. (3) Who should take the leadership for the agency? If it is true that the bureaucracy is becoming more politicized and political leadership is becoming more bureaucratized, then a greater mixture of career and noncareer combinations at the executive levels is probably necessary to produce greater flexibility in the government's effort to cope with the challenges of the 1970s and the 1980s. And regardless of the kind of mixture undertaken, the question of who has leadership is a point of contention between the political appointee and the careerist in the policy process.

Fifth, each individual has different basic values, which have as much of an impact on how he or she will act in the role of assistant secretary as does any expertise (management, technical, scientific, or otherwise) that he or she brings to the role. Political values, philosophical value systems, and basic moral stances have tremendous influence on which programs assistant secretaries champion, which ones they will simply monitor, and which ones they will attempt to sabotage. As Arnold Rogow said in his classic study of James Forrestal: "It is difficult to avoid the conclusion that in most policymakers personality needs, value systems, and policy recommendations are closely related."[4]

Sixth, an assistant secretary competes with other assistant secretaries in his or her agency and in other agencies for resources, attention, and status. Therefore, assistant secretaries must "fight like hell" for programs they believe in and champion programs their subordinates have expended much energy on. If they lose too many battles, their people may lose their enthusiasm for working hard, their support for the assistant secretaries, and their trust in the administration. As Dean Acheson once said, "A good administrator must 'fight like hell' to make sure that his policy recommendations are accepted so that those who follow him will continue to operate at a high level of effectiveness and commitment."[5]

Seventh, the post-Watergate environment made it politically attractive to develop a plethora of new structures concerning conflicts of interest, disclosure rights, ethics violations, ethical demands, codes of conduct, and similar phenomena, which we, as authors and citizens, believe are essential to maintaining the high integrity of public service. But this creates problems for individuals who are considering coming into the government to serve as effectively and efficiently as they can for a short period of time. The symposium discussion in this book indicates that one almost has to give up too much to serve in government in this day and age. This is not grousing or unreflective complaining; it is simply a fact that if the political system places too many barriers against people serving, we may find that fewer people of the highest caliber will come into government, while people of lesser quality may. Too many rules, procedures, and barriers may have an adverse effect on the more creative personality types who may fear that the letter of the law is overwhelming the spirit of the law.

Because the role of the assistant secretary is not as powerful as it was once thought to be, we must not only make government attractive in general, but we also must enrich the role of assistant secretary. People should perceive assistant secretaries as having some power and some capabilities to change the system. The symposium dialogue made it clear that for many, serving at the pleasure of the president is not as attractive as it used to be. This perception could lead to a denigration of government service per se, and it certainly could devastate the pracademic model. Somehow we must encourage the "best" people to travel between government and the larger society, to learn from both places so that government can operate more efficiently and more effectively.

Eighth, those who serve in government, both careerists and political appointees, operate in a political context whether they want to or not. Political values come into play through the electoral and bureaucratic processes to determine which programs will be supported and which ones scrapped. Conspicuous elected figures in the political system accept the fact that policymaking is a legitimate battleground for spirited political debate. But it appears that many individuals who enter that process see it as a business, management, or rational venture, rather than as a field on which different personalities, groups, and factions compete for their respective interests. As James Forrestal expressed it:

> I have always been amused by those who say that they are quite willing to go into government, but that they are not willing to go into politics. My answer, which has become a bromide with me, is that you can no more divorce government from politics than you can separate sex from creation.[6]

Politics is the name of the game. Politics is not bad. Politics is not necessarily dirty. In fact, in the time of the Greek city states, citizenship in the quest of political community was thought to be the highest developmental form of mankind. Once again individuals must be reminded that politics is the legitimate battleground in a democracy, wherein programs, politics, and resources are to be debated and determined.

Ninth, government work is difficult, and one must have expertise to contribute in the government policy process. However, the difficulty of government work is not only that much work has to be done well, but that the public has to be convinced that it is being done well. Again, to quote James Forrestal: "In other words there is a necessity both for competence and exposition and I hold it extremely difficult to combine the two in the same person."[7] This has tremendous implications for assistant secretaries, who must convince the president, their colleagues, and the public that they are doing a good job. Exposition of what one does is as important (if not sometimes more important) as merely doing a good job while hiding one's light under a bushel. It is one way to answer critics who demand that government get more quality, dedication, and hard work from its political and career employees. In essence, doing a good job and making sure that others know it is very important for leaders in a democratic government composed of complex bureaucracies.

Tenth, after listening to Mike Moskow and some of the others at the symposium, it appears absolutely essential that avenues be made available for high-caliber people to come into government. This is not a plea for the eighteen-month or the twenty-two-month assistant secretary. It is a plea that the arrangement in which people serve for periods of time and then return to the campus or to business be continued and supported as an integral part of the American policymaking process. This gives more people practical knowledge of what government can do and cannot do. It allows people to have short tenures so that they can take risks; it is important to have a cadre of individuals who can leave government without risking their careers. And it is important that the president of the United States be able to pick the best people available for the amount of time they are available. In this way, change will be infused into the upper levels of democratic government. The pracademic model is not only useful in terms of research on the policy process, it is also a useful operational model for carrying out government at the assistant secretary, under secretary, and even the secretary level.

The Federal Executive Institute and Government Leaders

The assistant secretaries' symposium was a confirmation of a basic goal of the Federal Executive Institute: to develop and increase government executives' ability to provide leadership, to process information, and to interact with others in creative decision making and administration. By bringing supergrades, political appointees, agency teams, and agency groups together, the FEI provides a residential environment where practitioners can teach and learn from each other and discuss mutual problems from different perspectives. We hope that assistant secretaries and others will take advantage of the FEI in the future to analyze government problems in an effort to make the government more vital, flexible, and dynamic. We hope that by focusing on the assistant secretary, we have been able to highlight some of the major managerial, executive, political, and policy-making problems and promises that exist in the modern American political system.

Hugh Heclo's book shows that the president's executive team is likely to be poorly organized. He says:

> If the American national parties and electoral process did automatically produce sets of mutually familiar and committed political executives led by the president, there would be little need to look beyond the presidency in search for political leadership, but that does not happen. In Washington administrative teams of political leaders in so far as they exist are created after rather than before a government is formed.[8]

The fact that most political executives must operate in what Heclo calls "a government of strangers" means that the FEI and similar organizations must help individuals at the assistant secretary level and, we hope, other levels as well, to build teams in their agencies and establish teamwork in their relations with the White House staff. This should be one of the principal tasks of political leadership in the bureaucracy of a democratic government. It is one of the principal tasks that we in the FEI take as our challenge.

Notes

1. Herbert C. Kelman, "Social-Psychological Approaches to the Study of International Relations: The Question of Relevance," in

International Behavior: A Social-Psychological Analysis, Herbert C. Kelman, ed. (New York: Holt, Rinehart and Winston, 1965), p. 588.

2. Special thanks to Graham T. Allison, *Essence of Decision* (Boston: Little, Brown & Co., 1971), for the insights noted in much of this section.

3. Hugh Heclo, *A Government of Strangers* (Washington, D.C.: The Brookings Institution, 1977).

4. Arnold A. Rogow, *James Forrestal: A Study of Personality, Politics, and Policy* (New York: Macmillan, 1963), p. 114.

5. Ronald J. Stupak, *The Shaping of Foreign Policy: The Role of the Secretary of State as Seen by Dean Acheson* (New York: The Odyssey Press, 1963), pp. 75, 112.

6. Quoted in ibid., p. 111.

7. Quoted in ibid., p. 110.

8. Heclo, *A Government of Strangers,* p. 11.

Epilogue: The Carter Model

I have promised the American people a fair, open, efficient and responsive government, carried out in the spirit as well as the letter of the law, and dedicated to the highest principles of our democratic society. You have been appointed to your present position to help fulfill this promise and I am grateful that you have found it possible to accept.

—Jimmy Carter

Although presidents are primarily concerned with policy formulation, inevitably they become heavily involved as well in the business of appointing key people to assist in policy formulation and to carry out policies and develop programs. Presidents have had different management philosophies, as exemplified in the Jacksonian spoils system, the staff systems of Roosevelt and Eisenhower, Nixon's attempt to centralize decision making, and now Carter's system. The presidents have differed not only with regard to the scope of the positions they have included in the political appointment process, but also in the kinds of criteria they have used for appointing people. They have of course been influenced by the culture of their times. In the Jacksonian era, it was not surprising that the political appointment process extended to virtually the entire federal bureaucracy; and it is not surprising that now it tends to be clustered in key policy-administrative and confidential-service staff positions.

Getting Control of the Bureaucracy

Although the president plays a major role in the kinds of political appointments made during his administration, his is not necessarily the dominant role, and it is certainly not the exclusive role. Other actors, in addition to cabinet secretaries and agency heads, include key political operatives in Congress and the campaign organization and on the White House staff. In the Carter administration, Hamilton Jordan, the president's assistant for political affairs, has had a major role in the appointment of key political officials.

Members of Carter's staff have been concerned with removing Nixon-Ford loyalists and appointing instead people who share their own ideology, political party affiliation, and personal loyalty to the president. To some, this last question has been determined by an individual's prior affiliation with Governor Carter or at least substantial involvement in the presidential campaign. This should not be surprising; in his capacity as campaign manager for Jimmy Carter's presidential election, Hamilton Jordan asked the help of numerous people throughout the states, and it is only realistic to expect that he would want to put in a good word for these people when it came time to pick people for key spots in the administration. Jordan has reason to expect to have this same role in a future presidential election campaign, and his task will be made easier to the extent that those who contributed in the last campaign were appropriately rewarded. Someone must look out for the president's political welfare. Distributing political benefits and placing loyalists in key spots is a part of that role.

Most administrations make strong efforts in the early months to gain control of the bureaucracy. The Nixon administration started slowly but then made a special priority of this.[1] It operated under the assumption that most high-ranking bureaucrats were Democrats and liberals and that it would be difficult to secure their loyalty—or even assistance—in implementing new programs. One significant administrative decision which contributed to gaining control of key field appointments, although it also related to Nixon's "new federalism," was to establish common geographic boundaries for most field offices of federal agencies. Previously, each department or agency had determined its own regional structure, and usually mayors and governors had to go to regional headquarters in several different cities to transact city or state government business. The effect of Nixon's uniform boundaries approach was that virtually all of the federal regional offices relevant to a particular city or state would be located in one city. The objective was not only to improve interdepartmental and intergovernmental coordination, but also to establish some degree of decentralization of federal decision makers. The other part of the equation was that Nixon hoped to appoint his people to these regional jobs to increase responsiveness to his administration.

The realignment of the regions resulted in the transfer of numerous high-ranking bureaucrats and new opportunities to appoint others. In general, Nixon was able to create a substantial number of regional vacancies and to appoint his people. The people appointed to positions as regional director and deputy director in the Departments of HEW, HUD, Labor, and Commerce in most cases were not career bureaucrats, but were recommended by congressional delegations in the states involved or by the political operators around Nixon.

Upon attaining power, Jimmy Carter's people wanted to make the regions more responsive. As governor of Georgia, Carter had not been very impressed with the federal regional operations. This is surprising since the southeast region of the federal government is located in Atlanta, the Georgia state capital, so that communication should have been direct and service should have been very effective. The role of the federal regions was carefully reviewed during the first year of the Carter administration, and some changes were made.

For example, the Departments of Agriculture and Interior no longer were considered to be regular members of the federal regional councils in the ten federal regions. The Law Enforcement Assistance Agency regions were abolished, as were secretarial representatives in the Department of Labor. HEW made its regional directors "principal regional officials," intended to convey the idea that they were now responsible for a representation role, not a management role. On the other hand, the Department of Commerce strengthened somewhat the role of its top regional officials.

One attempt to expand the responsiveness of the regions to the presidency involved extending the Nixon approach. Whereas President Ford had designated the regional directors of the Departments of Commerce, HEW, HUD, Labor, Transportation, the Small Business Administration, and the Environmental Protection Agency as NEA (noncareer executive assignment) appointments, President Carter had several other positions in some of those agencies converted to political status. In HEW, for example, the positions of assistant regional director for legislative and intergovernmental affairs and of assistant director for public affairs were made Schedule C positions.

Further, President Carter announced in November 1977 that he was extending the political appointment process to include the directors of other federal agencies in the regions. For example, the regional directors of the General Services Administration, the Community Services Administration, Defense Civil Preparedness Agency, and Action, which heretofore ostensibly had been career positions, were converted to political appointments, and Carter people were placed in those positions.

The president felt pressure both for and against this decision, which was announced in Executive Order No. 12021. The Democratic Congress, starved for political appointments during the eight years of the Nixon-Ford administration, pressed hard for extension of the number of political positions in the field. House Speaker Thomas P.

O'Neill, for example, had intense interest in seeing that more loyal Democrats were appointed to such positions in regional offices in Boston. Hamilton Jordan strongly supported this approach.

On the other hand, the chairman of the Civil Service Commission, Alan K. Campbell, was concerned with the image that the extension of the number of political appointments in the field would create.[2] Career bureaucrats are usually paranoiac regarding presidential transitions, and this was especially true after the Nixon years. Careerists feared not only policy changes but also a reduction in the number of key positions to which they might have access. In other words, Campbell did not necessarily object to the principle of having political appointees in these key field positions; however, he thought the timing was bad and that the career officials' confidence should first be gained.

Further, Campbell was presiding over a total review of the federal personnel system—the Personnel Reorganization Project, a major priority of President Carter. Campbell could not help but believe that the new personnel system would accomplish the same results, but in a much more satisfactory and positive manner. The Senior Executive Service proposed under Campbell's leadership would have abolished the distinction between political and career positions and resolved the flexibility problem in both headquarters and field offices of the federal agencies. Yet, to prevent a wholesale politicization of the federal executive ranks, the proposal also recommended that the total number of political appointments in the key supergrade positions be limited to the same proportions as currently existed—roughly 10 percent.

The logic behind this was that the Civil Service Commission had had great difficulty determining whether specific positions should be political or career positions. By removing the need to make such decisions and leaving the department secretaries free to make a particular position political on one occasion and career on another, management flexibility would be enhanced and criticisms from cabinet secretaries over the inflexibility of the federal personnel system would be reduced.

In addition, under the Campbell plan, career executives most likely would find it easier to be appointed to higher positions than those to which they can now aspire. In other words, since there would no longer be a distinction between career and political positions at the higher levels, career officials could be appointed to positions traditionally held by political appointees and, after a change in administration or policy, could be reassigned to other top-ranking career positions. Under the existing system, when career employees are appointed as assistant secretaries, they must give up their career status; and if a change of administration occurs, they are likely to be out of a job. The position of assistant secretary for administration is supposed to be an exception to this. However, in practice, ways generally are found to get around the allegedly career nature of this position as well.

Another change made by Campbell was to discontinue the Civil Service Commission's role of evaluating the qualifications of political appointees to NEA positions. This had been a sore point with many cabinet secretaries as they attempted to establish their offices. For example, Secretary of the Interior Cecil Andrus, who had been the governor of Idaho, brought a number of his top staff from Boise and offered them some key positions in the secretary's office. But in evaluating their qualifications, the Civil Service Commission determined that some of them did not have sufficient background to meet the qualification requirements for positions at these grade levels. Because Idaho pays relatively low salaries to its state executives, the argument could not be made that these individuals were actually working at a very high salary level and so were qualified for the federal positions.

Using outside salaries as an indicator of qualifications was a very special problem for the Carter administration. The situation was complicated by the president's attempt to increase the number of women and minorities in key executive positions. Many of these people were young and had gained their experience in nonprofit or educational institutions. Therefore, they had difficulty meeting the qualification standards for high positions in the federal government, because they had relatively few years of experience and because they had been earning relatively low salaries. The new Civil Service Commission—consisting of commissioners Campbell, Jule Sugarman, and Ersa Poston—responded to this challenge by initiating the release of a change in the Federal Personnel Manual through FPM letter no. 30 5-12, which asserted that upon certification by the cabinet secretary that a person was qualified for a particular level NEA or LEA (limited executive assignment) position, the Civil Service Commission would generally honor that certification as meeting the qualification requirement. This approach was carried over to noncareer positions in the Senior Executive Service proposal.

The Carter Assistant Secretaries

As early as June 1976, the Carter campaign set up a task force under Jack Watson to start identifying potential key political appointees for a Carter presidency. These talent hunters were open about the desire to increase the number of women and minorities in key positions. The results of this search were interesting. The task force planned to present the backgrounds of potential appointees to incoming cabinet secretaries, who could then select from among them. It was recognized, of course, that the secretaries might want to bring in some of their own people, but the hope was that a significant number of the appointments would result from the recruitment efforts of the Watson group.

In fact, presidents are not totally free in terms of their appointments to the cabinet. They must make allowances for the opinions of various interest groups in filling positions such as the secretary of labor, the secretary of agriculture, and the secretary of housing and urban development. Given the trade-offs necessary to establish the cabinet, and given the generally aggressive nature of persons who are appointed as cabinet secretaries, the recruitment recommendations of the Watson task forces were not followed very often. The secretaries wanted their own loyalists to achieve their programs, and it was difficult to convince them that they should give up those choices for political or other reasons proposed by the White House staff. Nevertheless, some appointments to assistant secretary positions resulted from the work of the task force.

The task force also was useful in helping to identify people to serve on the Carter "transition team," which was institutionalized to a greater extent than in prior administrations. Teams, appointed for every department and agency of the government, spent November, December, and January reviewing the operations of those agencies in an effort to brief the incoming cabinet secretary or agency head and to identify problems within the departments and agencies. In some cases, people from the transition team were then appointed to key positions in those agencies.

In any event, even though the Watson task force did not identify many of the individuals eventually selected by cabinet members, the whole operation—with its capacity to maintain information on the kinds of appointees being proposed for assistant secretary positions—resulted in greater attention to these selections. Cabinet secretaries were under great pressure to find other minorities and women if they did not choose those located by the task force. Overall, President Carter may have had a more significant impact on these appointments than his predecessors, at least in terms of the broad-based nature of the appointments.

Another major difference in Carter's process was that specific efforts were made to secure four-year commitments from assistant secretaries and under secretaries to cut down on turnover and enable the administration to perform more effectively. Only a handful of the new assistant secretaries failed to make this commitment. To some extent results have already been shown, in that during the first fourteen months of the Carter administration, only three assistant secretaries have departed. Several nominees were unable to secure Senate confirmation and one, Lawrence Woodworth of Treasury, died in office.

The role of the White House Personnel Office, headed by Jim King, was to support Hamilton Jordan in the identification and evaluation of candidates for assistant secretary positions. This office processed the many applications for political positions. Further, it had a very substantial role in decisions regarding Schedule C–type positions and many NEAs and LEAs selected during the Carter administration. King resigned in favor of an appointment to a regulatory commission in November 1977 on the basis that the peak workload was over and that only a few key positions were still open.

One of the presumed effects of the Watson task force on hiring new people for the administration and planning in detail for the transition was that Carter's cabinet secretaries would have a better briefing on their responsibilities and problems than prior secretaries had. They also would have available to them a preselected and politically cleared pool of potential appointees. It was assumed that this would enable the president to make nominations earlier in the administration and to have his team in place earlier than would normally be the case.

In fact, it did not work that way. The briefings received by the cabinet were generally useful. However, the cabinet was still reluctant to accept the transition team's slates of candidates for assistant secretary positions. In addition, there was some conflict within the Carter administration between the transition team and the political operation under Hamilton Jordan. The Watson groups reached out widely to professionals in the field, whereas the Jordan group was more closely aligned with those who had helped in the campaign and with Democrats in Congress. It was not possible to respond fully to either group, given the relatively small number of key jobs.

Generally speaking, the cohort of assistant secretaries in the Carter administration is younger and better educated and contains more women, blacks, Chicanos, and other minority appointees than prior assistant secretary cohorts. Further, there is a better distribution of university backgrounds than is usually the case. There are fewer lawyers, for example, and fewer appointees attended Ivy League universities (see Table E.1).

There are also relatively fewer veterans among assistant secretaries in the Carter administration, a reflection of the increase in the number of women nominated and appointed. Further, there was an increase in the number of former career officials appointed to assistant secretary jobs (see Table E.1). Before 1961, the number had been about 25 percent, whereas in the Carter administration, eighty-eight appointees, or about 60 percent of the total, were formerly career officials.

Many former career appointees who were able to stay in the administration changed (or had to change) their positions. For example, Alvin Alm went from assistant administrator of the Environmental Protection Agency to assistant secretary for policy and evaluation in the new Department of Energy. Likewise, William Heffelfinger moved from assistant secretary of transportation for administration to director of administration at Energy. These moves were facilitated by the need for a planning team of experienced officials to set up the new department. They went first for the planning job and then stayed to help carry it out. Fred Clark, former assistant secretary of administration for the Labor Department, was reassigned to the position of assistant to the commissioner, United States Customs Service; and John R. Ottina, who was HEW assistant secretary for administration and management, left his post for an Intergovernmental Personnel Act appointment with a local university.

Conclusion

The major changes in the composition of the assistant secretary cohort in the Carter administration are the greater diversity of backgrounds—especially the presence of more minorities and women—and the longer time commitment demanded by the president. These potentially very significant differences could mean that the Carter model will result in a difference in performance and output.

By 1981 the question of the length of time served by Carter assistant secretaries will have been determined. It may be useful to consider some potential impacts of a longer term. First, past history shows that political appointees at the assistant secretary level tend to think better of their career colleagues upon leaving federal service than they felt upon their arrival. The career people do not believe the improved

Table E.1   Socioeconomic Profile of
            Assistant Secretaries

	1933-1961 (average Roosevelt, Truman, Eisenhower)	1974 (Ford)	1978 (Carter)
Average age when appointed	48	n.a.	46
Percent women	1.0	4.2	17.2
Percent nonwhites	less than 1.0	3.4	18.6
Educational level attained	75% B.A. 50% grad.	n.a.	95.3% B.A. 74.6% grad.
Percent Ivy League educated	25% undergrad. 10% Harvard Law	n.a.	39.3
Percent lawyers	25.0	28.6	35.2
Percent former career civil servants	25.0	8.4*	60.7
Percent veterans	n.a.	n.a.	34.5**

Source: Dean E. Mann, with Jameson W. Doig, The Assistant Secretaries: Problems and Processes of Appointment (Washington, D.C.: The Brookings Institution, 1965); David T. Stanley, Dean E. Mann, and Jameson W. Doig, Federal Political Executives, 1933-1965: A Biographical Profile (Washington, D.C.: The Brookings Institution, 1967); and survey conducted by Thomas P. Murphy, January 1978.

* Civil service background in the Ford administration's summary meant that their civil service career was longer than any other type of position.

** However, 27 percent did not respond on this point.

image is due to *their* changing; they attribute it to the development of trust as the two groups work together and to the new learning of the political executives. Having one assistant secretary instead of two during a presidential term should mean that only half as much time will be devoted to orienting the new political executives. This could mean greater productivity and improved relations between career and appointed executives.

Second, the greater stability among assistant secretaries should help to overcome another institutional problem of the current political executive system—namely, that the assistant secretaries and their top political assistants do not have effective networks in the decision systems affecting their program areas. As indicated by the title of Hugh Heclo's book, these people constitute "a government of strangers." Longer terms mean that the whole second cycle of developing contacts and negotiating policies (which normally takes place in the last two years) would be abolished. Instead, the already Washington-wise assistant secretaries should be able to help each other to help their secretaries and the president to do a better job in the second two years than in the first two years. The problem of "the disappearing organizational memory" among political executives should be alleviated by the longer terms and by the conversion of many strangers into colleagues.

Granting the potential positive effects of greater longevity for assistant secretaries, the next question is the likelihood of these longer terms actually being achieved. First, of course, no administration has ever done a perfect job of recruiting. Not every assistant secretary can be effective, and not every one is first appointed to the position most appropriate for his or her specific talents. This means that some assistant secretaries will be asked to leave before the four-year commitment is fulfilled. It also means that this administration will probably have a greater opportunity than others to reassign assistant secretaries who were poorly placed at first or who outgrow their jobs. Whether the Carter administration makes a real effort to monitor these reassignments and even promote reassignments across departments will be one factor influencing the longevity record.

Second, the question of assistant secretaries' tenure will be influenced by the prospects for the president's extended tenure. If by 1979 or 1980 it appears that the president may be vulnerable in the primaries, some assistant secretaries will start looking for new jobs. But if his renomination and reelection seem assured, this will help to keep experienced assistant secretaries on the team.

Third, even if the president gives every appearance of being able to stay in office, this does not mean that the twelve cabinet secretaries will match his endurance—or even that he will want them to stay. Some serious policy differences are sure to develop, in addition to the inevitable personality differences. The departure of a cabinet secretary has a very direct influence on assistant secretaries, particularly if the secretary (rather than the White House) recruited them. And any new cabinet secretary will need to bring in a few assistant secretaries to help change policy directions and to provide psychological security. Needless to say, the factor of the president's political health will also influence the desire of at least some cabinet secretaries to leave before the conclusion of the first term.

Fourth, the nature of the backgrounds of the Carter executives will be important in terms of tenure. For example, many came from university faculties, and few universities are willing to grant leaves longer than two or three years. This means that after two or three years the assistant secretary will be under pressure to return to the university or voluntarily yield hard-won tenured faculty positions. Further, female and minority assistant secretaries, likely to be in high demand in the nongovernmental sector, may be offered attractive salaries that will lure them away prematurely.

On the other side of the equation, the Carter cohort includes fewer veterans, and so many will want to serve five years to have their federal retirement benefits vested—especially since they would be earning them with such a high three-year benefits computation base. Yet the Carterites who came from the career service would have no such pull factor operating after they have established their new "high three."

Another factor is that many of the Carter executives experienced a very substantial pay raise, due to the lower pay scales in the sectors from which they were recruited. These people will have trouble returning to their prior careers because they are likely to become addicted to their new standard of living and nonprofit, and educational institutions will no longer be able to afford them.

Finally, there is disagreement about the degree to which the president's party affiliation is significant in terms of the professional behavior of career executives. However, to the extent that this could be a cause of tension or policy differences, it ought not to be of critical concern in the Carter administration since it is generally agreed that most top career executives are Democrats.

Clearly, it is too early to reach conclusions about the longevity of Carter assistant secretaries or about the effect of the diversity of the Carter cohort on staying power. However, there appear to be some good reasons to expect that the tenures will be longer than the past average of eighteen to twenty-one months. This is especially likely to be true if President Carter looks like a winner in 1980 and if between now and then the administration takes some positive steps to reassign especially successful or inappropriately placed assistant secretaries. In short, the biggest single influence seems to be the president himself—his political prospects, his political executive development policy, and the degree to which those who made the four-year commitment feel that he has lived up to his end of the bargain. The assistant secretaries are the president's program directors, and so it is appropriate that he be the major factor in their continuation in office.

Notes

1. See Richard P. Nathan, *The Plot That Failed: Nixon and the Administrative Presidency* (New York: John Wiley & Sons, 1975) and Bradley H. Patterson, Jr., *The President's Cabinet: Issues and Questions* (Washington, D.C.: American Society for Public Administration, 1976).

2. Alan K. Campbell, "The Career Service and Responsible Government," in *Evaluating Governmental Performance: Changes and Challenges for GAO* (Washington, D.C.: Government Printing Office, 1975).

Appendix A:
Roster of Participants in
the 1976 Symposium

Alm, Alvin L.   Assistant Administrator for Planning and Management, Environmental Protection Agency

Blake, John F.   Deputy Director for Administration, Central Intelligence Agency

Bledsoe, Ralph   Professor, Federal Executive Institute

Bolduc, J. Paul   Assistant Secretary for Administration, Department of Agriculture

Boynton, Robert P.   Professor of Government and Public Administration, School of Government, American University, Washington, D.C.

Brotzman, Donald G.   Assistant Secretary of the Army (Manpower and Reserve Affairs), Department of the Army

Clark, Fred G.   Assistant Secretary for Administration and Management, Department of Labor

Connor, Judith T.   Assistant Secretary for Environment, Safety and Consumer Affairs, Department of Transportation

Cooper, Theodore   Assistant Secretary for Health, Department of Health, Education, and Welfare

Dembling, Paul G.   General Counsel, General Accounting Office

Feltner, Richard L.   Assistant Secretary for Marketing and Consumer Affairs, Department of Agriculture

Henry, Laurin L.   Professor, Woodrow Wilson Department of Government and Foreign Affairs, University of Virginia, Charlottesville, Va.

Hooker, Roger W., Jr.   Assistant Secretary for Congressional and

From Thomas P. Murphy, Donald E. Nuechterlein, and Ronald J. Stupak, eds., *The President's Program Directors: The Assistant Secretaries* (Charlottesville, Va.: The Federal Executive Institute, 1977).

Intergovernmental Affairs, Department of Transportation

Kolberg, William H.   Assistant Secretary for Employment and Training, Department of Labor

Macdonald, David R.   Under Secretary of the Navy, Department of the Navy

Morrill, William A.   Assistant Secretary for Planning and Evaluation, Department of Health, Education, and Welfare

Moskow, Michael H.   Under Secretary, Department of Labor

Mosso, David   Fiscal Assistant Secretary, Department of the Treasury

Orlebeke, Charles J.   Assistant Secretary for Policy Development and Research, Department of Housing and Urban Development

Patterson, Bradley H., Jr.   Assistant Director for Operations, Presidential Personnel Office

Rhinelander, John B.   Under Secretary, Department of Housing and Urban Development

Richardson, John, Jr.   Assistant Secretary of State for Educational and Cultural Affairs, Department of State

Scalia, Antonin   Assistant Attorney General, Office of Legal Counsel, Department of Justice

Taylor, David P.   Assistant Secretary of Defense for Manpower and Reserve Affairs, Department of Defense

Young, John D.   Assistant Secretary (Comptroller), Department of Health, Education, and Welfare

Appendix B:
Symposium Program Schedule

Wednesday, December 8, 1976

1:30 p.m.—3:00 p.m.   Arrival and Registration

3:00 p.m.—3:30 p.m.   Welcome and Introduction: Thomas P. Murphy, Director, Federal Executive Institute. Explanation of Themes for the Day: Patrick J. Conklin, Associate Director, Federal Executive Institute

3:30 p.m.—5:15 p.m.   Discussion of "Roles of the Assistant Secretary" in Executive Learning Teams

5:15 p.m.—6:00 p.m.   Social

6:00 p.m.—7:15 p.m.   Dinner

7:30 p.m.—9:00 p.m.   Executive Learning Team Reports to the Plenary on "Roles of the Assistant Secretary"—Discussion

9:00 p.m.—11:00 p.m.   Informal Discussion and Social Period

9:15 p.m.—10:15 p.m.   (Optional) Videotape on the President's Cabinet (Featuring Wilbur J. Cohen, Arthur S. Fleming, W. Averell Harriman, Bradley H. Patterson, Jr., Dean Rusk, Robert C. Weaver, and James E. Webb)

Thursday, December 9, 1976

7:00 a.m.—8:00 a.m.   Breakfast

8:15 a.m.—8:30 a.m.   Explanation of Themes for the Day: Donald E. Nuechterlein, Professor, Federal Executive Institute

8:30 a.m.—9:15 a.m.   "Political-Career Interface": John B. Rhinelander, Under Secretary, Department of Housing and Urban Development

From Thomas P. Murphy, Donald E. Nuechterlein, and Ronald J. Stupak, eds., *The President's Program Directors: The Assistant Secretaries* (Charlottesville, Va.: The Federal Executive Institute, 1977).

9:30 a.m.—11:00 a.m.   Discussion of "Political-Career Interface" in Executive Learning Teams

11:00 a.m.—12:00 noon   Executive Learning Team Reports to the Plenary on "Political-Career Interface"—Discussion

12:00 noon—12:45 p.m.   Lunch

12:45 p.m.—1:00 p.m.   Group Photograph

1:00 p.m.—1:45 p.m.   "Role of Assistant Secretaries in Policy Formulation and Implementation": Michael H. Moskow, Under Secretary, Department of Labor

2:00 p.m.—3:00 p.m.   Discussion of "Policy Formulation and Implementation" in Executive Learning Teams

3:00 p.m.—4:00 p.m.   Executive Learning Team Reports to the Plenary on "Policy Formulation and Implementation"—Discussion

4:00 p.m.—4:30 p.m. Summary and Wrap-Up: Thomas P. Murphy, Director, Federal Executive Institute; Patrick J. Conklin, Associate Director, Federal Executive Institute; Robert P. Boynton, Professor, School of Government, American University

Appendix C:
The Federal Executive Institute—
General Information

FEI Goals and Objectives

The Federal Executive Institute was established by Presidential Order on May 9, 1968. As an interagency executive development center of the United States Civil Service Commission, the Institute responds to the training and development needs of Federal executives, primarily at grade levels of GS-16 and above, or equivalent. It also serves selected executives at comparable levels in state and local governments.

The basic goals of FEI are:

- to promote active appreciation of the values of American Constitutional Democracy, such as the rule of law and the pursuit of human dignity;
- to foster understanding of and dedication to the responsibilities of public servants in a pluralistic and dynamic society;
- to develop and increase the executive's ability to provide leadership, to process information, and to interact with others in creative decision-making and administration;
- to facilitate the acquisition of knowledge relevant to the executive's political, social, and economic environments—for example, knowledge of self, of interpersonal, group, and social behavior, and of institutions and organizations (domestic and foreign).

To accomplish these goals, the Institute works primarily with the individual executives who constitute the one-half of 1 percent of civil

From Thomas P. Murphy, Donald E. Nuechterlein, and Ronald J. Stupak, eds., *The President's Program Directors: The Assistant Secretaries* (Charlottesville, Va.: The Federal Executive Institute, 1977).

servants at the top of the 2.8 million member civilian workforce. These executives fill responsible leadership positions in the multitude of specialized and general fields of governmental activities. Most have been promoted to high leadership positions after successful service in highly specialized career fields, and over 80 percent are responsible for program management. All are successful individuals, faced with heavy responsibilities for the future of effective, democratic government in an age of high technology, rapid change, and social complexity.

In an educational endeavor like that of the Federal Executive Institute, objectives in keeping with the above goals must be established and shared by individual executives who participate in Institute programs.

In short, the learning process is very largely one of setting individual objectives, planning for their accomplishment, implementing individual learning programs, monitoring progress toward objectives, evaluating results, and formulating new or revised objectives. The aim of the Institute is to provide an open learning environment which facilitates the process of development of the individual executive.

Executive Effectiveness Criteria

To assist executives in this learning process, several criteria common to executive effectiveness are identified as the basis of the Institute's several curricula, and those are outlined below under these three categories:

- The Environment of Federal Executive Performance.
- Management Systems and Processes.
- Interpersonal and Personal Executive Effectiveness.

Within the context of these effectiveness criteria, specific objectives toward which individual executives commonly work at the Institute include:

1. *Improved understanding of executive roles.* The behaviors expected of executives serve as standards of action. Role prescriptions in the literature of business and government executives and in actual practices of Federal executives are compared and contrasted with individual perceptions and behaviors.

2. *Strengthened individual capabilities.* FEI programs are designed to help strong people become stronger—to help individual executives assess existing strengths, interests, and needs, and to develop knowledge, skills, and programs for continued learning based on that assessment.

3. *Increased knowledge of management systems and processes.* Knowledge of current theories and practices of management and of their historic contexts in government and in business provides a framework for individual executive assessment, learning, and improved management behavior on the job. Consequently, this is an area of major emphasis in individual objectives-setting at FEI.

4. *Understanding of national needs and priorities.* Effectiveness as an executive means doing the right things, and that requires a basic understanding not only of agency goals and objectives but of the needs and priorities of the entire governmental system. Because of the interagency character of FEI programs and the high quality of executives selected as Institute participants, it is possible to explore current and future problems and prospects for the United States and the world and to relate general developments to specific situations which confront government executives. Because of these considerations, it is important that the participants at the Institute share approximately the same high levels of responsibility.

FEI Curriculum Components

Courses scheduled in various FEI programs are designed to facilitate executive improvement as provided for in Federal Personnel Manual Letter 412-2. The following required areas of Federal executive effectiveness are stressed:

I. The Environment of Federal Executive Performance; National Needs and Goals; the Governmental System.
  A. External Environment of Administration:
    1. Social, Economic, Political, and Governmental Forces and Institutions.
    2. Public Policies and Missions.
    3. Executive Personnel Systems.
  B. Internal Organization Environment of Administration:
    1. Administrative Organization, Processes, and Behavior.

    2. Alternative Organization and Management Models and Analysis.

    3. Federal Executive Roles.

II. Management Systems and Processes.
  A. Administrative Management:
    1. Financial Management.
    2. Personnel Management.
    3. Information Management.
  B. Program/Project Management:
    1. Objective Setting, Planning, Resource Assembly, Priorities Allocation.
    2. Program/Project Design, Implementation, Tracking, and Evaluation.

III. Interpersonal and Personal Executive Effectiveness.
  A. Self-Assessment and Self-Renewal.
  B. Leadership Styles and Skills.
  C. Communicating Skills.
  D. Counseling and Coaching Skills.
  E. Organization Change and Development Skills.

The range of objectives which an executive can establish and accomplish in a given FEI program depends primarily on the individual, but it is also influenced significantly by the length and basic design of the different programs. But whatever FEI program might be selected for an individual executive at a specific time, the above effectiveness criteria will serve as a guide to that person's long-term development as a Federal executive.

FEI Programs

Senior Executive Education Program

The seven-week Senior Executive Education Program is designed to meet the varied educational development needs of senior executives and of new executives who have had extended experience in government or as executives outside the Federal service. The program is structured in a way that encourages:

- Exchange of learning from the diverse experiences of executives.
- Individual assessment of self and objective-setting.
- Both variety and depth in the study of specific topics of

executive concern in the Federal Government—for example, the external and internal environment of Federal executive effectiveness, management systems and processes, and managerial skills.
- Self-renewal for experienced executives.

Executive Leadership and Management Program

The three-week residential program is designed to serve developmental needs of the executive at the critical time of initial entry into a Federal Government position at a grade level of GS-16 and above (or equivalent positions in other pay systems). As contrasted with the longer Senior Executive Education Program, which provides opportunities for both breadth and depth of study in a wide variety of course options relevant to executive effectiveness, this program concentrates on a few dimensions of roles, values, knowledge, and skills that are of the most crucial concern to individuals at the time of transition to executive ranks and in the early stages of the assumption of high-level Federal Government responsibilities.

One-Week and Follow-On Programs

One-week courses on single-issue topics are scheduled at intervals during the course of a fiscal year. These topics usually relate to organization development and multi-team building, in addition to areas of specialized interest in government. They are open to both FEI alumni and others at GS-16 levels and above.

Follow-on programs are scheduled for graduates of the Institute's seven- and three-week programs. Agencies are notified in advance of those persons eligible to attend.

New Directions at FEI

Currently, the Institute is exploring a series of new approaches to better serve the needs of its alumni; to develop broader capabilities to serve new clientele; and to expand its program offerings so as to be more proactive in facilitating interaction in the political-career interfaces within government, as well as academic-practitioner interfaces in the professional public administration context. The new major areas of emphasis include:

The Political Executives Program

FEI is working on ways to more effectively increase and enrich the political-careerist interfaces in the Federal bureaucratic environment. Examples of the thrust in this direction include the special Assistant

Secretaries Program held at the FEI in December, 1976, and the Special Organization Development and Multi-Team Building sessions for political executives and their teams scheduled to be held during 1977-78.

Intergovernmental Executive Development

The FEI has launched a campaign to cultivate its role as a catalyst for improved federal-state-local interrelationships, as well as increasing its visibility and capabilities to better serve its clientele out in the federal regions and in the field office areas. Thus, the Institute is placing renewed priorities on intergovernmental program designs at the FEI home location as well as expanding its outreach capabilities to perform programs at other geographical locations and, at times, even within agencies themselves. The successful Executive Development Days/West program conducted in San Francisco, California, in November, 1976, and the Denver Federal Executive Board program held in December, 1976, are examples of what may be expected from the FEI in the years to come.

External and Professional Relationships

The faculty and staff at the Institute are endeavoring to increase FEI's professional, academic, and governmental contribution through closer ties with the University of Virginia, the Federal Regional Councils, FEI alumni, and other relevant institutions and groups. In addition, faculty committees have been established to promote publications and to undertake impact analyses of FEI programs.

Some of these new undertakings will be a programmatic part of the Institute's Fiscal Year 1977-78 overall design, while others will be revised or maybe supplanted. In this era of rapid change, we at the FEI are continuing to be proactive in our adaptation to the new demands on individuals, government institutions, and the American democratic system. Hence, though FEI remains committed to its Federal supergrade clientele, the Institute will continue to do all it can to achieve its basic objectives in the most effective way possible. At the same time, FEI will search for new challenges and innovative programs to provide dynamic leadership in executive development and management training within the American political system.

Appendix D:
The Management of the
American Governmental System

In September [1976], *P.A. News and Views* invited Presidential Candidates Carter, Ford, Maddox, and McCarthy to submit brief statements on the topic, "The Management of the American Governmental System." Candidates Carter and Ford submitted statements prepared specifically for *P.A. News and Views*. Candidate McCarthy submitted a press release and an excerpt from a previous speech dealing with the subject, and Candidate Maddox thanked *P.A. News and Views* for the opportunity, but said he did not have the time nor the staff to reply.

The following are the statements of the three presidential candidates:

Statement of Jimmy Carter

On the campaign trail, a lot of promises are made by candidates for public office to improve economy and efficiency in government if they are elected. This pledge has a natural appeal to the financially overburdened taxpayer. But when winning candidates take office, they too often find that it's easier to talk about economy and efficiency in government than to accomplish it. I would like to share with you some of my ideas on how to carry out improved management of the federal government.

The basic difficulty facing the federal government today cuts across all other campaign issues. National problems and the government

From *P. A. News and Views* (published by the American Society for Public Administration), vol. 26, no. 10 (October 1976), pp. 1, 3, 4, 5.

programs and agencies intended to deal with them have become incredibly complex. To begin with, the federal government is ill-equipped to deal with a growing number of problems that transcend departmental jurisdictions. For example, foreign and domestic issues are becoming more interrelated; domestic prosperity and international relations are affected by our foreign agricultural policy, by raw materials and oil policies, and by our export policies, among others. *We must develop a policy-making and management machinery that transcends narrow perspectives and deals with complex problems on a comprehensive, systematic basis.*

In addition, the proliferation of programs and agencies, particularly in the past ten years, has inevitably created duplications, waste, and inefficiencies. There are over 83 federal housing programs, 302 federal health programs, and over 1,200 assorted commissions, councils, boards, committees, and the like. *We must undertake a thorough revision and reorganization of the federal bureaucracy, its budgeting system, and the procedures for analyzing the effectiveness of its services.*

The first step is to reshape the way we make federal spending decisions. *The federal government should be committed to requiring zero-base budgeting by all federal agencies.* Each program, other than income support programs such as social security, should be required to justify both its continued existence and its level of funding. We need to continue and expand programs that work and to discontinue those that do not. Without such a comprehensive review, it will be difficult to assess priorities and impossible to redirect expenditures away from areas showing relatively less success.

The heart of zero-base budgeting is decision packages, which are prepared by managers at each level of government, from top to the bottom. These packages cover every existing or proposed function of activity of each agency. The packages include analysis of the cost, purpose, alternative courses of action, measures of performance, consequences of not performing the activity, and benefits. These packages are then ranked in order of importance against other current and new activities, as a basis for determining what functions and activities are to be recommended for funding in the new budget.

Besides placing priority on spending programs and revealing more information about actual governmental operations, zero-base budgeting achieves one more important action: it forces planning into levels of government where planning may never have existed. It forces all levels of government to find better ways of accomplishing their missions.

Second, *we must commit ourselves to a greater reliance upon long-term planning budgets.* I propose that we adopt a three-year rolling budget technique to facilitate careful, long-term planning and budgeting. Too many of our spending decisions are focused just beyond our noses on next year's appropriations. "Uncontrollable" spending is only uncontrollable in the short run; spending can be controlled if the planning system builds in more lead time. The three-year rolling budget technique will also permit businessmen and public officials at the state and local levels to do a much better job in laying out their own plans, relying less on the need for more elaborate proposals of comprehensive planning.

Third, reforming the budget and planning process will not be enough unless we are also committed to insuring that programs are carried out with efficiency. Improving government's performance will require action on at least two other levels. *We must undertake the basic structural reforms necessary to streamline federal operations and to make the government efficient once again. And we need increased program evaluation.* Many programs fail to define with any specificity what they intend to accomplish. In Georgia, we applied rigorous performance standards and performance auditing. Such standards, which are working in state capitols around the nation and in successful businesses, should be adapted for use in federal departments and agencies.

Fourth, we must take steps to help insure that we have an open and honest government as well as an efficient and effective government. *An all-inclusive "Sunshine Law," similar to those passed in several states, should be implemented in Washington.* With narrowly defined exceptions, meetings of federal boards, commissions, and regulatory agencies should be opened to the public. *Broad public access, consonant with the right of personal privacy, should be provided to government files.*

The activities of lobbyists must be much more thoroughly revealed and controlled, both with respect to Congress and the Executive departments and agencies. Quarterly reports of expenditures by all lobbyists who spend more than $250 in lobbying in any three-month period should be required. *The sweetheart arrangement between regulatory agencies and the regulated industries must be broken up,* and the revolving door between them should be closed. Federal legislation should restrict the employment of any member of a regulatory agency by the industry being regulated for a set period of time.

Thus our first priority must be to improve both the process and structure of government. We seek a government that is efficient and effective, open and honest, and compassionate in achieving justice and meeting our critical national needs. Reorganization is not a dry exercise of moving around boxes in an organizational chart. It is a creative venture toward the better direction of the energies and resources of our government.

The reform I am seeking is not a retreat; it is a marshalling of our resources to meet the challenges of the last quarter of this century. The problem is not that program goals are unworthy; it is not that our public servants are unfit. What is at fault is that the structure and process of our government have not kept up with the times and a changing society.

In our fast moving world, the relationships among societal factors are indeed difficult to understand. Increases in world population, food shortages, environmental deterioration, depletion of irreplaceable commodities, trade barriers and price disruptions, arms buildups, arguments over control of the seas, and many other similar problems are each one serious in itself, but each has a complicating effect on the others.

As I stated at the outset, we must develop a policy-making and management machinery that transcends narrow perspectives and deals with complex problems on a comprehensive, systematic basis. Whether the issue is the cities, tax reform, energy, or transportation, *I am committed to forging a federal government which can successfully manage the modern complexities of America's third century.*

Statement of Gerald Ford

I commend the members of the American Society for Public Administration for your excellent work in helping to improve public management. I especially note with satisfaction your educational programs an efforts to exchange useful management information and experience with federal, state, and local governments.

The term "management" was not in use at the time of the framing of the Constitution, yet it is clear that management is what the drafters had in mind when they vested the president with the general executive powers and charged him to "take care that the laws be faithfully executed" (Art. II, Sec. 3). This "take care" clause conveys particularly well the fundamental responsibility of the president with respect to the management functions of planning, organizing, actuating, coordinating, and controlling, which are the necessary consequences of faithful and efficient execution of the nation's laws governing Executive Branch activities.

Over the course of almost 200 years, the role of the federal government has expanded and grown more complex. Each year new laws are passed by Congress which make the jobs of both the Congress and president more demanding. This is a direct reflection of what has happened in the country—the United States is a far larger, more complicated nation than that perceived by the founding fathers, and it demands a far more sophisticated federal government to administer national affairs.

Each president must cope with this complexity within the continuing constitutional framework of checks and balances. As president, I have pursued a broad range of initiatives in a constant effort to improve the quality of management in the federal government. My commitment to improved management of the governmental system is fully demonstrated in my legislative and budget programs. A few examples illustrate that commitment:

• I have proposed reform of the regulatory process to make regulatory agencies more effective and efficient in order to better serve the needs of the American people.

• I have placed increased emphasis on improving management in connection with the annual budget process. The yearly instructions to the agencies on developing their budget recommendations now require the agencies to do a better job in identifying program objectives, reducing paperwork, and assessing effects of inflation.

• I placed before the Congress in January legislative proposals to consolidate 58 categorical programs into four block grants. Together these 58 programs account for over $18 billion in federal spending for health, education, social services, and child nutrition. The defects in these programs and the obvious need for reform have been well documented.

• I have directed a comprehensive review of energy organization to assure the most effective long-term structure for managing energy and energy-related functions. The Energy Reorganization Act of 1974 established the Energy Research and Development Administration and the Nuclear Regulatory Commission, and the Federal Energy Administration to deal with the oil embargo and the energy crisis. It is generally recognized, however, that these actions were interim measures and that a more comprehensive plan would be necessary to deal with the entire range of federal energy problems.

• I have placed increased emphasis on intergovernmental relations through improved policy guidance and strengthening the

Federal Regional Councils. I look to the Federal Councils as a major force in our efforts to make government more efficient and responsive to the needs of the American people.

• I have proposed reform of the so-called Impact Aid Program. This initiative would ensure that school districts that are adversely affected by federal activities would receive offsetting support. At the same time, my proposal would not provide support where there are ancillary economic benefits provided through a federal presence or where there is no true burden resulting from federal activities.

• I have directed the establishment of a management orientation program for non-career executives who are new to the Executive Branch. The program has been established and is currently operational. This is a White House/OMB/Civil Service Commission enterprise which, through seminars and special reading materials, ensures that non-career executives, as they take office, are very well informed about how the Executive Branch and its central staff institutions work at the top level.

These are but a few of many, many examples where specific action has been proposed or taken to improve the governmental system. Perhaps the most important part of the total effort is our continuing work with the departments and agencies to "build in" effective management principles and practices in their major programs. Using the budget process, the Office of Management and Budget (OMB) circulars, and a variety of other techniques, we seek better program planning, clearer definition of program objectives, detailed, well-designed implementation plans and procedures, effective evaluation of programs, tighter financial controls, and improved management systems to support decision making.

The ongoing Presidential Management Initiatives effort, for which I have charged the Director of OMB to provide leadership, is an illustration of this point. At my direction, nearly all departments and agencies are currently seeking ways to improve their decision-making processes and organizational structures, to obtain better evaluations of their programs, to reduce the burdens imposed by federal reporting and regulations, to hold down overhead costs, to increase the use of the private sector in carrying out program functions, and to improve personnel management. These steps may appear unexciting to those who are constantly looking for dramatic new policy initiatives, but in the long run, the key to effective government is to make the programs we already have live up to their promise, by conducting them in an efficient and effective manner.

Statement of Eugene McCarthy

Washington, D.C., September 23, 1976—Independent presidential candidate Eugene McCarthy today characterized the Carter energy program as misconceived and inadequate. Said McCarthy, "There should be no separate department of energy since energy supplies, needs and use must be a part of general resources policy, which neither Ford nor Carter have." McCarthy continued, "The need is for a Department of Resources which would include, along with energy, agricultural production (not marketing), forestry, mines and minerals."

The Resources Department would be established according to a projected reorganization plan being prepared by the independent McCarthy. He would propose to reorganize the Executive Branch of the government into five basic departments. The other four would be:

• Commerce, which would include agricultural marketing, transportation, banking, regulatory agencies, postal services, housing, and labor.

• Justice, largely as now operating, with additional responsibility in the handling of tax cases.

• Foreign Affairs, which would include both State Department and military operations.

• Finance Department.

Finally, Eugene McCarthy would limit the number of independent executive offices which are self-contained and can be operated outside normal channels to those principally concerned with state, local, and federal government relationships.

The following are excerpts from an address given by Senator McCarthy to the 4th Annual AFL-CIO National Conference on Community Services in Chicago, Illinois, on June 1, 1959:

"We are guided by the fundamental rule of social philosophy, the principle of subsidiarity: that government should leave to individuals and private groups those functions which they can efficiently perform for themselves. But at the same time we must realize the right, the duty, of government to intervene when basic human welfare is at stake."

Appendix E:
Selected Reading Material
for Presidential Appointees

Campbell, Alan K. "Approaches to Defining, Measuring and Achieving Equity in the Public Sector." *Public Administration Review* 36 (September/October 1976):555-562.

_____. "The Career Service and Responsible Government." *Evaluating Governmental Performance: Changes and Challenges for GAO.* Washington, D.C.: Government Printing Office, 1975.

Cleveland, Harlan. *The Future Executive.* New York: Harper & Row, 1972.

Cronin, Thomas E., and Rexford G. Tugwell, eds. *The Presidency Reappraised.* 2nd edition. New York: Praeger Publishers, 1977.

Dodd, Lawrence C., and Bruce I. Oppenheimer, eds. *Congress Reconsidered.* New York: Praeger Publishers, 1977.

Drucker, Peter F. *Management: Tasks, Responsibilities, Practices.* New York: Harper & Row, 1974.

Fenno, Richard F., Jr., ed. *Congress: New Rules, New Leaders, Old Problems.* 1977-1978 edition. Washington, D.C.: National Journal, 1977.

Heclo, Hugh. *A Government of Strangers: Executive Politics in Washington.* Washington, D.C.: The Brookings Institution, 1977.

Hess, Stephen. *Organizing the Presidency.* Washington, D.C.: The Brookings Institution, 1976.

Holtzman, Abraham. *Legislative Liaison: Executive Leadership in Congress.* Chicago: Rand McNally & Co., 1970.

Kaufman, Herbert. *Administrative Feedback.* Washington, D.C.: The Brookings Institution, 1973.

Murphy, Thomas P. "Political Executive Roles, Policy Making, and Interface with the Career Bureaucracy." *The Bureaucrat* (Summer 1972):96-127.

Murphy, Thomas P., Donald E. Nuechterlein, and Ronald J. Stupak. *The President's Program Directors: The Assistant Secretaries.* Charlottesville, Va.: Federal Executive Institute, 1977.

Ogul, Morris S. *Congress Oversees the Bureaucracy.* Pittsburgh, Pa.: University of Pittsburgh Press, 1976.

Patterson, Bradley H., Jr. *The President's Cabinet: Issues and Questions.* Washington, D.C.: American Society for Personnel Administration, 1976.

Pechman, Joseph A., ed. *Setting National Priorities: The 1978 Budget.* Washington, D.C.: The Brookings Institution, 1977. (Editions are issued annually subsequent to submission of the president's budget.)

Rose, Richard. *Managing Presidential Objectives.* New York: Free Press, 1976.

Seidman, Harold. *Politics, Position, and Power.* 2nd edition. New York: Oxford University Press, 1975.

Stanley, David T., Dean E. Mann, and Jameson W. Doig. *Men Who Govern: A Biographical Profile of Federal Political Executives.* Washington, D.C.: The Brookings Institution, 1967.

U.S. Civil Service Commission. *Notes for Presidential Appointees.* Washington, D.C.: Government Printing Office, 1978.

Waldo, Dwight. "The Future of Management." *The Bureaucrat* (Fall 1977):101-116.

Wildavsky, Aaron. *The Politics of the Budgetary Process.* 2nd edition. Boston: Little, Brown and Co., 1974

Index